# THE FUTURE OF EU CONSTITUTIONALISM

Is there a real and meaningful future for EU constitutionalism? This collection explores this question in light of recent challenges to EU constitutional law; namely, the pandemic and the political schisms emerging across the European Union. The contributors explore the question through the prism of the five main pillars of EU constitutionalism: the constitutional values, the EU formal constitutional framework, its substance consisting of the EU political and economic constitution, and conclude by looking at the foundational concept of sovereignty (national and European) in a global realm. Drawing on expertise from both 'old' and 'new' Europe, it gives voice to the most fundamental question facing the Union in its second half century.

**Volume 116 in the Series Modern Studies in European Law**

**Modern Studies in European Law**

**Recent titles in this series:**

New Directions in European Private Law
*Edited by Mateja Durovic and Takis Tridimas*

Standing to Enforce European Union Law before National Courts
*Hilde Ellingsen*

The Relative Authority of Judicial and Extra-Judicial Review: The EU Courts, the Boards of Appeal and the Ombudsman
*Michal Krajewski*

Responsive Human Rights: Vulnerability and the ECtHR
*Corina Heri*

The Architecture of Fundamental Rights in the European Union
*Šejla Imamovic*

The EU and its Member States' Joint Participation in International Agreements
*Edited by Nicolas Levrat, Yuliya Kaspiarovich, Christine Kaddous and Ramses A Wessel*

The UN Convention on the Rights of Persons with Disabilities and the European Union: The Impact on Law and Governance
*Carmine Conte*

EU Criminal Law, Second Edition
*Valsamis Mitsilegas*

The EU as a Global Digital Actor: Institutionalising Global Data Protection, Trade, and Cybersecurity
*Elaine Fahey*

Exporting the European Convention on Human Rights
*Maria-Louiza Deftou*

Judicial Authority in EU Internal Market Law: Implications for the Balance of Competences and Powers
*Vilija Velyvyte*

The Changing European Union: A Critical View on the Role of Law and the Courts
*Edited by Tamara Capeta, Iris Goldner Lang and Tamara Perisin*

The Structural Transformation of European Private Law: A Critique of Juridical Hermeneutic
*Leone Niglia*

The Future of EU Constitutionalism
*Edited by Matej Avbelj*

**For the complete list of titles in this series see www.bloomsbury.com/uk/series/modern-studies-in-european-law/**

# The Future of EU Constitutionalism

Edited by
Matej Avbelj

•HART•
OXFORD • LONDON • NEW YORK • NEW DELHI • SYDNEY

HART PUBLISHING

Bloomsbury Publishing Plc

Kemp House, Chawley Park, Cumnor Hill, Oxford, OX2 9PH, UK

1385 Broadway, New York, NY 10018, USA

29 Earlsfort Terrace, Dublin 2, Ireland

HART PUBLISHING, the Hart/Stag logo, BLOOMSBURY and the Diana logo are trademarks of Bloomsbury Publishing Plc

First published in Great Britain 2023



A catalogue record for this book is available from the British Library.

A catalogue record for this book is available from the Library of Congress.

ISBN: HB: 978-1-50996-286-0
ePDF: 978-1-50996-288-4
ePub: 978-1-50996-287-7

Typeset by Compuscript Ltd, Shannon

To find out more about our authors and books visit www.hartpublishing.co.uk. Here you will find extracts, author information, details of forthcoming events and the option to sign up for our newsletters.

# ACKNOWLEDGEMENT OF FUNDERS

This book has been written within the framework of a research project dedicated to the integral theory on the future of the European Union, which was financially supported by the Slovenian Research Agency[1] and Nova univerza.

NOVA UNIVERZA

SLOVENIAN RESEARCH AGENCY

[1] Research project No.J5-1791 (A) 'An integral theory on the future of the European Union', https://eufuture.nova-uni.si/en/home/.

# CONTENTS

# LIST OF CONTRIBUTORS

**Daniel Augenstein** is Associate Professor in the Department of European and International Public Law at Tilburg University

**Matej Avbelj** is Professor of European Law at the New University in Ljubljana

**Federico Fabbrini** is Full Professor of EU Law at Dublin City University and PI of the Jean Monnet Centre of Excellence REBUILD

**Sacha Garben** is Professor of EU Law, College of Europe, Bruges and official (on leave) in the European Commission

**Alun Gibbs** is Associate Professor in Public Law and Director of the Centre for Law, Policy and Society within Southampton Law School at the University of Southampton

**Cormac Mac Amhlaigh** is Senior Lecturer in Public Law at the University of Edinburgh

**Giuseppe Martinico** is Full Professor of Comparative Public Law at the Scuola Superiore Sant'Anna, Pisa

**Katarina Vatovec** is Assistant Professor of European Law at the New University in Ljubljana

**Neil Walker** is the Regius Chair of Public Law and the Law of Nature and Nations at the University of Edinburgh

**Mattias Wendel** is professor of Public Law, EU Law, International Law, Migration Law and Comparative Law at Leipzig University

# 1

# What Future for EU Constitutionalism?

MATEJ AVBELJ

## I. Introduction

This volume grew out of a conference which was held at the New University in Ljubljana on 23–24 September 2021 within the framework of a research project dedicated to the Integral Theory on the Future of Europe.[1] The conference evolved around the central question of the future of EU constitutionalism. This academic focus was not a coincidence. On the contrary, the event took place against the backdrop of a Conference on the Future of Europe (hereinafter the Conference) that the EU institutions had launched a few months before, on 9 May. Starting off with a one-year delay due to the outbreak of the COVID-19 pandemic, the Conference, which had originally been planned to last for two years, now intended to provide a year-long conventional and digital forum in which the EU citizens could express their views, angst, expectations and desires with regard to the future course of development of the European Union.

This 'democratic experiment', as it was eventually branded by the EU institutions, had resulted out of political necessity, under duress of the unprecedented chain of crises in which the European Union has been entangled over the last decade and even longer. Admittedly, after the, at least ostensible, success of the enlargement, the EU has struggled with constitutional, political, economic, rule of law, democracy, humanitarian, security, public health, and again economic and security crises. As some of the crises appeared to be at least provisionally resolved and as the worst appeared to be behind the Union, a combination of man-made and natural disasters, typically occurring in an unanticipated manner, provoked another crisis that simultaneously reopened the wounds of the past crises, which, in reality, still have not fully passed. As a result, for more than a decade, the EU has been operating in constant full-crisis mode, moving ad hoc from one crisis-stricken competence field to another, mending the ship on the open seas in the hope of preventing it from sinking, while, *nolens volens*, losing the sense of its overall direction.

[1] 'The Integral Theory of the Future of Europe', Slovenian Research Agency Research Project J5-1791 (A), https://eufuture.nova-uni.si/en/home/. The volume also benefitted from the support of the Jean Monnet Chair on Pluralism in the EU co-funded by the EU.

However, in a short period between 2017 and 2019, at a moment of relative economic and political stability and just before the outbreak of the pandemic, a new national and supranational political consensus was formed and the decision was taken to engage with the future of the European Union in a direct, systematic and profoundly citizen-centred, democratic manner. In so doing, the expectations were, at least in some political circles,[2] driven extremely high, while at the same time the mandate of the Conference was relatively modest. By contrast with the Convention on the Future of Europe, which was held in 2002 and which possessed a constitutional, albeit somewhat usurped, mandate,[3] the Conference of 2021 was much closer to a mere process of democratic consultation. Its planned outcome was a citizens' report to the Joint Presidency of the Conference exercised by the European Parliament, the European Commission and the Council, which was to follow up on the report 'swiftly' and 'effectively' in accordance with the Treaties and the competences conferred therein.[4]

In short, not just the constitutional mandate, but the very constitutional language was notably absent from the Conference's discursive repository – and this was precisely the catalyst behind the Ljubljana conference and the present volume resulting out of it. Namely, while everyone, the national and supranational stakeholders alike, insisted that it was necessary and appropriate to debate, as openly and as democratically as possible, the object and purpose of integration, its values, concrete policies and the institutional changes necessary to achieve them, not even excluding, a priori and ex ante, a Treaty change, reference to the 'C' word was missing. In that way, the EU hit a double paradox. On the one hand, the national and supranational insistence on the need for a Conference with a strong democratic pedigree was a sign of awareness that the issues the Conference ought to have dealt with were in fact of fundamental – that is, constitutional – importance for the future of the Union. Moreover, the unanticipated developments running in parallel with the Conference, most recently and most horrifying the Russian aggression in Ukraine, led to formal and informal political initiatives and adopted measures in the economic, humanitarian and above all military domains that had been utterly unthinkable on the supranational level just a few months ago.

In other words, the European Union has been, as a result of endogenous and exogenous crises, de facto and again by stealth turning not only into an ever closer and more perfect union economically (monetary, fiscal and banking), but also with regard to health, energy, security and defence. All of the crises the EU has been subject to over the last decade and a half have thus tossed the EU into a situation comparable to a constitutional moment. That is in a context whereby the

[2] Speech by Emmanuel Macron at Université La Sorbonne, 26 September 2017; speech by Emmanuel Macron at the award of the Prix Charlemagne, Aachen, 11 May 2018; Emmanuel Macron, 'Lettre Pour Une Renaissance Européenne', 4 March 2019.

[3] P Norman, *The Accidental Constitution: The Story of the European Convention* (Brussels, EuroComment 2003).

[4] https://futureu.europa.eu/pages/about.

overall social circumstances change so much that they also entail a change in the constitution of the polity at stake. Yet, despite the transformative events which have clearly and directly impacted on the EU's small 'c' constitution, there has been no attempt to launch a big 'C', ie a formal constitution-making process that would openly, transparently and with popular endorsement, on the national and supranational level, replace the EU's unwritten constitution with a written one, and at the same time reconstitute its small 'c' constitutionalism, formally turning the Union into a constitutional, but non-statist polity.

It was against this backdrop that the participants at the Ljubljana conference queried what future there is for EU constitutionalism. Could it be that the latter will, at best, remain a tacit, small 'c' constitutionalism? While, of course, eventually the answer to this question boils down to political realism, namely to what is objectively possible in practice, given the diverging interests between different EU Member States and supranational institutions, it is important to understand that the EU formal, big 'C' Constitution is not precluded conceptually. To the contrary, this volume, like the conference on which it draws, insists that, despite the negative historical experience, nothing in the nature of constitutionalism as a concept stands in the way of the European Union eventually adopting a constitution, and so turning its tacit and silent constitutionalism into an explicit big 'C' project.[5]

Furthermore, the past crises of European integration, which have been left in suspense rather than resolved, might make the case for explicit constitutionalisation of the EU even stronger today. At the same time, and this is where the point related to political realism kicks back in, it is by no means certain that constitutionalism is a normatively and empirically viable alternative for shaping the future of the European Union. And while this cannot be known until it is tried, this book examines whether a refined, pluralist approach to EU constitutionalism – perhaps also within the framework of the Conference on the Future of Europe or its aftermath – could succeed in revitalising the EU, with all of its legal, democratic, political, economic and federalist conceptual novelties.[6]

## II. The Argument of the Book

The book is substantively, though not formally, divided into five sections. The first section opens with this prologue and is followed by an introductory chapter, containing a keynote by Neil Walker. This sets the scene for a theoretical debate on EU constitutionalism that thereafter develops across nine chapters, broken down into four sections addressing the main substantive dimensions of EU constitutionalism: the constitutional values of the Union (section two); the EU's formal (section three) as well as political and economic constitution (section four); whereas the final

[5] M Avbelj, 'Revitalisation of EU Constitutionalism' (2021) 46 *EL Rev* 3.
[6] ibid.

section (section five) takes up the foundational concept of modern constitutionalism: the question of sovereignty in the EU.

Neil Walker, in his introductory chapter, engages with the above-mentioned paradox of EU constitutionalism, its past, present and future. He notes that while the constitutional debate in the EU has always been with us, it has so far had little institutional success in terms of big 'C' constitutionalism. This has led to the overall decline of optimism relating to the prospects of EU constitutionalism's institutional and legitimacy-conferring potential, and yet, at the same time, it is quite likely that the constitutional discourse perseveres and continues to shape the evolution of the EU also in the future. This paradox of simultaneous inevitable omnipresence of the (tacit) constitutional debate and its lack of concomitant explicit institutionalisation, which at the same time constantly remains (im)plausible, necessary and in and of itself potentially also insufficient, presents for Walker the burden as well as the allure of the European constitution.

This burden is not easy to dispose of, as has, inter alia, been confirmed also by the Conference on the Future of Europe, which, unlike the 2002 Convention, has engaged not only with the ontological, but also with the very existential questions of the European Union. Nevertheless, Walker notes that, like in the earlier proto-constitutional engagements in the EU, in the Conference too the instrumental and purposive function of the constitution remained at the forefront, whereas the ontological and the integrative functions were sidelined. While, from a purely pragmatic perspective, this has always made perfect sense, as the nature of the EU and our capacity to conceive ourselves as belonging to a shared (political) community have typically proven to be extremely divisive, at the same time the unprecedented internal and external challenges the EU has been faced with might not be successfully addressed without resolving in common, and hence constitutionally, also the ontological and integrative dimensions of the EU. In this way, according to Walker, the EU Constitution remains both the burden of and the allure for European integration.

Having set the scene by Walker's introductory chapter, the book continues with a section dedicated to the EU constitutional values. The chapter by Alun Gibbs picks up precisely where Walker leaves off. Rather than succumbing to the mainstream praise about the centrality of the common values for the viability of the European Union, Gibb's chapter advocates a much more nuanced, even somewhat sceptical approach. It does so, first, by clearly delineating between the juridical, legitimacy-reinforcing and membership-enhancing functions of the common values in the EU. This is followed by questioning the actual potential of the common values in their different guises to contribute to the formation of the EU as a 'political form', especially due to its indeterminacy, which flows directly from the unresolved issue of sovereignty understood in broader political, rather than just legal terms. Here, Gibbs, dwelling on what Walker has described as the integrative function of the constitution, worries that the EU has so far failed to develop truly common EU values. Instead, the EU has drawn quite mechanically from the statist tradition and, to the extent it has managed to sever itself from it, it has in terms of common values overly satisfied itself with a mere market-based rationale. The chapter concludes that while the common values might not hold all the answers for the future of the EU, the latter does depend on them too, and especially on the capacity of EU citizens to develop 'authentic forms of common action', which could be, in the thinnest sense at least, identified also in the Conference on the Future of Europe.

The chapter by Matej Avbelj centres on the same question of the role of common values in ensuring the viability of European integration, albeit on a lower level of abstraction, by concentrating on the current deep value fissures in the EU that, quite unhelpfully, broke out at a time when the actual and genuine commonness of the common values was needed more than ever before. How to close that value gap, which is much less visible on paper, but increasingly bites in the practices of several EU Member States? The chapter suggests that the answer might also be found in the constitutional register, indeed in launching the process of big 'C' constitutionalism which could help generate the necessary constitutional culture for preserving the unity of integration despite its (growing) diversity, but not necessarily in the contemporary unitary, one-size-fit-all form. Perhaps, the chapter concludes, the future formal big 'C' constitutional settlement could come in the form of an EU of concentric circles, which would give a better expression to the value differences between the Member States and consequently allow for more flexible constitutional arrangements. By agreeing to disagree in common also about the common values, the EU might be, to many counterintuitively so, better able to ensure its own viability.

Having examined the value-based foundations of EU constitutionalism, the following two chapters touch upon the EU formal constitution with the autonomous EU legal order and its core principles of primacy, direct applicability, direct effect and loyal cooperation at its heart. While the EU formal constitutional framework, structured around those principles, has been well established, its nature has simultaneously remained at least theoretically contested between the so-called pluralists and monists.[7] However, with several recent rulings of the national constitutional courts,[8] this contestation has also taken a very practical shape. The chapters by Mattias Wendel and Giuseppe Martinico both look at this problematique, albeit from two very different angles.

Mattias Wendel concentrates on the most recent challenges of the German Constitutional Court (Bundesverfassungsgericht, BVerfG) to the autonomy of

[7] M Avbelj and J Komárek (eds), *Constitutional Pluralism in the European Union and Beyond* (Oxford, Hart Publishing 2012); G Davies and M Avbelj (eds), *Research Handbook on Legal Pluralism and EU Law* (Cheltenham, Edward Elgar 2018).

[8] Czech Constitutional Court case of 31 January 2012 Pl ÚS 5/12, *Slovak Pensions*, English translation, www.usoud.cz/en/decisions/20120131-pl-us-512-slovak-pensions/; Danish Supreme Court Case No 15/2014, *Dansk Industri (DI) acting for Ajos A/S v The estate left by A* 2 BvR 859/15; Polish Constitutional Court, K 3/21 Assessment of the conformity to the Polish Constitution of selected provisions of the Treaty on European Union; German Federal Constitutional Court Judgment of 5 May 2020, English translation, www.bverfg.de/e/rs20200505_2bvr085915en.html.

EU legal order and, in particular, its capacity to determine its own competences (*Kompetenz-Kompetenz*). While the BVerfG has for five decades now been a front-runner in the judicial dialogue between the Court of Justice of the European Union (CJEU) and its national counterparts, which has contributed to several (to many, welcome) developments in EU law, in the recent public sector purchase programme (PSPP) conflict the overwhelming majority of scholars believed that the line had been crossed.[9] Not only did the BVerfG for the first time reject the application of the CJEU ruling as ultra vires, it did so for reasons that were less than convincing. However, Wendel's chapter, unlike the mainstream appreciation of the ruling, takes a more balanced and therefore more nuanced approach.

In examining how the conflict came about and unfolded through two decisions of the BVerfG, involving a diplomatic interaction between the European Commission and the German federal government, with a prior (in)direct mending of the issue in the triangle between the European Central Bank, the German legislative, executive powers and the Bundesbank, the issue has been finally removed from the table. In so doing, the clash between the BVerfG and the CJEU, as Wendel reminds us, is not a sign of a failure of the European Union as a distinctively pluralist polity, it is a confirmation of its ongoing pluralist character. The latter is not susceptible to any 'ultimate answer', be it in substantive terms or formally by way of creating new institutions; rather, it requires fitting procedures based on a continued dialogue. While the BVerfG behaviour in the PSPP conflict failed to live up to the highest standards of this dialogue, to say the least, the rest of the EU and national institutions compensated for this failure by overcoming it through 'constructive misunderstandings'. In fact, the latter might not just hold promise for the future of the European Union; it is also something that all those systems that could not be described as unitary have been characterised by.

That is precisely the gist of the chapter by Giuseppe Martinico. He engages in a thorough historical analysis of the contribution of Thomas Jefferson's legal and political thought to the development of American federalism. This subject is, perhaps counterintuitively, highly topical in the context of the debate on the future of Europe. The European federal thought, and in particular the development of European integration to the extent it has been shaped by federal ideas, has always been influenced, at least indirectly, and for better or worse, by the US federal experience.[10] And in this rich repository of federal ideas and practices, the influence of Thomas Jefferson has been studied much less than the contribution of other thinkers and stakeholders of the time, in particular the authors of the Federalist papers.

[9] DR Kelemen, P Eeckhout, F Fabbrini, L Pech and R Uitz, 'National Courts Cannot Override CJEU Judgments: A Joint Statement in Defense of the EU Legal Order' *Verfassungsblog* (26 May 2020), https://verfassungsblog.de/national-courts-cannot-override-cjeu-judgments/.

[10] M Avbelj, 'The Pitfalls of (Comparative) Constitutionalism for European Integration' (2008) Eric Stein Working Paper 1, https://csesp.files.wordpress.com/2015/05/eswp-2008-01-avbelj.pdf.

Against this backdrop, Martinico's chapter thus inquires whether the constitutional controversies with regard to the EU formal constitution, as spurred by the BVerfG PSPP ruling, really signified the rupture of the integration. Not unlike Wendel's response discussed above, Martinico's answer is also much more optimistic than the views held by the rest of the academia. Drawing historical parallels with the US nullification crises, in which Thomas Jefferson, albeit tacitly, played an important role, Martinico argues that the BVerfG's opposition to the CJEU amounts to nothing other than a confirmation of the federal nature of the EU. It is in this federal dynamics that the future of Europe will play out, paying close attention to the persuasiveness of the arguments the national constitutional courts cite in the event of conflict with the CJEU. In this way, the sometimes thin line between the constructive constitutional pluralism and the arbitrary solipsistic reactions of the national authorities, perhaps even rooted in the proto-authoritarian practices, can be preserved and the special, admittedly federal albeit not statist, character of the EU upheld.

The section on the formal EU constitution is followed by the exploration of its political and economic sides. In chapter seven, Sacha Garben takes up three constitutional problems of the European Union, which are reflected in the EU political constitution. The first is about the lack of popular, democratic endorsement of the autonomous legal order of the EU, as the CJEU has developed it with the plethora of other principles making up the EU's formal constitution. The second constitutional problem boils down to the inappropriate normative hierarchy of fundamental values of the Union, in which, due to the specific genesis of EU constitutionalism, the fundamental economic freedoms are clearly prioritised, in particular, over fundamental social rights. Finally, the third constitutional problem lurks in avoidance of the ordinary legislative procedure (the so-called Community method) in favour of intergovernmental decision-making (the Union method) at the expense of the democratic guarantees required by the EU's political constitution.

Garben's chapter clearly does not exercise any self-restraint as it requires that for a sound, viable future of EU constitutionalism it is necessary to resolve all three constitutional problems at once. The partial approach, staying faithful to the traditional *modus operandi* of political incrementalism, is precluded, as in the author's opinion the only legitimate alternative that remains is to reverse the course of integration and essentially give up on the EU's constitutional ambitions. The political stakes of EU constitutionalism are therefore extremely high already in and of themselves. Adding to that the underlying economic basis of the integration, the complexity of the constitutional future of the EU increases even further.

To obtain a holistic understanding of the contemporary and future challenges of the European Union, it is thus indispensable to engage also with the economic predicaments of the EU constitution. This is a task that the chapter by Federico Fabbrini embarks upon. Tracing the economic developments in the European Union, Fabbrini argues that the changes implemented in the economic architecture of the EU in response to the COVID-19 epidemic constitute a veritable paradigm shift. The Next Generation Europe programme (NGEU) has ensured the EU's own fiscal capacity, based not on an increased common budget, but on a common debt. Already in its present status, as a temporary economic instrument, it raises several important constitutional questions, whose pertinence only grows stronger with a view of turning the NGEU in a permanent feature of the EU economic constitution.

Fabbrini consequently admits that all the changes in the EU economic constitution that resulted as a reaction to the COVID-19 emergency situation have significantly rebalanced the economic and monetary legs of the Economic and Monetary Union to the extent that they would require constitutional adjustments, lest they be rolled back. This constitutional readjustment in the EU economic constitution would therefore need to be followed up by a similar move in the EU political constitution, increasing the effectiveness and the overall legitimacy of the European constitutional project, in whose absence there can be less than little hope for a viable future of the European Union.

Typically, when addressing the legitimacy of the EU as one of the decisive factors of its viability, the theory and practice of EU law and politics are overwhelmed by pessimism and negative expectations about what the future might bring. Cormac Mac Amghlaih's chapter, which rounds up this section on the EU political and economic constitution, makes an important difference. He argues that despite all of the doom and gloom pervading the EU social as well as scholarly atmosphere, the EU not only does still exist, but it has also clearly succeeded, sometimes with more, sometimes with fewer difficulties, to stand against the crises that it has faced. Since the EU *Eppur Esiste!*, Mac Amghlaih argues that there is an apparent discrepancy between the way the EU socio-political reality is perceived and the way it actually is in practice.

The root cause of this mismatch between the way of thinking about the legitimacy of the European Union and its actual functioning according to Mac Amghlaih's chapter lurks in the political moralist approach to political legitimacy in the EU. Rescinding the moralist approach in favour of a political realist approach to legitimacy, as developed in the political philosophy of Bernard Williams, allows us to discover that the EU as a supranational polity has so far successfully responded to the questions of the existence of supranational authority that have eluded or escaped the national realm. Once the question of the actual existence of the supranational authority has been successfully answered, then the disagreement about the sources of the legitimacy of the hence established authority are not only completely normal, but are even expected, in particular in an in-between polity such as the EU, and cannot be taken, as per the moralist account of legitimacy, as a sign of a polity's malaise. As a result, the future of EU constitutionalism might actually be much brighter than when perceived through a conventional political moralist lens.

Finally, the future of EU constitutionalism to a great extent also depends on the actual capacity of the EU to preserve and advance its supranational authority – in short, its ability to assert and plausibly exercise its sovereignty. To what extent and for which purposes the EU has been able to do that are the questions that Daniel Augenstein and Katarina Vatovec explore in their chapters, albeit in relatively contrasting ways. Augenstein's discussion of EU sovereignty paints quite a sobering picture. He demonstrates that the bolstering of EU sovereignty internally could result in a neoliberal emptying of Member States' democratic welfare-state regimes, while externally it could lead to the imposition (or attempts thereof) of mainly economic EU regulatory standards upon the rest of the globe. Neither would be democratic or in accordance with the cosmopolitan aspirations of human rights protection.

Nevertheless, Augenstein concludes on a positive note, stressing that the functional sovereignty the EU has developed cannot and should not be equated with the neoliberal project of imposing the private over the public and shielding global markets from democratic oversight. He insists that these trends should be resisted and therefore charges the future of EU constitutionalism with the task of ensuring that internally the EU is not just about the common market, but the market that EU citizens have in common, while externally EU regulatory globalisation should be accompanied by the constitutionalisation of foreign citizens' rights, giving them a voice and enabling them to hold the EU accountable in front of its courts.

If, for Augenstein, the evolution of EU sovereignty, especially if mobilised essentially for neoliberal economic purposes, could thus also be a threat to national and global constitutional values, the chapter by Katarina Vatovec adopts a much more affirmative approach to EU sovereignty. Having mapped the historical development of sovereignty, its ills and virtues in the context of European integration, her chapter celebrates the political aspirations to EU sovereignty which have emerged and been strengthened in the political narratives over the last decade. This is so since EU sovereignty can be chiefly conceptualised as a shield against the interests, incursions or even direct threats stemming from other entities in an increasingly interconnected global world.

This shield conception of European sovereignty is explicated using a case study of the EU's capacity to counter the extraterritorial application of foreign legislation. The case study demonstrates that in a globally interconnected world, composed of territorial sovereigns (states) and functional sovereigns (public, hybrid and private regimes and entities), the EU can and should play an important role, ensuring that its constitutional principles, values and commitments are actually ensured in practice too. Therefore, the chapter concludes that there is a clear need for European sovereignty, whose viability requires moving beyond the present sovereignty talk towards a comprehensive and efficient normative response in practice. That this is not just an academic lofty ideal is more than brutally proved by the Russian aggression in Ukraine, which poses the first direct, but also, as the chapter notes, the ultimate test for the viability of European sovereignty.

## III. The Constitutional Epilogue for the Future of Europe?

As the short synopsis of the content of this book in the preceding paragraphs has demonstrated, once more the present and the future of the European Union are clearly not free of any challenges. To the contrary, despite the fact that the EU does indeed still exist and has relatively successfully coped with the many crises it has faced over the last decade and a half, it is nevertheless clear that the present status quo, marked by incremental politics of pragmatic muddling through the concrete challenges as they arise, has grown increasingly unsustainable. It therefore appears that the process of European integration is coming ever closer to a tipping point at which something will need to happen to shift the integration into a higher gear, to a qualitatively higher level that will enable the Union and its Member States to cope better with the man-made and natural disaster tests they shall face.

That this impression is not just an entirely subjective feeling of the editor of this volume is confirmed by the political discourse that has accompanied the conclusion of the Conference on the Future of Europe. What follows from that high-level political, both national and supranational, debate is that the closing of the Conference was not considered the end of a process of unprecedented democratic deliberation, but a prelude to something bigger yet. The European Parliament thus openly demands Treaty change, and expects the leaders of the Member States to call for a convention to revise the Treaties.[11] The Commission continues to remain faithful to the Monnet method of pragmatic problem-solving and to fine-tuning the Union, using all the flexibilities afforded by its existing legal framework to better deliver for its citizens and the Member States. In so doing, however, it does not exclude Treaty change, but simultaneously insists that opening of the Treaties should not be an end in and of itself.[12]

The Member States have left the Conference relatively divided. There are those who are apparently wary of any bigger changes, let alone a rupture of or clear discontinuity with the present status quo.[13] There are others which appear, especially due to the major upheaval wrought upon Europe by the Russian aggression in Ukraine, more ambitious,[14] but still fall short of proposing any decisive step forward and hence also away from the way things have usually been done in the Union over the course of the last several decades. The only exception seems to be

[11] www.europarl.europa.eu/news/en/headlines/priorities/eu-future-conference-follow-up/20220603IPR32122/parliament-activates-process-to-change-eu-treaties.

[12] https://ec.europa.eu/commission/presscorner/detail/en/IP_22_3750.

[13] www.government.se/information-material/2022/05/non-paper-by-bulgaria-croatia-the-czech-republic-denmark-estonia-finland-latvia-lithuania-malta-poland-romania-slovenia-and-sweden/.

[14] The German coalition agreement, however, explicitly calls for a European constitutional convention as a follow-up to the Conference on the Future of Europe that would lead to the establishment of the European Federal State; see www.politico.eu/wp-content/uploads/2021/11/24/Koalitionsvertrag-2021-2025.pdf, para 4421.

France, whose president spoke openly of political reorganisation of the European continent in which the EU would no longer be an exclusive club, but would be one in which all European countries that are committed to democracy and the rule of law and are currently not members of the EU could find their place.[15] Following this proposal, a European political community next to the EU should come into existence, in which Ukraine, Moldova, Georgia, the Western Balkan states and the UK again could take part with the EU Member States. This would simultaneously permit the EU to proceed along its integrative path, in the scope of the membership that would be feasible, and that would also, thanks to more active differentiation strategies in place, allow for its more efficient functioning.

In conclusion, it can be anticipated that the circumstances, both internal and external to the European Union, which will continue to cause increased deepening of EU integration, at a pace not witnessed before, will also cause the burden of the European constitution, to revert again to Neil Walker, to continue to mount. The need to democratically legitimise the already existing scope of integration, in terms of both its depth and breadth, on the supranational level will only grow further with additional 'unions', be it in health, energy, security or defence, being transferred to the supranational plane. At the same time, the conflicting interests of the Member States, and their concerns about their identity as well as about the potential '*Entstaatlichung*' will multiply too. The burden of EU constitutionalism will thus keep growing, but so too will the need for it to be discharged. It is therefore not an exercise in futurology to predict that in the near, though perhaps not the very near, future, the EU will need to adopt a new constitutional settlement. This will be a heavy legal, political, indeed an overall extremely demanding, social task. If this short theoretical treatise, whose purpose has been to elucidate the main elements of the multilayered EU constitutionalism and the challenges that the future holds for it, makes this task only slightly easier and therefore more feasible, then this volume's aims and ambitions will have been achieved.

[15] https://presidence-francaise.consilium.europa.eu/en/news/speech-by-emmanuel-macron-at-the-closing-ceremony-of-the-conference-on-the-future-of-europe/.

# 2

# The Burden of the European Constitution

NEIL WALKER

## I. Three Questions

Why, with varying degrees of intensity, has the European Union constitutional debate always been with us in some shape or form over recent decades? (Question One) Why, despite this sustained attention, do optimistic views remain so scarce on the ground, either as to the prospects of the successful production and ratification of a canonical big 'C' Constitutional document or, even if such a prospect were to be realised, as to the likelihood of that documentary achievement augmenting the legitimacy of the EU? (Question Two) Yet why, nevertheless, is it so difficult to imagine the debate over a written constitution for the EU just fading away and being consigned to the dustbin of history? (Question Three)

These questions have acquired a renewed urgency as we contemplate the latest attempt to 'reset'[1] the European project. The Conference on the Future of Europe (the Conference)[2] – a joint venture of the European Parliament, the Council and the European Commission, concluded its work in May 2022. It has been a European initiative with quite radical polity-wide ambitions, yet, like many before, without explicit constitution-making intent. But, also like many before, it is an initiative around which constitution talk has circulated. It is, moreover, a venture born in a period when the official discourse of the EU had become notably more defensive. The Conference's role was portrayed as one responding to a series of profound challenges to the EU's very viability as a political community – around fiscal questions, migration, common European values and, with Brexit, even membership – rather than, as has so often been the progressive mood music of the past, one exploring new frontiers and building on 'success'. Indeed, it hardly overstates the novel significance of the new political mood to say that whereas at the (often only tacitly acknowledged) heart of many previous reckonings lay the key *ontological*

[1] R Youngs, *Europe Reset: New Directions for the EU* (London, Bloomsbury 2018).
[2] https://futureu.europa.eu/?locale=en.

question – what kind of entity was the EU meant to be, and what institutions and aims were most appropriate to that kind of entity? – in this new phase the ontological question has often been joined to an even more basic *existential* question – how is the EU *at all* capable of surviving in any recognisable form?

In this regard, we should note the telling headline of the Joint Declaration launching the Conference – 'Engaging with citizens to build a more *resilient* Europe'.[3] Similarly eloquent of the prevailing political atmosphere, we should also note that the opening of the Conference, initially intended as an early venture of the new, post-2019 elections EU political regime, was delayed for a year to the spring of 2021 due to yet one more crisis of political capability of the depth and seriousness that prompted the initiative in the first place – namely, that presented by the onset of the coronavirus pandemic. And as the Conference drew to a close, once again unanticipated events, and the searching light they shine on the credentials of the Union's claim to a distinctive political identity and agency, came to the fore – this time in the form of Russia's invasion of Ukraine.

Posed anew in the turbulent context of the Conference project, the most basic answer to the three opening questions lies in what I call the *burden* of the European Constitution. The idea of a self-proclaimed big 'C' European Constitution, and of 'constitutionalism' generally, including small 'c' non-canonical constitutionalism,[4] means many different things to many different people with many different aspirations. This is not just a question of our disagreeing over what a constitution (small 'c' or big 'C') should or can do in any particular case, such as the specific values that it should enshrine or the precise balance and relationship between different organs of government. Rather, it signals a deeper disagreement over the *kinds of things* that a constitution can or should generally do, or that should be given greater emphasis or accorded top priority. And it is just because of the variety of kinds of things a constitution can do that so many diverse constituencies become invested in the constitutional debate, or at least remain or become not indifferent to it – particularly in the face of investment by rival constituencies. This answers Question One.

Yet it is precisely that variety, and the deep differences and disagreements that it produces, which also suggests the answer to Question Two. Note that I do not claim the burden is one that is *impossible* to discharge, just very burdensome. Perhaps doomed to failure, but perhaps not. What is more, and here lies the answer to Question Three, even if a constitutional solution appears but a distant prospect, it is not clear what else, if anything, would be fit for the mix of key purposes that such a solution would serve. The social and political forces that sustain and regularly 'revitalise'[5] the EU constitutional debate are powerful and constant, and just as it

[3] https://ec.europa.eu/info/sites/default/files/en_-_joint_declaration_on_the_conference_on_the_future_of_europe.pdf.

[4] See, eg N Walker, 'Big "C" or Small "c"?' (2006) 12 *European Law Journal* 12.

[5] M Avbelj, 'Revitalisation of EU Constitutionalism' (2021) 46 *EL Rev* 3.

remains very difficult to see how a successful EU Constitution can be produced, given the diversity of aspirations associated with these forces, the very intensity of these forces and their various motivational attractions to at least some part of the constitutional register means that it is also very difficult to see the legitimacy of the EU being enhanced in the long run *without* recourse to the high (or big 'C') notes in the constitutional register.

## II. Constitutional Functions

To explain briefly, a c(C)onstitution does three main kinds of things, or has three main kinds of functions.[6] We can say, additionally, that the very act of constitution-making often involves a key presupposition. Where that presupposition can be relied upon, a fourth kind of function is implicitly performed, and where that presupposition cannot be relied upon, the claim that is made in its stead – the gambit it offers – presents a more active version of that fourth kind of function. What are these functions?

First, the constitution has an *instrumental design* function. This refers to the basic normative content of the formal constitutional text, or, in the absence of a canonical document, the informal or unwritten constitutional rules. These establish the machinery of government within a polity, prescribing the institutional means by which policy ends may be realised, including various rights-based constraints and inter-branch checks that limit institutional capacity.

Secondly, a constitution has an *integrative* or communitarian function. Through a variety of means – involvement in the constitution-making process; investment in the 'sacred' text itself and its founding; ongoing participation in and valorisation of the institutional life it frames, the political subjectivities it specifies (both offices and citizenship) and the key norms it articulates; the collective memorialisation of the constitutional record, etc – the constitution operates as a cultural vector concerned with the process of social integration. In other words, the integrative function helps invest the institutional architecture with the requisite social energy. Through this function, the constitution conveys and nurtures a set of meanings that encourages those addressed and affected by its design to develop and sustain a sense of the entity constituted as one in which they, in concert with other members, come to identify themselves, in some measure at least, as a community of engagement in a common form of political life (rather than simply possessing certain contingently overlapping interests).

[6] Often writers focus on only two main functional sets. See, eg the distinction between the 'legal-institutional' and the 'socio-political' dimension in M Avbelj, 'Can European Integration be Constitutional and Pluralist – Both at the Same Time?" in M Avbelj and J Komarek (eds), *Constitutional Pluralism in the European Union and Beyond* (Oxford, Hart Publishing, 2012) 381; see, similarly, the distinction between the 'normative' and the 'integrative' functions of constitutions, D Grimm, 'Integration by Constitution' (2005) 3 *International Journal of Constitutional Law* 193.

Thirdly, and, for reasons I return to shortly, often somewhat overlooked or neglected in the literature, the Constitution has a *purposive* function. It is a means by which a fundamental normative orientation for the polity can be endorsed. This endorsement may consist of a statement of primary values, key objectives or state directives, whether market-based or socialist, or based upon some religious creed. It may also be expressed or implicit in more specific policy-centred provisions of the constitutional text, an increasingly evident feature as a more detailed style of constitutional drafting has come to prevail over the course of the twentieth and twenty-first centuries.

Fourthly, the constitution typically involves the presupposition of sovereign statehood. That is to say, the mere act and fact of constitution-making normally offers an implicit answer to the question of what kind of polity it is. Yet, where that implicit answer is not plausibly available, any constitutional initiative must instead face, as a matter to be resolved, what we have dubbed the *ontological* question of what kind of (non-state) polity it aspires to be.

How do these various functions – instrumental, integrative, purposive and ontological – tend to sit together in the national constitutional context? Here, the quotidian preoccupation is typically with the instrumental design function. As noted, the performance of the ontological function – the assertion or assumption of the status of a sovereign state polity – is implicit in the very success of the act of constitution-making. The integrative function, concerned with the provision of the basic political–cultural software without which the sovereign authority assumed by the ontological claim cannot translate into viable political community and effective political capacity, is also often relatively uncontroversial. While the subject of much symbolic ceremony, some other event in the more or less distant past – war, revolution, etc – will generally already have set the contours of the polity and asserted it as a legitimate site for a common political life amongst its citizenry. The Constitution is merely reinforcing that assertion, or is at most co-constitutive.[7]

The centrality of the instrumental design function, then, is predicated on the acceptance of polity status and viability, and, therefore, on a sense that the ontological and integrative questions have already received basically affirmative answers. So institutional architecture moves front and centre. This is even the case in many first constitutions, where the *pouvoir constituant* is engaged for the first time and the integrative project may still be relatively new and unsettled. But it is more emphatically true of reform constitutions where, typically, the threshold integrity

[7] In Michel Rosenfeld's very general taxonomical terms, the US model is an outlier, giving unusual priority to the constitution in that in the American experience the original document predated and helped precipitate much of the work both of state building and (cultural) nation building. His two more common models are the German model, where the nation precedes both state and constitution, and the French model, where the state comes before the nation and constitution; see M Rosenfeld, *The Identity of the Constitutional Subject* (London, Routledge, 2010) ch 5.

of the polity is no longer in question[8] and some kind of overlapping consensus has developed over the need for – though not necessarily the content of – institutional reform. In most national constitutional moments, then, most of the overt constitutional action, including most of the conflict and controversy, tends to surround the detail of instrumental design.

The purposive function of the national constitution, for its part, tends also, like the integrative and ontological functions, to be somewhat muted, and again that has to do with how and where the very idea of statehood figures in the modern political imagination. A key feature of this is the default open-endedness of the basic idea of political sovereignty that underpins state constitutional authority.[9] The modern notion of sovereignty presupposes a comprehensive and exclusive concentration of authority in the institutions, roles and capacities established by the constitution – a compendious *pouvoir constitué* derived from the people's or the nation's equally compendious original *pouvoir constituant*. Under the sign of sovereignty, then, the jurisdictional scope prescribed by the constitution is constitutively incapable of being subject to any external constraint. The constitution is the only source of the limitations of its power. Sovereign authority implies *Kompetenz-Kompetenz*, and this, in turn, supports a tendency not to self-inhibit the kinds of purposes for which that authority might be deployed.

What follows from this? To begin with, the purpose-guiding words used in the preamble and in the main body – typically its early provisions – are often bland and general, referencing universal ideals such as peace, justice, equality, liberty, democracy and solidarity. They are often non-justiciable, and to the extent they have any interpretive function this is likely to be permissive rather than prohibitive of state action. For its part, the broader economic orientation of the polity is often taken for granted and unspecified, and in principle secondary to and dependent upon the all-embracing authority of political sovereignty.[10] What is more, such purposes and governing ideals as are textually articulated are typically wrapped up in a series of attributions to the national people and its aspirations, and so in significant measure submerged within or at least closely coupled with the integrative function. And even where more explicit and detailed, as most prominently in certain socialist and theocratic constitutions, the first setting and articulation of the purposive function often coincides with the founding of the polity. Here too, therefore, the purposive function is closely linked to the pursuit of the integrative

[8] This need not be the case. In my home state it is difficult to imagine the task of any 'reform' of the UK constitution as primarily concerned with anything other than restoring the integrity of the UK in the face of the very real prospect of secession by Scotland and, perhaps, Northern Ireland and Wales. See, eg N Walker, 'Our Constitutional Unsettlement' [2014] *PL* 529.

[9] See, eg N Walker, 'The Sovereignty Surplus' (2020) 18 *International Journal of Constitutional Law* 370.

[10] See, eg N Walker, 'Where's the 'E" in Constitution? A European Puzzle (2020) Edinburgh School of Law Research Paper 14, SSRN: https://ssrn.com/abstract=3642534 or http://dx.doi.org/10.2139/ssrn.3642534.

function; and as with the integrative function, and indeed also the ontological function, textual constitutional endorsement of basic purpose is more concerned to provide juridical reinforcement and to guide practical implementation of a claim already made and successfully asserted in the course of transformative political events than it is to supply an original assertion and direction.

However, as the recent interest in the operation of 'transformative' constitutionalism in South Africa, South America and, albeit less intensely, also in Northern systems, such as post-war Germany, indicates, all this need not be so.[11] Constitutional purpose does not have to be simply reflective of a prior political reality, nor a mere appendage to and general embroidery of national identity and integrative ambition. Polities with a long prior history of integration and institutionalisation *can* have their normative orientation reset through processes in which constitutional change is pivotal. This requires a new 'constitutional commitment to broad-scale social transformation, aspiring ultimately to a better and more equal society'[12] – a commitment that typically involves the state itself in a proactive role and also normally prescribes effective ways of holding powerful private parties to account to avoid frustration of the transformative project. We should not, however, overstate the importance of this. In the national context, the transformative paradigm remains the exception to a norm of constitutional purpose as textually permissive but unlikely to disrupt the broadly settled contours of operation of the polity.

## III. The Distinctiveness of the European Union

In the EU, much is different. It can seem superficially that this is not true. As in the national case, the most prominent constitutional register is that of instrumental design. Indeed, Joseph Weiler's well-known designation of the EU in the early 1990s as a 'constitution without constitutionalism'[13] plays to the fact that in the EU there had long been a quite myopic concentration on the instrumental function to the neglect of others. Supranational Europe clearly possessed from its 1950s inception much of the institutional architecture we are long acquainted with from the state constitutional context. Indeed, as the architecture filled out over the decades, in many ways it became even more familiarly state-like. Innovations such as the directly elected European Parliament (1979), the Charter of Fundamental Rights (2000) and a gradually increasing parliamentary role in the appointment of the executive Commission (1992–2009) borrowed directly from the state template.

[11] See, eg M Hailbronner, 'Transformative Constitutionalism: Not only in the Global South' (2017) 65 *African Journal of Comparative Law* 527; the term 'transformative constitutionalism' was coined by Karl Klare with reference to the post-Apartheid South African Constitution; K Klare, 'Legal Culture and Transformative Constitutionalism' (1998) 14 *South African Journal of Human Rights* 146.

[12] Hailbronner (n 11) 540.

[13] JHH Weiler, *The Constitution of Europe* (Cambridge, Cambridge University Press, 1999) ch 1.

But, for a long time, this restless institutional innovation coexisted with only very modest and uneven development of EU-wide political self-consciousness. And so, whereas in the national context preoccupation with design questions normally signals both that the ontological question of polity type and standing is settled and that the integrative question of engaged membership has already received an important threshold resolution and is now largely a matter a reinforcement and consolidation, in the EU such preoccupation has tended to signal the very opposite.

The relative neglect of any explicit attention to the integrative function of political self-identification, still less to the ontological question of the very nature of the EU polity, speaks to a variety of quite different considerations. Certainly, in the early days of supranationalism, it may simply have revealed the remoteness of any strongly integrationist prospect – and, indeed, the absence of a policy agenda whose delivery would require the levels of mutual solidarity and solidarity associated with a robust sense of collective identity – and so a consequent indifference to its consideration. Alternatively, and increasingly so over the life of the EU, from the Messina Conference of 1955 to the 1992 project and the Treaties of Maastricht and Amsterdam four decades later, such relative neglect of matters of politically integrative ambition and polity status spoke to a sense that these matters would be so controversial and divisive that to make them central to any holistic reform initiative, and to any 'constitutional' conversation around such an initiative, might be fatal to the very prospects of that initiative.

Even by the time of the Constitutional Treaty project of the early 2000s, attention to these deeper constitutional functions remained limited and uneven. Tellingly, for all its unprecedentedly explicit constitutional credentials and ambitions, these were more *grasped* by Giscard d'Estaing as President of the Convention than they were *granted* by the Council or sponsored by any of the other institutions.[14] Many constituencies, faced with the growing dysfunctionality of the normal intergovernmental (IGC) reform process so recently highlighted by the meagre returns of the Treaty of Nice, were much more motivated by the opportunity for institutional reform that the increased gravitas, resources and deliberative potential that the unusually grand setting of a Convention allowed than by any desire to face directly the integrative and ontological questions that tended to be associated with an overtly constitutional initiative. Indeed, famously, even after the Constitutional Treaty was aborted in 2007 in response to the failed referendums in France and the Netherlands, the vast majority of its design provisions were revived and lived again – and continue to operate today – in the subsequent constitutionally silent Lisbon Treaty.

Yet, there is also evidence in the Constitutional Treaty, and in its generative convention, of institutional reform supplying a proxy battle ground for the broader

[14] See, eg P Norman, *The Accidental Constitution: The Story of the European Convention* (Brussels, EuroComment, 2003).

polity questions. More sceptical national audiences sought to cut down the polity-formative and integrative ambitions of the EU by reference to limits imposed by a competence catalogue and the Charter of Fundamental Rights, while more pro-integrationist elements sought to deepen the polity identification of the EU citizenry osmotically through expansion in state-like areas such as home affairs, foreign policy and social policy. In addition, the very constitutional explicitness of the mandate, and of Giscard d'Estaing's development of it, also signalled the inevitability of some measure of direct consideration of the polity questions, and the increased desire of at least certain parties to grasp that nettle. And, in so unfolding, the constitutional debate only tended to underline how contentious these matters remained, and how much their raising might stoke, even mould, tribal divisions. As regards the integrative function, the very Convention process, although itself a way of fuelling a sense of common political engagement, also revealed tensions between those with strong ambitions for a deepening of common commitments and those suspicious that the cultural dividend of any considered common dialogue could lead in a federalist direction. As regards the ontological function, a closely connected set of concerns were evident. So deeply rooted is the connection between statehood and constitutional authority in the modern political imagination that the open ontological question of the kind of polity the EU might become tended to be reduced in public discourse to the closed state/non-state binary. That is to say, those who sought to treat the very fact of written Constitutional anointment as a symbol of the independent polity maturity of the EU exposed themselves to the criticism of those who sought – ultimately successfully, once the Treaty entered the harsh waters of national ratification – to treat such an ambition not as an exploration of the identity of a new type of polity, but merely as a 'state-like' – or, rather, superstate-like – existential threat to national sovereignty.

To complicate the picture further, as with the integrative and ontological function, the purposive function stands in a different and more awkward relation to the EU and its constitutional standing than it does in the case of many states. Whereas, in the state context, normative purposes are either implicit or couched at a high level of abstraction, or, where more concrete and explicit, either baked in with the founding of the polity or part of a post-founding transformative initiative, the EU offers another pattern. Its supranational purposes, and in particular the founding functionally restricted emphasis on continental market values and objectives, are quite concrete and explicit, yet preceded the integrative work of developing of the EU as a political community.[15]

This has opened up another set of opposing incentives and another arena of contention in European constitutional debate. On the one hand, there are those for whom the fact that the EU's prospectus as a continent-wide free market 'club good' from which all would benefit as a matter of mutual self-interest preceded any project of deep attachment to it as a political community in its own right remains

[15] See, eg T Isiksel, *Europe's Functional Constitution: A Theory of Constitutionalism beyond the State* (Oxford, Oxford University Press, 2016).

the very basis of their support. From that basis, they might either wish to maintain their preference in a merely small 'c' constitutional context or, as we saw some indication of during the Constitutional Treaty debate, freeze and consolidate their particular version of integration in a big 'C' settlement.[16] On the other hand, there is the European Left, split between those who share an understanding of the EU as a capitalist club but make an opposite (ie negative) evaluation, and are wary of the further constitutional entrenchment of that state of affairs;[17] and those for whom the fact that the purposive orientation of the EU preceded its deepening as a political community suggests that the former is still fluid, and is capable of reform, and constitutional consolidation, in a radically social democratic direction.[18] Here, we find the various different constitutional functions strategically rejoined. This is so because for many of this persuasion, perhaps most prominently Yanis Varoufakis's DIEM25 movement,[19] a big 'C' focus on a wide pre-settlement participation is vital not only to bring about through its final *product* a commitment to deepening of common social democratic purpose and the institutional design supports for this, but also to foster through the very inclusiveness of its *process* the sense of community integration and stable polity identity that would lend legitimacy to a political project whose more ambitiously distributive purposes would necessarily invite greater levels of individual or group sacrifice for the common good.

## IV. Conclusion

It is no surprise, then, that any new 'out-of-the-box'[20] initiative for remaking Europe, such as the Conference on the Future of Europe, should begin on the ground of institutional and policy reform. The EU's polity trajectory has always been one of incremental adjustment and adaptive growth. Where the modern sovereign state begins with a constitutional framework of compendious legal and political authority in which wide-ranging institutional innovation and policy growth may be accommodated, the EU has ploughed the opposite furrow. The ongoing development of its specific institutional architecture and policy competences have not been sanctioned by any wider constitutional authority, but have instead supplied the very measure of its constitutional progress. Rather than its shifting particular manifestations being anchored in a stable general authority, the stepwise accumulation of these particulars has always provided its net

[16] For a fuller discussion, see eg N Walker, 'Europe's Constitutional Momentum and the Search for Polity Legitimacy' (2005) 3 *International Journal of Constitutional Law* 211, 225–33.

[17] See, eg M Wilkinson, *Authoritarian Liberalism and the Transformation of Modern Europe* (Oxford, Oxford University Press, 2021).

[18] As Jürgen Habermas has often argued; see in particular J Habermas, 'Why Europe Needs a Constitution' (2001) 11 *New Left Review* 5. For Habermas's evolving views on the subject, see N Walker, 'Habermas's European Constitution: Catalyst, Reconstruction, Refounding' (2019) 25 *European Law Journal* 508.

[19] https://diem25.org/en/.

[20] F Fabbrini, 'The Conference on the Future of Europe: Process and Prospects' (2020) 26 *European Law Journal* 401, 401.

constitutional standing and profile.[21] For the EU, in other words, legal and political power has been an aggregative achievement rather than a holistic endowment. Where the EU has sought to move beyond this incremental pattern and grapple with deeper and more general constitutional questions – in particular, questions of integration and polity identity – as it did in the case of the Constitutional Treaty, it has tended to confront unresolved basic differences of political ambition and uncharted complexities. This leaves us with a dilemma. Do we avoid or marginalise these broader questions, which have brought much trouble, or do we reckon that in the long run, and perhaps even in the fairly short-term, the legitimacy of the European Union depends on them somehow being confronted and resolved?

Some sense of that dilemma, and the tension associated with it, can be glimpsed in the work of the Conference. On the one hand, particularly through the Working Groups feeding into the Conference Plenary, we can see a strong focus on policy development, and, to a lesser extent, institutional reform. The policy themes ranged widely across climate change and the environment; health; economy and social justice; the EU in the world; rule of law and security; digital transformation; migration; and education, culture and sport, while there was also a focus on the question of the adequacy of Europe's democratic institutions. On the other hand, through the work of the national panels, the European citizens' panels and the multilingual digital platform, there was also an effort, unprecedented in its depth, to provide an experimental template of how a more expansive form of citizen engagement might work on a supranational scale. So, alongside the pursuit of the EU's trademark instrumental and purposive functions, we see some attention to the kind of political-culture-building activity that is also central to the integrative function. Yet it is not apparent that these different functional priorities are well reconciled. There remains a tension between the top-down dispositive prerogative of the three institutions (Council, Parliament and Commission) that make up the Joint Presidency and the emphasis on bottom-up participation;[22] and a related unresolved trade-off, reflected in post-Conference discussions across the institutions and civil society over the appropriateness of a programme of Treaty reform to implement the Conference proposals, between the Conference conceived of as a vehicle for concrete reform and as a participatory forum for reflection and the generation of new forms of democratic capacity.[23]

[21] This is nicely captured in Kaarlo Tuori's depiction of EU constitutional development as involving the successive emergence of various 'sectoral' constitutions – economic, social and security – alongside the juridical and political orders. In these terms, Europe has required so many partial constitutional orders, and such a baroque architecture, just because it lacked the founding legitimacy that would have produced a single encompassing settlement. See K Tuori, *European Constitutionalism* (Cambridge, Cambridge University Press, 2015).

[22] Fabbrini (n 20).

[23] See, eg S Fabbrini, JE Fossum, M Gora and GE Wolff, 'The Conference on the Future of Europe: Vehicle for Reform Versus Forum for Reflection?' *Bruegel Blog* (June 2021), www.bruegel.org/2021/06/the-conference-on-the-future-of-europe-vehicle-for-reform-versus-forum-for-reflection. On post-Conference proposals by the institutions to pursue Treaty reform, see, eg P Blokker, 'Experimenting with European Democracy; Citizen-driven Treaty change and the Conference on the Future of Europe' *VerfBlog* 2022/6/21.

Looking beyond a Conference of quite limited constitutional ambition, and one that in any case has tended to be overshadowed by the crises that bookmarked its existence, how do we envisage the underlying dilemma playing out in the future? Two things are undeniable. On the one side, Europe has so far survived its progressive immersion in 'events-politics'[24] and the various existential threats this has brought. 'Eppur Esiste', as my colleague Cormac Mac Amhlaigh puts it.[25] We should not, therefore, underestimate the resilient strength of the Union's *Sonderweg*.[26] Its special emphasis on the more mundane design and purposive functions speak to a 'thin' version of constitutionalism that has long served it.[27]

On the other side, however, the various crises of recent years – of fiscal capacity and responsibility, of border security, of the rule of law and democracy, of membership of the Union, of public health and now of defence – all speak to the historical imbalance in the development of the Union's constitutional functionality. On the one hand, they all involve a tangible sense of an EU-wide 'shared predicament'[28] that would not have arisen in earlier decades. For it is only with the busy engagement of instrumental and purposive constitutional functions to develop a swathe of significant new institutional capacities and policy competences, in particular from the Treaty of Maastricht onwards, that these issues have begun to crystallise as common predicaments: that the question of the EU's responsibility for the mutualisation of debt and the redistribution of risks and resources arises; that the EU becomes an integrated Area of Freedom, Security and Justice with its own borders to regulate and population movements to monitor; that it assumes a measure of direct responsibility for the democratic credentials and legality standards of its members; that it becomes viewed as the kind of politically significant entity from which exit begins at least somewhat to resemble, in its material and reputational implications, secession from a sovereign state; that it can be understood as the lead player in the coordination of a transnational response to an unprecedented social emergency; and that it comes to be viewed as a geopolitically significant and militarily relevant entity in a globally ramified conflict. On the other hand, it is far from clear how well equipped the EU is to develop the common response that such shared predicaments would seem to invite. Rather, each of these can be seen to showcase and to underline unresolved questions of the degree of common

[24] For the contrast between the EU's traditional 'rules-politics' and its increasing engagement with 'events-politics', see L van Middelaar, *Pandemonium: Saving Europe* (Liz Waters trans, Newcastle, Agenda, 2021).

[25] C Mac Amhlaigh, 'Eppur Esiste!: Legitimacy and Longevity in the EU's Long Decade of Crisis', ch 9 below.

[26] JHH Weiler, 'In Defence of the Status Quo: Europe's Constitutional *Sonderweg*' in JHH Weiler and M Wind (eds), *European Constitutionalism beyond the State* (Cambridge, Cambridge University Press, 2003).

[27] See, eg P Craig, 'Constitutions, Constitutionalism and the European Union' (2001) 7 *European Law Journal* 125.

[28] N Walker, 'Europe's Constitutional Overture' in NW Barber, M Cahill and R Ekins (eds), *The Rise and Fall of the European Constitution* (Oxford, Hart Publishing, 2019) 177, 192.

cause that it is possible and desirable for the European states and citizenry to find. And, it should be added, many of the more robust rhetorical responses we hear from European leaders in acknowledgement of these new challenges, such as the recently renewed investment in an idea of European 'sovereignty' merely beg rather than answer the same questions.[29]

If this reminds us of how formidable the polity-building task remains, we should also recall the limits of any constitutional contribution. The lesson of the emergence of the modern state, lest we forget, is that the deeper work of polity generation often precedes the moment or phase of explicit constitutionalisation, and that the integrative function, and even more so the ontological function, associated with constitutionalisation should normally be understood more as reinforcing elements than as original factors.[30] Yet, even with the caveat that we should not expect too much of a constitutional rebalancing at the EU level, and that these deeper constitutional functions must always find traction in underlying social and political processes, it would seem collectively self-defeating to close off the constitutional route. For it remains difficult to see how satisfactory answers to the insistent questions about how and to what extent the EU should embrace its common predicaments can be found other than through a serious common engagement in both generating the effective means and determining the feasible limits of its integrative potential, and in addressing the related ontological question of the kind of polity the EU ought ultimately to become. To seek *in common* to resolve these questions of Europe's common path remains both the allure and the burden of the European constitution.[31]

[29] See in particular the 2017 Sorbonne speech of President Macron of France, 'New Initiative for Europe', 26 September 2017, www.elysee.fr. For discussion, see S Barbou des Places, 'Taking the Language of "European Sovereignty" Seriously' (2020) 5 *European Papers* 287; with early reference to developments in sovereignty discourse following the Russian invasion of Ukraine, see SR Larsen, 'Imagining Europe' *German Law Journal* (forthcoming).

[30] See, eg M Loughlin, 'What Is Constitutionalisation?' in P Dobner and M Loughlin (eds) *The Twilight of Constitutionalism?* (Oxford, Oxford University Press, 2010) 47.

[31] Central to any constitutional project of discovering what Europeans might resolve to put and to do in common that does not simply revert to a state-building enterprise is a requirement to supply a conception of Europe's constituent power, and the representation of that conception of constituent power in the constitution-making process, that moves beyond the unitary conception of 'the people' intrinsic to the statist model. This takes us to the terrain of the 'dual constituent power', introduced by Habermas as a way of respecting the joint role of the as yet 'unconstituted' European 'people' and the already constituted European states (and citizenries) in the construction of the European Union. See, eg J Habermas, 'Citizen and State Equality in a Supranational Political Community: Digressive Proportionality and the *Pouvoir Constituant Mixte*' (2017) 55 *Journal of Common Market Studies* 1781; see also M Patberg, *Constituent Power in the European Union* (Oxford, Oxford University Press, 2020); Walker (n 18).

# 3

# Common Values, Europe's Indeterminate Nature and Enduring Sovereignty

ALUN GIBBS

## I. Introduction

Does the articulation of common values in the European Union indicate the maturity of the post-state political form? Alternatively, are common values emblematic of the uncertainty or instability surrounding the question of 'political form'? These questions are at the centre of this chapter's investigation into the role of common values. The aim is to be able to offer an understanding of the connection between common values and the issues associated with the 'polity' construction of the European Union. Although common values have different sorts of functions with the wider institutional practice of the European Union and have been prominent in the juridical architecture of the Treaties and the jurisprudence of the Court of Justice, the argument developed here is that it is in the structural or constitutional – 'polity-building' – where we can locate more uncertainty as to the kind of role and contribution that common values can engender. Using common values in this kind of polity-building sense to enhance or develop the 'political form' of the European Union must be understood as a different kind of activity to the juridical one. Common values can provide a focal point for the development of collective sense of social solidarities and identity which enables the finding of novel forms of institutional understandings. In this sense, they can be understood as an aspect of the way that uncertainties over political form are acknowledged. However, this will require making common values work through concrete issues (crises) developing dialogue and authentic forms of common action. Does the European Union possess the deeper resources to look beyond both its market-driven politics and the tendency to draw from the state tradition in order to cultivate common values that are capable of sustaining commitment to a common political life? The answer is unclear, but this is the terrain upon which the European Union will need to stake its constitutional future.

The first part of this chapter looks at the emergence of common values as an important plank of the post-documentary approach to legitimacy and governance in the European Union. In this phase, common values can be articulated in terms of three dimensions: a juridical standard; an aspect of membership that the European Union shares values with a liberal state tradition; and finally, as constitutional values. Overall, common values aim to give determinacy to the European Union as an emerging site of governance beyond the state. However, the second and third parts of this chapter consider the question of political form and sovereignty in order to argue that the legitimacy problems facing the European Union are complex and cannot straightforwardly be resolved by appeal to common values.

## II. Europe's Common Values

References to the common values of the European Union take shape as political and legal integration acquires a degree of maturity. Stephen Weatherill outlines how the original Treaty of Rome in 1957, in its preamble, contained the aspirational goal of an 'ever closer union', but that the main focus of the subsequent Treaty Articles was not so much the articulation of governing common values but the general parameters of 'economic activity' in the common market.[1] A fundamental transformation can be traced if we accelerate to the Lisbon Treaty of 2009.[2] Common values form a central plank of the post-Constitutional Treaty reform, whereby formal legal measures become a focal aspect of augmenting the legitimacy of the European Union. With the maturity of the political project, we find that common values have acquired a central significance and have moved beyond the theme of economic activity within the architecture of the internal market. Article 2 TEU locates the European Union as a values-based or 'values driven'[3] system, articulating a commitment to 'the values of respect for human dignity, freedom, democracy, equality, the rule of law and respect for human rights'.[4] Allied to this, the European Union indicates that these commitments to foundational values are indeed common or shared as they have a common origin in the emergence of *modern* constitutionalism in the state tradition: 'these values are common to the Member States in a society in which pluralism, non-discrimination, tolerance, justice, solidarity and equality between women and men prevail'.[5]

[1] S Weatherill, *Law and Values in the European Union* (Oxford, Oxford University Press, 2016) 393.
[2] For a more detailed treatment of the historical trajectory of common values in the EU founding Treaties, see ch 4 of this volume.
[3] Weatherill (n 1) 394.
[4] Consolidated Version of the Treaty on European Union [2012] OJ C326, Art 2.
[5] ibid.

Although Article 2 might seem to be a symbolic articulation of the common values that are pledged to future EU governance, it is nevertheless apparent that it sits within a sophisticated juridical architecture which looks to establish enforceable general principles of European law. Article 6 TEU directs and recognises the rights, freedoms and principles set out in the Charter of Fundamental Rights and is given legal effect through the CJEU.[6] In addition, Article 7 TEU sets out an enforcement mechanism by which sufficiently serious breaches will be subject to sanction against a Member State. It is in this *juridical* dimension that common values might credibly be seen to have the most practical impact – in encountering the crises in Poland and Hungary, the European Union institutions have engaged in the legal enforcement of common values – particularly in relation to rule-of-law standards and the independence of the judiciary.[7] In two important recent judgments, the Court of Justice of the European Union (CJEU) has reinforced the view that the common values outlined in Article 2 are foundational to and underly the nature of the European Union as a political and legal project, and as such acquire normative force.[8] As the Court phrased it, 'the European Union must be able to defend those values, within the limits of its powers as laid down by the Treaties',[9] and rejected a submission by Hungary and Poland that the common values articulated in Article 2 could not be clearly identified so as to make them enforceable. Whilst the common values of the European Union enjoy a juridical pedigree from the Treaties, the judgments make it clear that the normative force of common values derives from their underlying character – the fact these are embedded in the historical enfolding of the experience of political life in the European Union. This is a significant matter and opens a way of exploring common values beyond the juridical claims.

The CJEU has emphasised that the fundamental constitutional values of the European Union are shared and can be derived from the Member States' traditions.[10] Common values are understood to be part of claims of *membership* in the sense that maintaining that a political entity is committed to the practice of modern constitutionalism entails the articulation of a set of common values which are presupposed to be an integral aspect of this tradition. This is further exemplified in the way that human rights[11] have emerged as an increasingly significant part

[6] Case C-617/10 *Åklagaren v Hans Åkerberg Fransson* ECLI:EU:C:2013:105, [2013] ECR I-0000.

[7] Z Körtvélyesi, 'The Illiberal Challenge in the EU: Exploring the Parallel with Illiberal Minorities and the Example of Hungary' (2020) 16 *European Constitutional Law Review* 567; L Pech and KL Scheppele, 'Illiberalism Within: Rule of Law Backsliding in the EU' (2017) 19 *Cambridge Yearbook of European Legal Studies* 3; A Sajó, *The Emergence of the Illiberal State: Ruling by Cheating: Governance in Illiberal Democracy* (Cambridge, Cambridge University Press, 2021).

[8] Case C-156/21 *Hungary v Parliament and Council* ECLI:EU:C:2022:97; Case C-157/21 *Poland v Parliament and Council* ECLI:EU:C:2022:98.

[9] ibid para 145.

[10] Case 29/69 *Stauder v City of Ulm – Sozialamt* EU:C:1969:57, [1969] ECR 419; Case 4/73 *J Nold, Kohlen-und Baustoffgrosshandlung v Commission* ECLI:EU:C:1974:51, [1974] ECR 507.

[11] A von Bogdandy, 'The European Union as a Human Rights Organization? Human Rights and the Core of the European Union' (2000) 37 *CML Rev* 1307; L Betten and N Grief, *EU Law and Human Rights* (Harlow, Longman Publishing, 1998).

not only of the Treaty commitments, but also in the jurisprudence of the CJEU.[12] In this way, we might observe that common values are akin to 'calling cards' – part of claiming that democratic governance and modern constitutional practice are integral to the credentials of the European Union as a maturing governing space.

Both the 'juridical' and 'membership' dimensions of common values can also be indicative of a maturing confidence about how values fit or are integral to a common constitutional space[13] at the European level. That common values can also be understood as *constitutional* values demonstrates a connection to the idea of a common European legal and institutional space framed by democratic solidarities or commitments (*demos*) that are an aspect of values as 'polity building'.[14] The lack of a European-level *demos* has been cited as a factor in the question of the European Union's political legitimacy,[15] and has in part stemmed from the way that the *demos* is often framed around the national homogeneous solidarities – linguistic, cultural, religious, for example.[16] Conceiving common values as part of the constitutionalising of the European Union can be seen, therefore, as a way to meet the 'no *demos*' charge, the argument being that shared fundamental political and social values are a means of putting things in common so as to underpin the emergence of the constitutional space at the European Union level even in the absence of the kind of homogeneous solidarities that have framed the national polity.

In this section, we have explored three ways in which common values in the European Union can be viewed as the unfolding of a stable and mature political form at the post-state level: first, they can be used as a juridical device to ensure overall Member State allegiance; they can also be seen as a commitment to constitutional values in order to counter the argument that democratic legitimacy stems from the 'thick' social solidarities exhibited in the nation as a political form; finally, they can be presented as membership – a presupposition that the maturing governance practices of the European Union must be based on the shared values which have underpinned the Member States as modern constitutional democracies. These ways of considering common values are interlocking and related to the extent that common values aim to give determinacy (or at least answer a claim to indeterminacy) to the European Union as an emerging site of governance beyond the state. How successful this can be is analysed in the next section.

[12] Most importantly emphasised in Joined Cases C-402/05 P and C-415/05, *P Kadi and Al Barakaat International Foundation v Council and Commission* EU:C:2008:461, [2008] ECR I-6351.

[13] MW Gehring, *Europe's Second Constitution: Crisis, Courts and Community* (Cambridge, Cambridge University Press, 2020) ch 4.

[14] N Walker, 'In Search of the Area of Freedom, Security and Justice: A Constitutional Odyssey' in Walker (ed), *Europe's Area of Freedom, Security, and Justice* (Oxford, Oxford University Press, 2004), which highlighted the importance of the role of values and polity building in the creation of the area of freedom, security and justice in the Amsterdam Treaty.

[15] See, eg *Maastricht-Urteil* [1994] CMLR 57; the 'Lisbon Judgment', *Bundesverfassungsgericht*, Second Senate of 30 June 2009 in Joint Cases 2 BvE 2/08, 2BvE 5/08, 2 BvR 1010/08, 2BvR 1022/08, 2 BvR 1259/08 and 2 BvR 182/09 (Lisbon Treaty).

[16] D Grimm, *Constitutionalism: Past and Present* (Oxford, Oxford University Press, 2016).

## III. Uncertainty of Political Form and Sovereignty

One of the important constitutional assumptions underlying the reliance on European common values is that these foundational principles allow the institutional structure or framework to develop, perhaps in response to differing crises,[17] in order to vindicate wider legitimacy claims about the European Union. With common values in place and accepted, institutional practice and reform to augment the constitutional space will follow.

A prominent counter argument to this rests on the claim that the European Union's common values are 'too thin', in the sense that it lacks the social prerequisites for a kind of democratic legitimation in the state.[18] Above all, this kind of argument is about the uncertainty of whether common values that have their roots in the 'national' political form are readily applicable to the European Union. Shared solidarities are complex, and it is difficult to sustain a plausible case that the common values can *never* vindicate the deeper feelings of 'commonality' that can sustain something like the legitimation of institutional or constitutional practice in the European Union. For many, the recent illustration that in the midst of the Ukraine War the President of Ukraine sought to make a formal application for membership provided a potent illustration that European Union common values can and do carry an existential weight.[19]

It is possible, however, that a more challenging question emerges from the articulation of common values in the European Union which would be along the lines of how does the assertion of common values fit (and do they?) as part of wider discussions about the *sovereignty*? What this raises is not directly how the common values that might legitimate the various kinds of governing or institutional practices at the European Union level can achieve this; instead, the question concerns whether common values resolve the instability or uncertainty over 'political form'. This term requires some measure of unpacking, and particularly needs focused attention around the relationship between sovereignty and legitimacy.

Political form means the ability to shape and configure the fundamental structures and meanings that determine collective political life.[20] As indicated in Pierre

[17] J Habermas, *The Lure of Technocracy* (Cambridge, Polity Press, 2015); G Ross *The European Union and Its Crises through the Eyes of the Brussels' Elite* (London, Palgrave Macmillan, 2011); O Cramm and S Hobolt (eds), *Democratic Politics in a European Union under Stress* (Oxford, Oxford University Press, 2014); J White, *Politics of Last Resort Governing by Emergency in the European Union* (Oxford, Oxford University Press, 2019); M Dawson, H Enderlein and C Joerges, *Beyond the Crisis: The Governance of Europe's Economic, Political and Legal Transformation* (Oxford, Oxford University Press, 2015); J Lawrence, 'The EU in Crisis: Crisis Discourse as a Technique of Government' (2014) 44 *Netherlands Yearbook of International Law* 187; L Spieker, 'Breathing Life into the Union's Common Values: On the Judicial Application of Article 2 TEU in the EU Value Crisis' (2019) 20 *German Law Journal* 1182.

[18] Grimm (n 16) 293.

[19] Heads of state of the European Union gave a symbolic commitment indicating that 'Ukraine belongs to our European family', informal meeting of heads of state or government, Versailles, 10–11 March 2022, www.consilium.europa.eu/en/meetings/european-council/2022/03/10-11/.

[20] For accounts of political form, see N Gibbs, 'Post-Sovereignty and the European Legal Space' (2017) 80 *MLR* 812; P Manent, *An Intellectual History of Liberalism* (New Haven, Yale University Press,

Manent's work on political theory, political form is akin to a vessel by which the meaning and practice that constitute collective political life, or the civic association, take shape: city, empire, nation state – these are illustrations of political form. As Nathan Gibbs points out, in the context of examining political form and the European Union, political form can be understood as shaped by two principal dynamics of human agency in the formation of collective political life: *historicity* and *finitude*. The former develops an understanding that the background, social narrative and context determine how we understand the legitimacy of emerging political form, the latter that questions of legitimacy of the political form are not determined at the outset, but are both embedded in the social practice of a civic association and require a commitment to the *open-ended* nature of the formation of collective political life (that is to say, the type of political form exhibited).

Uncertainty over political form in the EU can be traced to the difficulties with understanding claims about sovereignty. In 1992, Neil MacCormick gave the Chorley Lecture, in which he outlined the 'post-sovereign' way to understand claims of legal authority, creating in the process a much broader school of thought in EU scholarship – constitutional pluralism.[21] What is interesting about MacCormick's work is the certainty that what must be confronted with the deepening integration of the EU is what is 'beyond the sovereign state'.[22] As Wilkinson explores, recent crises at both national and Union level have placed significant doubts on any assertion that debate has moved beyond the sovereignty paradigm:

> [W]hat begins at Maastricht as a set of mere irritants grows through the euro crisis phase into a full-blown crisis of post-sovereignty and of constitutional pluralism. Sovereignty claims now re-emerge both 'from below', in regard to the so-called 'populist' surge in the nation-state (in the core of Europe as well as in the periphery) and 'from above' [in the EUs response to various crises].[23]

What is compelling in Wilkinson's analysis of the problem is that MacCormick's work on constitutional pluralism and moving beyond the sovereign state created a truncated picture of sovereignty, in that it leaned towards a view of ultimate claims of legal authority within a largely positivist methodological framework.[24]

1996); P Manent, *A World Beyond Politics?* (New Haven, Yale University Press, 2006); for a similar idea of a political regime, see A Gibbs, 'The Horizons of the Constitution: Politeia, the Political Regime and the Good' (2016) 27 *Law and Critique* 83.

[21] For an overview, see M Avbelj and J Komárek (eds), *Constitutional Pluralism in the EU and Beyond* (Oxford, Hart Publishing, 2012).

[22] N MacCormick, 'Beyond the Sovereign State' (1993) 56 *MLR* 1: 'On this view, our passing beyond the sovereign state is to be considered a good thing, an entirely welcome development in the history of legal and political ideas.'

[23] M Wilkinson, 'Beyond the Post-Sovereign State?: The Past, Present, and Future of Constitutional Pluralism' (2019) 21 *Cambridge Yearbook of European Legal Studies* 6.

[24] ibid 8.

The consequence is the suppression of a *political* conception of sovereignty, where this is understood in terms of the material conditions of the political constitution,[25]

> the formation of polity unity in conditions of plurality, various and competing institutions and their relative strengths and weaknesses, the solidity or fragility of social relations, and the various and conflicting political objectives pursued by the European polity and Member States.[26]

Whether we focus on the 'material' conditions of the political constitution or the question of 'political form', the diagnosis is a similar one: namely, the apparent suppression, and therefore destabilisation, of a political sense of sovereignty becomes part of a wider crisis of legitimacy in the EU.[27]

The legitimacy crisis of the European Union rests upon a stable means of shaping and configuring the fundamental structures and meanings that determine collective political life – that is, a stable 'political form'. A principal challenge has been the problem of sovereignty. As legal authority, it has been unstable, as competing claims of sovereign determination are made at Member State and European level and the attempt to shift the focus to post-sovereignty has been inconclusive. A plausible mode of inquiry, following that developed by Wilkinson, is to understand the modalities of the political conception of sovereignty, which has often been sidelined in discussions that have focused on a legalistic picture of sovereignty. Taking the inquiry in the direction of considering political sovereignty, the connection with political form becomes clearer.

## IV. Enduring Sovereignty – Sovereignty and Political Form

Recent scholarship in constitutional theory – looking in particular at the historical foundations of the modern state[28] – reveals the complex ways in which sovereignty must be seen in a 'political' sense and as bound up with the historicity and finitude of the emergence of the state as a distinct 'political form'. Early secular conceptions of public authority in the state broke with the theological and hierarchical claims of legitimacy of the medieval church and the kingship – the so-called politico-theological problem.[29] To achieve this transformation

[25] M Goldoni and M Wilkinson, 'The Material Constitution' (2018) 81 *MLR* 567.
[26] Ibid; Wilkinson (n 23) 13.
[27] M Wilkinson, 'Authoritarian Liberalism in the European Constitutional Imagination: Second Time as Farce?' (2015) 21 *European Law Journal* 313 – where economic liberalism pursues technocratic rather than democratic ends.
[28] See, eg M Loughlin, *Foundations of Public Law* (Oxford, Oxford University Press, 2010); D Lee, *Popular Sovereignty in Early Modern Constitutional Thought* (Oxford, Oxford University Press, 2016); D Lee, *The Right of Sovereignty, Jean Bodin on the Sovereign State and the Law of Nations* (Oxford, Oxford University Press, 2021).
[29] Manent, *An Intellectual History of Liberalism* (n 20).

of political authority required a complex modification of the juridical framework of natural law – away from its rootedness in the Aristotelian notion of human nature as communal towards the view that human nature was solitary and required the artifice of political authority for security.[30] Equally important was the emergence of the field of politics in its own right, as the practice and maintenance of the state, the 'Machiavellian moment'.[31] Out of these efforts, an essentially absolute idea of political authority emerged – a sovereign and also a unit of the political 'the state'.

Martin Loughlin traces this history of sovereignty to its early modern foundations, and highlights a key figure for particular attention – Jean Bodin.[32] In Bodin, we find a distinction between government and sovereignty[33] that becomes central to subsequent writers about the state. For Bodin, a sovereign people can delegate its sovereignty to form an apparatus of governing whilst retaining the original source of sovereignty during moments of crisis of government.[34] In the *Methodus*, Bodin provides a historical perspective to point out that we cannot hope to get at what sovereignty means simply by examining the governmental and institutional practices of different regimes of power. What is required is to look behind this power (the *imperium* behind the *imperium*). For Bodin, sovereignty becomes a higher-order power in the conceptualisation of the state, a kind of power that is necessary in order for the state to exist and persist or endure through changes to its governmental form. In this way, sovereignty can be understood to 'carve out' the boundaries of an autonomous space in which collective political life can develop, endure over time and account for the ultimate legitimacy upon which the governing apparatus rests. By ensuring that political sovereignty guarantees the autonomy of the political, it provides a stable basis for the political form (of the state).

Deliberately or otherwise, the political form of the modern state constituted a significant background to the formulation of the political conception of sovereignty in the EU. Possibly the clearest illustration is also the most well known, and concerns the juridical statements of the nature of the sovereign legal order of the European Union in the early case law of the CJEU. Alongside the claims of the 'new legal order'[35] and the legal relationships that flow from it is an assertion about the political nature of sovereignty that echoes the formulation of the political form in the state, in particular the finitude of sovereignty in its unlimited duration:

> By creating a community of unlimited duration, having its own institutions, its own personality, its own legal capacity and capacity of representation on the international

[30] ibid.

[31] C Lefort, *Machiavelli in the Making* (Evanston, Northwestern University Press, 2012)

[32] Loughlin (n 28) 56–62.

[33] This distinction becomes in time the constituent and constituted power idea in the 18th century. For a comprehensive history, see L Rubinelli, *Constituent Power: A History* (Cambridge, Cambridge University Press, 2020).

[34] Lee, *Popular Sovereignty in Early Modern Constitutional Thought* (n 28).

[35] Case 26-62 *NV Algemene Transport- en Expeditie Onderneming van Gend & Loos v Netherlands Inland Revenue Administration* ECLI:EU:C:1963:1, [1963] ECR 1.

> plane and, more particularly, real powers stemming from a limitation of sovereignty or a transfer of powers from the states to the community, the member states have limited their sovereign rights, albeit within limited fields, and have thus created a body of law which binds both their nationals and themselves.[36]

*Costa*'s formulation of sovereignty echoes that early modern development of the political conception of sovereignty. We can see the drawing of a contrast, a distinction between government institutions and practices and the political sovereignty upon which this rests. It is also possible to find in this passage the notion of the unlimited duration of the political form, resembling closely Bodin's meaning, in the sense of a delegation by Member States of the primary 'political' kind of sovereignty. Hence, it is possible to suggest that formulation expresses the *existence of a constitutional order through time*, which is of unlimited duration, because it is a political grant of sovereignty rather than merely juridical. It is an unexpected and indeed unstable assertion. The Court of Justice is borrowing from the state constitutional tradition an idea of political sovereignty in the shape of a claim to unlimited duration, but without a robust understanding or space for the emergence of the political form in the European Union. Of course, it is not this single judgment of the CJEU that sets in motion the crises of legitimacy associated with the polity-building dimension of the European Union. However, the language used becomes illustrative of the wider and deeper confusions of thinking over sovereignty and political form which gather over time and arguably reach a zenith with the efforts at a documentary constitution in 2005.[37] It is this unstable tension between a claim of political sovereignty and the indeterminacy of political form that causes the turn towards articulating a space of common values. In the final part of the chapter, I outline some concluding thoughts as to whether or not the reliance on common values provides a meaningful way past these problems.

## V. Conclusion: Do Common Values Hold the Answer?

Whilst the European Union articulates a political sense of sovereignty based on the state constitutional tradition, it is also axiomatic that this rests, as indicated in the previous section, on the uncertain foundation of political form. The political form of the unified state is unable to assuage wider legitimacy concerns in the European Union and, as we have analysed, the 'post-sovereignty' of legal or juristic authority has also not led to a stabilisation of political form. Returning to the central theme of the chapter – common values – it might be prudent now to ask whether the gradual development and strengthening of the political and legal importance of 'common values' might be viewed as a means to gradually

[36] Case 6-64 *Flaminio Costa v ENEL* ECLI:EU:C:1964:66, [1964] ECR 585.
[37] Draft Treaty Establishing a Constitution for Europe [2003] OJ C169.

augment the forms of political solidarity of the European Union and to develop a common constitutional space which might answer the uncertainty of political form.

Whereas 'common values' augment the legitimacy of the formal institutional and integration governance of the European Union in the ways outlined earlier in the chapter, it is difficult to assert that common values alone can resolve the deeper kind of legitimacy crisis associated with uncertainty over 'political form'. This does not mean 'common values' are not important to this dimension. Recalling that political form is the human agency involved in shaping and configuring the fundamental structures and meanings that determine collective political life, common values can provide a focal point for the development of a collective sense of social solidarities and identity which enables the finding of novel forms of institutional understandings. Doing so requires the use of common values to work through concrete issues (crises) developing dialogue and authentic forms of common action – different from the understanding of common values as juridical/legal standards.

Among the many challenges this strategy faces, one of the clearest is that common values have intentionally been construed around the state constitutional tradition – shared values derived from Member States. Locating and developing distinct common values that are shared because they derive from the shared political experience at the level of the European Union will require imagination, dialogue and reflection. A second consequence follows from this: in order to understand how shared political experience can lead to common values, it will be necessary to conceive how the political commitments in the European Union can be broader than the market-centred politics and functional instrumentalism that accompanies questions of governance.

The new deliberative, albeit constitutionally silent, project of the European Union, the Conference on the Future of Europe, has been launched with the explicit intention of reflecting on the historical evolution of the Union and fostering the distinct solidarities upon which the future depends.[38] There was acknowledgement that the conference took place against a backdrop of crises – which, in the first place, has raised different types of legitimacy concerns for the European Union, but has equally prompted functional questions about delivery for citizens. As explored in this chapter, the common values sit within a 'wider' legitimacy crisis, which revolves around the form of the polity itself. The commitment in the Future of Europe is to a bottom-up process of citizen consultation. It is hoped that the conscious efforts to move beyond the elite-driven process of constitutional legitimation that characterised the previous efforts 20 years ago will lead to developing dialogue and authentic forms of common action.

[38] Joint Declaration of the European Parliament, the Council and the European Commission on the Conference on the Future of Europe Engaging with citizens for democracy – Building a more resilient Europe [2021] OJ C91I.

# 4

# Values, Constitutionalism and the Viability of European Integration

MATEJ AVBELJ

## I. Introduction

This chapter examines the question of impact of common values on the viability of European integration and the role of constitutionalism, as a discourse of imagination and conceptualisation,[1] in it. It is a large question that, even before taking it up, requires some clarification and a narrowing of focus. Our theoretical assumptions should therefore be spelled out first. We proceed from the hypothesis that any form of social cooperation requires some sort of agreement, either explicit or implicit, on the conditions for starting the cooperation, for conducting the cooperation and about the outcomes the cooperation should ideally result in. These conditions are typically set because those engaged in a particular form of social cooperation find them of value. They are thus value-based conditions – in other words, the common values of cooperation.[2] As they are present at three different stages of cooperation – at its input, throughput and output – they are hereinafter labelled as input, throughput and output values of cooperation.

Our second hypothesis is that the values of cooperation, their type and the degree of their actual presence or absence influence the viability of cooperation. Under the notion of viability of cooperation can be understood the capacity of cooperation to actually get going, its capacity to last and finally to achieve, as much as possible, the object and purpose for which it has been created. If a form of cooperation runs short of delivering on its anticipated outcomes, if, in its daily operation, it does not comply with the preset standards and if those who cooperate no longer comply with the conditions that had been set for their cooperation so that the input, throughput and output values are in decline, undermined or even

[1] JHH Weiler and JP Trachtman, 'European Constitutionalism and Its Discontents' (1996–97) 17 *Northwestern Journal of International Law and Business* 354, 359.

[2] C Callies, 'Europe as Transnational Law – the Transnationalisation of Values by European Law' (2009) 10 *German Law Journal* 1367, 1381, noting that 'integration depends on values'.

inexistent, the viability of cooperation decreases too. Finally, my third hypothesis is that while the viability of cooperation is thus also, but not exclusively, dependent on the existence of common input, throughput and output values, the degree of existence of these values as well as their content and type, ie what kind of values these should be, hinges on the intensity of a given form of social cooperation. The more intense a cooperation, the greater the need for common-value foundations across all three domains of cooperation: input, throughput and output. And vice versa, of course.

The chapter thus builds against the backdrop of these three abstract hypotheses, to focus concretely on the viability of European integration and the impact of common values thereof. The process of European integration is an example of an intense form of social cooperation not just between individuals, but also between the states. Furthermore, the intensity of cooperation inside the process of European integration has increased over the years, which has in turn also required widening and deepening of the shared-value foundations. However, as the shared-value foundations were about to widen and deepen, profound value fissures between the North and the South, but in particular between the West and the East, have emerged as a disadvantage of the integration's viability.

Today, the EU is going through a difficult time, with the deepening of the integration requiring increasingly solid common-value grounds, which have, however, in recent years been weakened instead. The challenge, both theoretical and practical, that the EU is facing is thus how to close the value gap to meet the demands of a progressing integration. Possible strategies include: strengthening the common values for more integration; rolling the integration back to fit the actual limited scope of common values; or investing in variable geometry to adapt the depth and breadth of the integration to the existing value variations between the Member States while preserving the Union as a whole. In short, the question that poses itself is: how much and which values ought to be shared at a particular stage of integration? And, related to that, taking into account the existing actual scope of common values, how much integration can the EU actually afford?

Our argument shall, accordingly, proceed as follows. First, we will study the historical trajectory of European integration in order to examine how the deepening and widening of the integration process, in which the very character of the integration has been transformed, has impacted on the degree of required shared-value foundations, as well as how the need for such foundations has affected the dynamics of the integration process. Secondly, having conducted the historical analysis, we will concentrate on the present in order to describe and understand the contemporary value fissures in the European Union. This reflection will allow me, in the third step, to turn to the future in order to examine the viability of the three visions of the future of the EU – the status quo vision, the status quo ante vision and the reformist vision – in light of the existing or required shared-valued foundations. Finally, the chapter will conclude by examining the appropriateness and utility of couching the presented theoretical, and above all practical, dilemmas of the relationship between common values and the viability of European integration in a constitutional language. Can constitutionalism, as a discourse of imagination and conceptualisation,[3] be used as a vehicle for striking an integration–value balance that will contribute to the viability of the European Union?

## II. Historical Value-Based Trajectory of European Integration

This section studies the evolution of the proclaimed common values of the European Union by concentrating on the texts of the founding treaties and of the solemn declarations that were issued by the leaders of the EU or its institutions when the latter reached important, symbolic milestones. The values will be analysed following the above-proposed theoretical scheme differentiating between input, throughput and output values. The input values are the values that are set as a precondition for entering the integration process. They typically require a certain quality on behalf of the candidate states and their commitment to specific ideals that the integration shall personify. The throughput values are the values that guide the EU decision-making process *lato sensu*. Finally, the output values are the goals and objectives for which the EU has been created and which ought to be maximised to the greatest possible extent.

Our analysis inevitably starts with the Schuman Declaration of 9 May 1950, which is in symbolical terms the founding act of the integration. As such, it has also provided a profound value basis for the process of integration that it sought to launch.[4] The emphasis of the Schuman Declaration, however, has almost entirely rested on the output, and to a much lesser extent on the throughput values of the integration. The input values were only implicit at best. As the main output value of the integration according to the Schuman Declaration was the assurance of lasting peace, the only input value-based requirement, which was again no more than implicit in the logic of the desired output, was that all participating countries be peace-loving nations. Beyond that, the Schuman Declaration failed to posit any other input value requirement. As indicated, its value orientation was predominantly directed towards the output values, among which lasting peace was an independent output value, an innate value in whose function there was another output value: the economic value of a rising living standard. The Schuman Declaration thus set up the integration process essentially as a utilitarian project that was geared to the amelioration of the economic situation across Europe, which would, in turn, contribute to lasting peace. The main throughput value that should steer this process was a value of solidarity, which was admittedly stipulated both as a means as well as a goal of the integration. The conventional

[3] Weiler and Trachtman (n 1).

[4] Schuman Declaration, https://european-union.europa.eu/principles-countries-history/history-eu/1945-59/schuman-declaration-may-1950_en.

international relationship between the participating states was to be complemented by a supranational element in the form of the High Authority, which was set up to act independently, promoting not national interests, but the interests of the newly established supranational community that could, incrementally, through concrete steps and across a larger time span, lead to the creation of a European federation.[5]

The first founding treaty of European integration, the Treaty Establishing the European Coal and Steel Community, *in toto* reflected the value framework stipulated by the Schuman Declaration. Its conception of the integration was thus utilitarian and economic, in which the economic means contributed to peace through concrete steps of cooperation between the participating states, without prescribing almost any input and throughput values. These initial, relatively shallow value foundations of European integration were importantly enriched six years later, with the adoption of the Treaty Establishing the European Economic Community. Its value orientation remained utilitarian, directed towards economic output in the form of a constant improvement of the living and working conditions of individuals to which the creation the common market should contribute.[6] However, the economic values were also complemented by political values, which were reflected in the determination of laying down the foundations for an ever closer union between the peoples of Europe.[7] Furthermore, the paramount output value of peace was joined by the value of liberty, and both were also used as input values as the Treaty explicitly called on other nations of Europe that partake of the two values to join in the common effort.[8]

Thirty years later, in the first truly noteworthy amendment to the founding treaties brought about by the Single European Act,[9] the value foundations were deepened yet further. While the emphasis remained on the output values, where the exclusively economic outputs were newly joined by the requirement of social cohesion and environmental protection, and the commitment to the ever closer union was strengthened in the explicit pursuit of the European unity,[10] the real change was made at the level of the throughput and output values. In their functioning, the European Communities were to promote democracy, respect human rights and ensure compliance with the law. An explicit reference was also made to the democratic peoples of Europe. In so doing, the values of democracy, human rights protection and the rule of law gradually crept in as preconditions for the integration's functioning as input values, as well as values that the Communities should observe in their own functioning (throughput values).

[5] ibid.

[6] Treaty establishing the European Economic Community, https://eur-lex.europa.eu/legal-content/FR/TXT/PDF/?uri=CELEX:11957E/TXT&from=EN.

[7] ibid.

[8] ibid.

[9] Single European Act [1987] OJ L169.

[10] ibid Art 1.

The described value deepening was by no means coincidental. It was prompted by the judicial dialogue between the Court of Justice of the European Union (CJEU) and the national constitutional courts addressing the fact the European founding treaties initially did not contain any provision on the protection of fundamental human rights,[11] while at the same time the CJEU had already developed the doctrine of primacy of EU law, requiring that EU law takes precedence over national laws. As EU law was thus not bound by human rights protection standards, national laws were permeated by human rights norms that, to quote the German Federal Constitutional Court, 'incorporate an objective scale of values which applies, as a matter of constitutional law, throughout the entire legal system'.[12] As a result of this discrepancy in human rights protection between EU law and national law, the former's primacy over the latter became jeopardised. The national constitutional courts namely conditioned the primacy of EU law by the latter's protection of human rights, which would be comparable to the national standards.[13] The CJEU thus had to react, so it moved to develop unwritten EU standards of human rights protection to fill the then existing textual void in EU law. Accordingly, following the established jurisprudence of the CJEU, starting with its decision in *Nold*:[14]

> Fundamental rights form an integral part of the general principles of law, observance of which [the Court] ensures. For that purpose, the Court draws inspiration from the constitutional traditions common to the Member States and from the guidelines supplied by international treaties for the protection of human rights on which the Member States have collaborated or of which they are signatories … The European Convention on Human Rights (ECHR) has special significance in that respect.

This anything but uncontroversial jurisprudential development in the hands of the CJEU was supported by the Member States and the then Community institutions, which adopted a number of soft law instruments aimed at proclaiming and safeguarding human rights and other shared values of the European Union. In a Declaration on European Identity, adopted by the then nine Member States in 1973, the core elements of European identity were identified in the protection of the principles of representative democracy, the rule of law, social justice and the respect for human rights. These were stipulated both as throughput and input values to which the economic progress, as the original output value, was declared

[11] JHH Weiler, 'Methods of Protection: Towards a Second and Third Generation of Protection' in Cassese et al (eds), *Human Rights and the European Community: Methods of Protection* (Baden-Baden, Nomos, 1991) 555.

[12] Case *Lüth*, BVerfGE 7, 198, para 1: 'eine objektive Wertordnung, die als verfassungsrechtliche Grundentscheidung für alle Bereiche des Rechts gilt'.

[13] Case *Solange I*, BVerfGE 37, 291, 29 May 1974.

[14] Case 29/69 *Stauder v City of Ulm – Sozialamt* EU:C:1969:57, [1969] ECR 419; Case 11/70 *Internationale Handelsgesellschaft mbH v Einfuhr- und Vorratsstelle für Getreide und Futtermittel* EU:C:1970:114, [1970] ECR 1125; Case 4/73 *J Nold, Kohlen- und Baustoffgrosshandlung v Commission* ECLI:EU:C:1974:51, [1974] ECR 507.

as instrumental.[15] While preserving the maintenance of peace as the essential output value of the integration,[16] the output value of the united Europe was specifically pointed out too. It was portrayed as a building block of European civilisation, whose essential part is also the diversity of European cultures,[17] which ought to be preserved in its rich variety.[18] Europe should also engage closely, and preferably with one voice, with the outside world, which adds cosmopolitanism to the catalogue of the EU throughput values.[19]

In 1977, the European Parliament, the Council and the Commission, in a joint declaration, explicitly confirmed that human rights, as protected in the jurisprudence of the CJEU, are and will continue to be respected by the European Communities and their institutions.[20] Human rights have thus ever since been legally and politically turned into the central throughput values of the integration, as standards that guide the functioning of the European institutions. The political deepening and widening of the common values, however, reached climaxes in 1984 and 1989, with the adoption, first, of the draft European Union Treaty and, second, of a Resolution on Fundamental Rights and a Declaration of Fundamental Rights and Freedoms. These documents were non-binding, programmatic acts adopted by the European Parliament whose content fully anticipated, and was in many ways also verbatim incorporated into, the Treaty on European Union as adopted in Maastricht and amended in Amsterdam, Nice and finally Lisbon, including the Charter of Fundamental Rights, which was finally made binding in 2009.

Since the mid-1980s politically and since 1993 in a binding legal manner, the initially shallow shared-value foundations of European integration gave way to a comprehensive framework of input, throughput and output values of the EU. Article 2 TEU, which today enumerates the common values of the EU, has thus had a decades-long period of gestation and is an outcome of a deliberate process involving cooperation and full commitment on behalf of the Member States and the supranational institutions. Today, accordingly:

> The Union is founded on the values of respect for human dignity, freedom, democracy, equality, the rule of law and respect for human rights, including the rights of persons belonging to minorities. These values are common to the Member States in a society in which pluralism, non-discrimination, tolerance, justice, solidarity and equality between women and men prevail.[21]

[15] Declaration on European Identity (Copenhagen, 14 December 1973) para 1, www.cvce.eu/content/publication/1999/1/1/02798dc9-9c69-4b7d-b2c9-f03a8db7da32/publishable_en.pdf.

[16] ibid para 1.

[17] ibid para 3.

[18] ibid para 1.

[19] ibid part II.

[20] Joint Declaration by the European Parliament, the Council and the Commission concerning the Protection of Fundamental Rights and the ECHR [1977] OJ C103.

[21] Consolidated Version of the Treaty on European Union [2012] OJ C326, Art 2.

The common values contained in Article 2 TEU are the alpha and omega of the integration, and at the same time they set the standards for its functioning. Drawing from the cultural, religious and humanist inheritance of Europe, these common European values have become universal and stand as a source of inviolable and inalienable rights of the human person.[22] By way of the Copenhagen criteria,[23] adopted in 1993, the respect of these values is also one of the key criteria for accession to the EU. First envisaged in the 1984 Draft Treaty on European Union, since the Treaty of Amsterdam in 1997, the EU law also provides for a sanctioning mechanism in case these common values come under a systemic threat or are actually systemically undermined in the Member States.[24]

The value of peace has remained a paramount output value from the very beginning of the integration process to the present day. The same role is played by the value of 'an ever closer union', which has been pursued since 1957 while observing the principle of subsidiarity and paying heed to the national identities of the Member States. All these common values, contained in the legally binding founding treaties, have been repeatedly confirmed in solemn political declarations, such as the Berlin Declaration,[25] marking the fiftieth anniversary of the Treaty of Rome, and the Rome Declaration 10 years later.[26] The EU has thus matured into a community of values. The current president of the European Commission, Ursula von der Leyen, described these 'great European values' as being 'part of our soul, part of what defines us today'.[27] Most recently, the Court of Justice of the European Union, sitting *en banc*, ruled that the values contained in Article 2 TEU 'define the very identity of the European Union as a common legal order'.[28] They are the input, throughput and output values of European integration, which the EU institutions are called upon and must be able to defend within the limits of their Treaty powers.[29] These values are inexhaustible and must be complied with by the Member States not only at the moment of accession to the EU, but throughout their membership in it.[30]

[22] ibid.

[23] https://eur-lex.europa.eu/legal-content/EN/TXT/?uri=LEGISSUM%3Aaccession_criteria_copenhague.

[24] Treaty of Amsterdam [1997] OJ C340, 10/11/1997, Art F.1.

[25] Berlin Declaration, 50th anniversary of the Treaty of Rome, https://europa.eu/50/docs/berlin_declaration_en.pdf.

[26] Rome Declaration, https://ec.europa.eu/commission/presscorner/detail/en/STATEMENT_17_767 25.3. 2017.

[27] U von der Leyen, State of the Union Speech 2021, https://ec.europa.eu/commission/presscorner/detail/en/SPEECH_21_4701.

[28] Case C-156/21 *Hungary v European Parliament and Council* ECLI:EU:C:2022:97; Case C-157/21 *Poland v European Parliament and Council* ECLI:EU:C:2022:98, para 127.

[29] ibid.

[30] ibid para 126.

## III. Contemporary Value Fissures in the EU

Judging by the texts of the founding treaties and the many solemn declarations issued over the years by the Member States and the EU institutions, the common-value foundations of the European Union are formally hard as a rock and there is little controversy surrounding them. The common values are imposed and accepted by the candidate states; they shape the functioning of the Union, which is supranationally controlled by the CJEU as well as the constitutional courts in the national dimension. Eventually, the common values that enter the integration process and guide its conduct are also part of its outcome. What goes in also comes out of the integration process. However, this simple formula is too simplistic to reflect the actual value landscape in the EU,[31] especially since the outbreak of the global financial and the ensuing economic crisis in 2008. This crisis had devastating economic effects across the Union, but it was its southern belt, stretching from Portugal to Greece, that was affected particularly badly. Greece was for months on the brink of bankruptcy, whereas other southern EU economies were only kept afloat thanks to the financial aid by the newly created ad hoc EU credit mechanism.[32] However, these freshly minted loans did not come for free; rather, they were accompanied by strict conditionality, which was a hallmark of the main method for resolving the economic crisis: the method of austerity.

The most immediate effect of the economic crisis was a complete depletion of the EU outcome legitimacy. A profound recession caused the lowering of living standards, which meant that the main output value of economic welfare was seriously undermined. The political decision to 'remedy' the crisis by way of austerity chipped away at another important throughput value: solidarity. Instead of solidarity, the EU witnessed the language and practice of deep division between the centre and the periphery, between the allegedly economically progressive, prudent, but frugal North and the economically backward, reckless, even lazy and not law-abiding South. Not only did the economic crisis reinforce the divisions between different economic visions of the EU – between a welfare state-oriented transfer union and a more neoliberal camp – it has also stirred strong social divisions. Names were called, prejudices renewed and reinforced. Resentment was widespread, running from the North to the South and vice versa. In this way, the economic crisis exacerbated already existing divisions between two economic models: one based on labour, and present in the East and in the South, whose competitiveness derived from cheaper workforce, the other based on capital, services and free movement of goods, located in the North or in the Centre, which essentially benefited from the economy of scale resulting out of removal of protectionist measures. The blacklist of prejudices already containing

[31] ibid.

[32] For an overview, see A de Gregorio Merino, 'Legal Developments in the Economic and Monetary Union during the Debt Crisis: The Mechanisms of Financial Assistance' (2012) 49 *CML Rev* 1613.

Polish plumbers, Romanian and Bulgarian 'welfare tourists', and Latvian and Estonian social dumping was complemented by lazy Greeks, irreparable Italian *dolce far niente* etc.

The described decline in the utilitarian output values and the undermining of the throughput value of solidarity caused by the economic depression was exacerbated by the uncontrolled mass migration of 2015. This provoked a humanitarian as well as a security crisis, which led to the collapse of the Schengen regime and the breakdown of the common EU asylum policy. Like in the economic crisis, the so-called periphery – the Member States controlling the external borders of the EU – was affected the most. Neither the EU nor the so-called core EU Member States were capable or ready to extend their solidary to alleviate the burden of migration that had been long seen coming. Consequently, the dissatisfaction not just with the EU, but also with the traditional national political class, was deepened further. While this was felt most in the periphery and in the Member States that had joined the EU since 2004 and lacked a long democratic tradition, it did not leave the core EU Member States unaffected either. To the contrary, across the EU the parties of the political centre lost support in favour of the radical political fringes to both the right and left sides of the political spectrum. Not only did this create a lot of room for political experimentalism, resulting in the emergence of new faces and single-issue ad hoc political parties, it also provided a lot of space for demagogy and for the rise of populism.[33] This was initially economic populism, as a reaction to the economic crisis. It later grew, as a response to the migration crisis, into xenophobic populism, until it matured in a speech act advocating a whole new political order branded as illiberal democracy.[34] Its emergence signalled the beginning of a profound crisis of constitutional democracy.

For the first time since the demise of totalitarianism in Europe, elected politicians, supported by pundits, political and legal philosophers, as well as parts of the civil society, developed a wholesale justification for a political and value-based system rejecting the underlying liberal values of a constitutional democracy.[35] As an antipode to liberal democracy, illiberal democracy in value-based terms opposes the centrality of an individual. It rejects individualism and replaces it with a family-focused approach as the central building block of a nation, understood first in cultural, and only later in civic, terms. In this sense, the advocates of illiberal democracy promote the tradition as widely understood, of collective values

[33] JW Müller, *What Is Populism?* (Philadelphia, University of Pennsylvania Press, 2016).

[34] In describing the 'illiberal democracy', I draw on the speeches, declarations and writings by political and academic critics of a liberal democracy, among whom there are several explicit advocates of illiberal democracy. These views have been described and usefully gathered in a paper by G Halmai, 'Illiberalism in East-Central Europe' (2019) EUI Department of Law Research Paper 5, http://hdl.handle.net/1814/64967.

[35] V Orbán, Speech at Băile Tuşnad (Tusnádfürdő) of 26 July 2014, https://budapestbeacon.com/full-text-of-viktor-orbans-speech-at-baile-tusnad-tusnadfurdo-of-26-july-2014/; V Orbán, Speech at the 30th Bálványos Summer Open University and Student Camp, https://visegradpost.com/en/2019/07/29/orbans-full-speech-at-tusvanyos-political-philosophy-upcoming-crisis-and-projects-for-the-next-15-years/.

conducive to strengthening the nation, and assign at least an equal weight to the duties of the individuals as they do to their rights. Illiberal democracy is monist in an organisational and institutional sense, but this organisational monism is just a reflection of the value monism it serves. If the object and purpose of liberal democracy is the flourishing and self-fulfilment of individuals, which makes liberal democracy a priori pluralist both in its point of departure and its outcome, illiberal democracy is monist because it is concerned with the preservation and thriving not of individuals, but of a community known as a nation. While, in a liberal democracy, a nation is one of the environments in which individuals can fulfil their conception of a good life, if they so please, in an illiberal democracy, an individual is rather instrumental to the nation, which by way of a democratic majority prescribes the norms, rules and values of a good life that ought to be followed by the people as a whole. This instrumentalist conception of an individual also begets an instrumentalist conception of the law. Consequently, law becomes a tool to rule with, *gubernaculum*, rather than a limit on power, *jurisdictio*, which should ensure non-arbitrariness, equality in and before the law as well as the protection of fundamental human rights.[36]

By way of a speech act advocating for an illiberal democracy that since 2010 has certainly gained traction in many parts of the EU, but in particular in Central and Eastern Europe,[37] a schism has occurred right at the heart of the EU throughput and input values. The rule of law, democracy, human rights protection, pluralism and the protection of minorities, once undisputed primordial values of the integration and a standard of functioning both of the Member States and the EU institutions, not only came into question, but were tossed into the middle of a fierce *Kulturkampf*, in which nothing short of the very identity of Christian Europe was allegedly at stake. As a result of this systemic value breakdown, the EU institutions launched an Article 7 TEU procedure against Poland and Hungary due to a clear risk of a serious breach by the two countries of the EU fundamental values referred to in Article 2 TEU. The EU and its Member States have been thus embroiled in a conflict about the fundamental values that ought to be respected by each and every Member State at the moment of their accession to the EU and that the EU has been, as part and parcel of its distinctive soft power identity, proud to promote abroad. The fundamental values meltdown and the conflicts surrounding it consequently also undermined the output values of the EU, and its capacity to uphold its own fundamental values at home and to promote them abroad. The very soul of Europe that consists, as we have seen, of these 'great European values' has thus been divided, if not broken.

[36] For the distinction between the instrumental and limitation conceptions of the (rule of) law, see G Palombella, 'The Rule of Law beyond the State: Failures, Promises, and Theory' (2009) 7 *International Journal of Constitutional Law* 422, 451.

[37] For an overview, see W Sadurski, *Poland's Constitutional Breakdown* (Oxford, Oxford University Press, 2019); M Avbelj and J Letnar Černič, *The Impact of European Institutions on the Rule of Law and Democracy: Slovenia and Beyond* (Oxford, Hart Publishing, 2020); B Magyar, *Post-Communist Mafia State: The Case of Hungary* (Budapest, Central European University Press, 2016).

However, what was indeed broken, and not just divided, was the fundamental federal value of the European Union, according to which the latter has been destined since 1957 to form an 'ever closer union between the peoples of Europe'. The removal of this clause was part of David Cameron's deal with the EU, in an attempt to redefine the status of the UK in the Union. The deal, however, did not succeed in quelling the Euroscepticism of the majority of British voters as they decided in a referendum – also under the impact of all of the above-described EU crises, which significantly undermined the EU output legitimacy – not only to abandon the clause on the 'ever closer union', but to quit the union itself. For the first time in EU history, the process of widening the integration was reversed. The EU lost a strategically important Member State, a champion of economic integration with the single market at its peak. This yet again undermined the Union's output capacity, but also the credibility of its federal genus, its capacity to exist as a common whole. Indeed, with Brexit at the top of all the described value fissures, the very viability of the EU was not just potentially, but also concretely at stake.

Nevertheless, and contrary to some expectations, this strategic external shock in the ensuing Brexit negotiations stimulated the EU Member States to act as one, thereby at least to some degree reinforcing the unity of the Union. However, the latter quickly and completely unexpectedly came under a significant new stress, with the outbreak of the COVID-19 pandemic tossing the EU into a profound public health crisis. This was initially approached in an old-fashioned, protectionist, nation-state manner, threatening the collapse not only of Schengen, but also of the single market. However, the EU Member States, demonstrating that they nevertheless had learned something from the mistakes committed during the preceding crises, relatively quickly decided to combine their strength, to act together and reinforce the Union actions even in those fields that have traditionally been reserved for the Member States, such as the protection of public health. At the same time, this incipient health union was supported by growing fiscal powers of the EU, which was given a green light to raise substantial credits on behalf of the Union for its Member States.[38] The emerging public health union and the developing fiscal union as its corollary, contrary to Brexit, reinforced the so-called federal ethos of the EU. However, the deepening of the integration, and the competence of the EU to penetrate ever further into the socio-political and legal substrata of its Member States, concomitantly exposed deeper value fissures among the Member States. As more integration tends to require greater value homogeneity across the input, throughput and output spectra of the functioning of the Union, the extent of the actual value heterogeneity, to some extent also deliberately reinforced for short-term political gains, became visible. In short, the Union hit at a paradox. Despite being expected – indeed, called upon – to do more for its Member States, the undergirding common value basis of the EU has shrunk, making that objective politically less feasible or even impossible.

[38] B de Witte, 'The European Union's COVID-19 Recovery Plan: The Legal Engineering of an Economic Policy Shift' (2021) 58 *CML Rev* 635.

## IV. Values and the Future of the EU

The described deepening of the value fissures inside the European Union raises the question of how much integration between the EU Member States is actually possible? How much can these apparently objectively and subjectively diverse states, even when it comes to the fundamental values of the Union, do together and in what kind of legal-institutional way? After the British vote in favour of Brexit and even before the crisis of constitutional democracy reached the present level of gravity, the European Commission not only raised this question, but also attempted to respond to it. In its White Paper on the future of Europe,[39] published in 2017, the Commission presented five different scenarios for the future development of the integration. The first scenario, tagged 'Carrying on', was essentially about the preservation of the current state of the integration.[40] The second scenario, 'Nothing but the single market', basically envisaged scaling back the integration to its original economic roots.[41] The third scenario, 'Those who want more do more', suggested that while some Member States could carry on as they were, others would deepen the integration among themselves to more effectively respond to the monetary, fiscal, security and defence challenges.[42] In the fourth scenario, the Commission proposed that the EU, within the ambit of conferred competences, did less, but more efficiently. Finally, in the most ambitious scenario, 'Doing much more together',[43] the European Commission foresaw that the Member States would decide to 'share more powers, resources and decision-making across the board'[44] and hence push the integration significantly beyond its existing scope.

It is submitted that the five scenarios proposed by the European Commission can be effectively divided into three visions of the future of the European Union: the status quo ante vision, the status quo vision and the reformist vision.[45] Pursuant to the status quo ante vision, the integration process should be rolled back and some of the existing competences returned to the Member States. 'Nothing but the single market' is part of this vision, as its strives to shrink the present scope of competences to those of the single market only, conceding that even that would gradually apply exclusively to goods and capital.[46] The scenario 'Doing less more efficiently' also belongs to the status quo ante vision, albeit only nominally or at first glance. Not unlike the subsidiarity principle, it announces the sharpening of the EU focus to what it is really efficient at – leaving the rest of the competences to

[39] European Commission, 'White Paper on the Future of Europe' COM (2017) 2025, https://ec.europa.eu/info/sites/default/files/white_paper_on_the_future_of_europe_en.pdf.
[40] ibid 16.
[41] ibid 18.
[42] ibid 20.
[43] ibid 24.
[44] ibid.
[45] For an earlier discussion, see M Avbelj, 'What Future for the European Union' (2017) WZB Discussion Paper SP IV-802, 5, https://bibliothek.wzb.eu/pdf/2017/iv17-802.pdf.
[46] European Commission (n 39).

the Member States. However, it is clear from the Commission's description of the scenario that the fields of competences where the EU is believed to be more efficient are much more numerous than those which the Member States should take over again. For this reason, the 'Doing less more efficiently' scenario could also be seen as a continuation of the tradition of the integration by stealth,[47] and hence forming part of the status quo vision.

The latter is most clearly endorsed by the 'Carrying on' scenario. This is, after all, visible already in its name. However, the traces of the status quo vision could also be identified in the scenario that advances the idea of an enhanced differentiated integration. Judging by the experiences from the past, the attempts at differentiated integration were rarely successful because of the strict conditions the Treaties subject it to, as well as because of a general reluctance of the supranational institutions and the less keen Member States to differentiate inside EU law.[48] Should this practice remain unchanged, it would be expected that even the scenario 'Those who want more do more' would only perpetuate the status quo. In the opposite case, if differentiated integration is actually much more effectuated in practice than in the past, it could also unlock the status quo and grow into a scenario belonging to the reformist vision of the future of the EU.

The reformist vision is represented by the scenario labelled as 'Doing much more together'. This rejects the status quo ante vision as an unfeasible alternative and insists on moving decisively beyond the present status quo by deepening the integration in the economic, security, defence and therefore also political spheres. The European Commission's White Paper admittedly remains rather elusive as to how far the deepening of the integration should go. What is clear, however, is that the envisaged deepening is not an end in and of itself, but a means for an effective response to the present crises of the integration and hence should ensure the EU's viability in the longer run.

Having presented the three visions of the future of the EU, what can be said about their feasibility in light of the conditions in which the common values of European integration, as described in the preceding section, currently find themselves? The most straightforward response to that question can be given with respect to the status quo ante vision. Returning to the single market, presumably just in goods and capital, would be a fitting solution to the current breakdown in the EU common values. The crisis of constitutional democracy would thus be resolved as the required degree of shared throughput values, their quality and intensity would be lowered significantly. To trade in goods and capital, as the global trading relations attest, the countries involved do not need to be fully fledged democracies, based on the rule of law, with an impeccable human rights record. This means that the currently existing degree of EU common values exceeds that which would be required by the status quo ante vision. This is

[47] G Majone, *Dilemmas of European Integration: The Ambiguities and Pitfalls of Integration by Stealth* (Oxford, Oxford University Press, 2009).

[48] M Avbelj, 'Differentiated Integration – Farewell to the EU-27?' (2013) 14 *German Law Journal* 191.

certainly true for the input and throughput values, while the output values would hinge on the economic performance of a thus rolled backed integration. Here, a degree of scepticism would, however, be warranted, being mindful of the external economic, political and geo-strategic shocks that, as a rule, the EU single market in the past has not been able to cope with in the absence of supranational regulatory, political, monetary and fiscal cushioning measures. As these would simply not be available under the status quo ante vision, this could also adversely affect the output values of the thus scaled-back Union.

With regard to the status quo vison of the future of the EU, the current scope of EU common values certainly suffices for carrying on with the integration process in the usual way. That scope includes: normal decision-making under the shadow of perpetual crises, political incrementalism, half-baked political compromises, conflicts about the fundamental values, political use and abuse of (minor) differences between the Member States and European political parties, combined with a true joining of forces in the time of necessity, all of which are also reflected in the fissures in the EU common values. While these are still strong enough to sustain the status quo, the latter might no longer be, in and of itself, sufficient to ensure the integration's viability in light of the challenges faced by it. The viability of EU integration requires deepening of its legal, economic, security, defence, public health and therefore also political and democratic foundations.

This is what the reformist vison of the future of the EU calls for, but it cannot deliver given the existing ruptures in the most fundamental EU input and throughput values. While the reformist vision of the EU thus appears necessary, its realisation requires mending the lacking and crumbling value foundations, which also prevent the growth of a political momentum and support for the reformist breakthrough. The institutionalisation of the reformist vision of the future of the EU patently requires a significant investment in the shared-value foundations of the EU across all of its three dimensions: input, throughput and output. In the next section, I explore whether the launching of a formal constitution-making process in the EU could close that value gap and provide the stimulus, content and framework for a reformist vision of the integration's future.

## V. Constitutionalising the Future of the EU

We begin by relying on a broad conception of constitutionalism, which does not have only a formal-legal dimension, but also includes a socio-political and a philosophical dimension.[49] Accordingly, constitutionalism is a legal, political, economic

[49] M Avbelj, 'Can European Integration Be Constitutional and Pluralist – Both at the Same Time?' in M Avbelj and J Komárek (eds), *Constitutional Pluralism in the EU and Beyond* (Oxford, Hart Publishing, 2012) 378.

and cultural discourse of conceptualisation and imagination,[50] which, if appropriated by the public institutions, civil society and the citizenry at large, turns society into a polity. It constitutes political unity out of social plurality, without exhausting the latter. Constitutionalism, thus broadly conceived of, is therefore much more than a text of a particular constitution, and much more than the institutions that the constitution inaugurates. Constitutionalism is about all of that, but it is also about culture. Following Pučnik, culture is understood here as a comprehensive system of technology that contains and constantly reconstitutes a society by way of unlimited and often unrelated, piecemeal and particularistic actions of individuals (and institutions) who are simultaneously a source and a product of this cultural technological process.[51] Constitutionalism is part of a culture; it is dependent on it, but at the same time is constitutive of it. Constitutionalism is also one of the main technological tools for socio-cultural engineering. In short, while culture begets constitutionalism, constitutionalism also (re)constitutes it in return.[52]

It is on this cultural aspect of constitutionalism that we lay our hopes for mending the value fissures in the EU. The idea is that the tacit, small 'c' constitutionalism,[53] which has marked the development of the integration so far and which has, not infrequently, progressed by stealth, is replaced by an open, deliberate, explicit and inclusive process of constitution-making in the EU. This process could, ideally, lift democratic attention from the exclusively national to the supranational domain too, gradually giving rise to transnational political, democratic and hence also constitutional culture. In this constitution-making process, it is hoped, the existing value fissures would be debated in the open among the national and supranational institutions, as well as among the citizens in and between the Member States. This process could be as inclusive as the present Conference on the Future of Europe had been envisaged, but unlike it, it would not be just a broad, largely informal democratic consultation, but a formal and binding process with a clear constitutional mandate. In this way, it would formally determine which of the input, throughput and output values that have been so prominent in the binding and declaratory texts of the European Union are in fact supported by its citizens and their Member States. A thus-conducted constitution-making process would hence serve as a litmus test of the EU constitutional culture, of the common values that are actually, rather than just nominally, present inside the EU constitution. However, once these values were included in the text of a constitution, they would be formally constitutionalised and therefore endowed with a normative power that would, in turn, guide and shape the functioning of the EU in the future, including by generating its requisite constitutional culture. In so doing, the value fissures could be gradually mended, overcome and closed.

[50] Weiler and Trachtman (n 1) 359.

[51] J Pučnik, *Kultura, družba in tehnologija* (Inštitut dr Jožeta Pučnika, 2008) 27–45; see also M Avbelj, 'Constitutionalization of Jože Pučnik's Political Thought' (2021) 29 *Acta Histriae* 191.

[52] For a discussion, see S Obermeyer, *Integrationsfuktion der Verfassung und Verfassungsnormativität* (Berlin, Duncker & Humblot 2008).

[53] N Walker, 'Big "C" or Small "c"' (2006) 1 *European Law Journal* 12; see also M Avbelj, 'Revitalization of EU Constitutionalism' (2021) 46 *EL Rev* 3.

This is, of course, the best-case scenario, which is far from certain. The opposite outcome of a formal constitution-making process could be envisaged too. Rather than assuaging the cracks in the common values of the EU, it could open up a Pandora's box instead. Putting all the existing deep-value disagreements on the table and engaging with them openly is no guarantee that they will actually be resolved. They could be exacerbated further, growing so acute as to prevent the launch of the formal constitution-making process, as the very agreement for its initiation would be lacking. In the worst-case scenario, the disagreements could also lead to the dissolution of the Union or to additional exits of Member States. Nevertheless, the disagreements, even if very acute, as long they stop short of dismantling the EU, could also be taken as an opportunity, including for reforming the European Union.

If it turns out that differences even with regard to the most fundamental input, throughput and output values between the Member States run so deep that they no longer have a meaningful common denominator, then it is certainly more advantageous to lay them out in the open and recognise them, rather than to wage increasingly exhausting political fights to the detriment of the relationships between the Member States and the Union as a whole. At a certain stage, as the saying goes, it can be far more productive to simply agree to disagree.[54] This is all the more so when the repository of EU law provides a solution for it in the form of differentiated integration. As envisaged by the scenario 'Those who want more do more', the Member States could agree to launch a formal constitution-making process that would recognise the existence of profound value differences among them and devise appropriate constitutional solutions for them. The European Union could thus be transformed into a common whole consisting of several concentric circles characterised by different intensities of integration. The core EU would be made by the present eurozone countries. This would grow into a veritable economic, security, defence and political union, a federal Europe – not a state, but a union, with a formal, written constitution. Beyond it, a treaty framework could be agreed which would permit a lower intensity of integration, down to the single market or even just a customs union, which could also accommodate as different interests and characteristics as those of Britain, Turkey, Ukraine and the Western Balkan states.[55]

## VI. Conclusion

The preceding discussion on common values, on common institutional solutions for a common future of the EU, even on the basis of a new constitution-making

[54] See also JC Piris, *The Future of Europe: Towards a Two-Speed EU* (Cambridge, Cambridge University Press, 2012).

[55] Compare also with the speech of Emmanuel Macron at the closing session of the Conference on the Future of Europe: www.elysee.fr/en/emmanuel-macron/2022/05/09/closure-of-the-conference-on-the-future-of-europe.

process which might eventually lead to a differentiated integration, to a European Union of several concentric circles inside a common whole, only makes sense if a commitment to this common whole is (still) genuinely present in the integration. The experience of similar projects in European history confirms that any project of integration requires an integrationist culture. The deeper the integration, the more entrenched and widely shared this culture should be. What is required for the project of European integration, which could be best described as a non-statist federation,[56] is therefore a federal culture. This has been defined as a shared understanding, a shared belief system,[57] a federal creed,[58] even federal morality[59] – in short, a common public ethos which is about the defence of the federal cause, consisting of an equilibrium between the federal and national authorities and the boundaries on which this federal balance rests.[60] Essentially, this federal culture among the citizens of the EU should prevent, by way of a civic commitment to the common whole, the federal level from encroaching on the competences of its Member States, while the latter should not shirk their responsibilities under EU law.[61]

However, the required federal culture faces a challenge which is not unlike that experienced by Baron Munchausen when he had to save himself from quicksand. He allegedly did so by pulling himself out by his bootstraps. The federal culture could be deepened by a formal constitution-making process, but for the latter to be launched, it must be presupposed that a federal cultural already exists to a degree at which a threshold for its formal constitutionalisation can be crossed. Furthermore, this federal culture should be embraced by the people living in the EU, who would need to 'feel federal',[62] committing to the integration 'as an end, as a good for its own sake'.[63] They should consequently, in advance and as a result, conceive of themselves, in an internally and externally pluralist manner,[64] not exclusively as members of the national polity, but also concurrently as members of the supranational polity. This *pouvoir constituent mixte*, as Habermas has dubbed it,[65] is, however, in turn dependent on some degree of federal culture, whose continuous source it will then be.

[56] M Avbelj, 'Theory of European Union' (2011) 36 *EL Rev* 818.

[57] R Maiz, 'Beyond Institutional Design: The Political Culture of Federalism (A Normative Approach)' in AL Basaguren et al (eds), *The Ways of Federalism in Western Countries and the Horizons of Territorial Autonomy in Spain*, vol 1 (Berlin, Springer Verlag, 2013) 100.

[58] M Grodzins, *The American System* (Chicago, McNally, 1966) 314.

[59] M Burgess, *The Success and Failure of Federation* (London, Routledge, 2006) 288 speaks about the moral basis to federalism.

[60] J Bednar, *The Robust Federation, Principles of Design* (Cambridge, Cambridge University Press, 2009) 218–19.

[61] ibid.

[62] Burgess (n 59) 281.

[63] ibid.

[64] Maiz (n 57) 97.

[65] J Habermas, *The Crisis of the European Union: A Response* (Cambridge, Polity, 2012); J Habermas, 'Democracy in Europe: Why the Development of the EU into a Democracy Is Necessary and How It Is Possible' (2015) 4 *European Law Journal* 546.

To square this circle is thus certainly not an easy task. The Conference on the Future of Europe as a Union-wide democratic consultation could, at least to some degree, help in identifying the extent to which this federal culture exists. Again, it is quite likely that its presence will not be very strong and that it will, on the top of that, also vary significantly among the different EU Member States. If so, this would be yet another confirmation that for moving beyond the existing, admittedly unsustainable, status quo to a reformist vision of the future of the EU, flexible solutions inside a common whole would be called for. Formal constitutionalisation at the EU's core, supported by the existing federal culture, would be combined with a preserved treaty framework for the competencies and policies in which the less integrationist Member States and their citizens with weaker federal culture would be more loosely integrated and yet would still form part of the EU's common whole. A thus-constructed European Union of concentric circles, which would exhibit constitutional, international and in-between *sui generis* characteristics, could grow increasingly viable in time, provided that common EU movements, ideologies and narratives[66] were mobilised among its citizenry in the latter's national and supranational capacity.

[66] Maiz (n 57) 100.

# 5

# Constructive Misunderstandings – How the PSPP Conflict was Eventually Settled and How it Reflects Constitutional Pluralism

MATTIAS WENDEL

## I. Introduction

In retrospect, the ferocity of the outrage may seem astonishing. After the German Federal Constitutional Court had announced its much-discussed ruling of 5 May 2020[1] on PSPP,[2] well-founded criticism was hyped up by war rhetoric. Some called the decision a 'bombshell ruling',[3] others even went so far as to state that the Court had gone 'nuclear'.[4] The fact that these terms were used so lightly bears witness to how much their original meaning had already faded by that time. In the EU, the reality of war had largely disappeared from life. What remained were idioms. Expressions that had once primarily designated violent death and mass destruction transformed increasingly into metaphorical terms for social conflicts of a different kind.

Reviewing the debate on the PSPP ruling through today's eyes, after the tragedy of war has returned to Europe, one looks back to a happier time, a time when war rhetoric was cheap and when many, too many, took peace in Europe for granted and considered the EU's proclaimed aim 'to promote peace'[5] an anachronism.[6]

[1] BVerfG, Case 2 BvR 859/15 *PSPP I* (5 May 2020), English translation, www.bundesverfassungsgericht.de/SharedDocs/Entscheidungen/EN/2020/05/rs20200505_2bvr085915en.html.

[2] The European Central Bank's Public Sector Purchase Programme (PSPP).

[3] See P Inman, 'Jolt to Eurozone as German Court Warns against Central Bank Stimulus' *The Guardian* (5 May 2020) www.theguardian.com/business/2020/may/05/jolt-to-eurozone-as-german-court-warns-against-central-bank-stimulus; T Marzal, 'Is the BVerfG PSPP Decision "Simply Not Comprehensible"?' *Verfassungsblog* (9 May 2020) www.verfassungsblog.de/is-the-bverfg-pspp-decision-simply-not-comprehensible.

[4] L Guttenberg, *Twitter* (5 May 2020) www.twitter.com/lucasguttenberg/status/1257592204308164609.

[5] Art 3(1) TEU.

[6] Convincingly emphasising the continuing importance of the aim to promote peace, see FC Mayer, 'Die Europäische Union als *Rechtsgemeinschaft*' (2017) 70 *Neue Juristische Wochenschrift* 3631.

Hence, when this chapter tells the story of how the PSPP conflict was eventually settled and how it reflects the pluralist constitutional architecture of the EU, it does so against the backdrop of a fundamentally changed context, a context that shows that the framework in which the PSPP conflict unfolded was a highly civilised one and should by no means be taken for granted.

The aim of this contribution is to examine the way the PSPP saga was brought to an end and how the open conflict between the Federal Constitutional Court (Bundesverfassungsgericht, BVerfG) and European institutions has impacted on the constitutional architecture of the EU. The *spiritus rector* of this volume has raised several insightful questions in this regard. Did the PSPP conflict lead to a disruption of the constitutional foundations of the EU? Has it 'finally resolved' or 'irretrievably broken' the nature of the European constitutional order? Did it force us to abandon a pluralistic understanding of European constitutional law?

To answer these questions (or at least give an approximation), the settlement of the PSPP conflict will be reviewed in detail as a first step. The decision of 5 May 2020 has been covered by countless studies[7] – critical,[8] affirmative,[9] dialectical[10] – and does not need to be reiterated here in detail. Instead, the focus will be on further developments, in particular the second PSPP decision of 29 April 2021,[11] as well as the infringement proceeding that was initiated on 9 June 2021 by the European Commission and then, following a short reply by the German Federal Government (Bundesregierung), closed on 2 December 2021. Ultimately, the European Commission and the Federal Government have, on the basis of a constructive misunderstanding, pointed the way to a more fruitful and continuous dialogue (see section II). In a second step, it will be argued that the PSPP conflict and its resolution should not be seen as the end, but rather as an expression of constitutional pluralism, albeit a poorly articulated and badly tempered expression on the part of the BVerfG under both European and domestic constitutional standards. The BVerfG's highly questionable performance should be the starting point for learning lessons about the cooperative dimension of constitutional pluralism in the EU (see section III).

[7] See the contributions in the special sections: (2020) 21 *German Law Journal* 944; (2020) 31 *Europäische Wirtschaftszeitung* 491; (2021) 19 *International Journal of Constitutional Law* 179.

[8] *cf* I Pernice, 'Machtspruch aus Karlsruhe' (2020) 31 *Europäische Wirtschaftszeitung* 508; FC Mayer, 'To Boldly Go Where No Court Has Gone Before' (2020) 21 *German Law Journal* 1116; H Sauer, 'Substantive EU Law Review Beyond the Veil of Democracy' (2020) 16 *EU Law Live* 1; D Sarmiento, 'Requiem for Judicial Dialogue' (2020) 16 *EU Law Live* 9.

[9] See D Grimm, 'A Long Time Coming' (2020) 21 *German Law Journal* 944; KF Gärditz, 'Herrschaftslegitimation und implizite Identitätskontrolle' *Verfassungsblog* (21 May 2020) www.verfassungsblog.de/herrschaftslegitimation-und-implizite-identitaetskontrolle; F Schorkopf, 'Antwort auf eine entgrenzte Politik' *Frankfurter Allgemeine Zeitung* (8 May 2020) www.faz.net/einspruch/ezb-urteil-des-bundesverfassungsgerichts-entgrenzte-politik-16760094.html.

[10] U Haltern, 'Revolutions, Real Contradictions, and the Method of Resolving Them' (2021) 19 *International Journal of Constitutional Law* 208.

[11] BVerfG, Case 2 BvR 1651/15 et al *PSPP II* (29 April 2021), English translation, www.bundesverfassungsgericht.de/SharedDocs/Entscheidungen/EN/2021/04/rs20210429_2bvr165115en.html.

# II. How the PSPP Conflict was Eventually Settled

## A. From PSPP I to PSPP II

The PSPP ruling of 5 May 2020 was a highly paradoxical decision in several respects, be it in terms of law or context.[12] The BVerfG's reasoning, according to which both the Court of Justice of the European Union (CJEU, the Court) and the European Central Bank (ECB) had manifestly exceeded their competences under the Treaties, was contestable to such a remarkable degree that the ruling failed to meet the high constitutional standards that the BVerfG had itself established for ultra vires review. Striking examples of the Court's questionable reasoning are its peculiar reconception of the principle of proportionality under Article 5(4) TEU as a principle governing the delimitation (but not the exercise) of EU competences[13] and its methodologically hardly consistent approach that better motivation and substantiation on the part of the ECB could ultimately turn an obvious transgression of competences into a lawful act[14] and hence transform an act of economic policy into an act of monetary policy.

The first PSPP ruling was also paradoxical with regard to its legal outcome. Due to the specific procedural setting of the case – and similar to the case law on Outright Monetary Transactions (OMT)[15] – the BVerfG had to pronounce itself on an alleged unconstitutional inactivity of the Federal Parliament (Bundestag) and the Federal Government. The contested measures at EU level, ie the *Weiß* ruling and the PSPP programme, were only indirectly subject to constitutional review. What the BVerfG finally decided was that both the Bundestag and the Bundesregierung had violated the constitution[16] by failing to take 'suitable steps' against an alleged failure of the ECB to conduct and substantiate a test of proportionality.[17] The paradox of this legal outcome already lay in the fact that both parliament and government are prohibited under Article 130 TFEU and Article 88 of the German Basic Law to exercise political influence on the ECB and the Federal Bank (Bundesbank). But even if these provisions on the ECB's independence were not applied to the extent that the ECB allegedly acted ultra vires, a key conceptual problem still remained. It was hardly possible to prescribe, in terms

[12] For more detail, see M Wendel, 'Paradoxes of Ultra-Vires Review: A Critical Review of the PSPP Decision and Its Initial Reception' (2020) 21 *German Law Journal* 979.

[13] BVerfG, *PSPP I* (n 1) paras 119, 127, 139.

[14] BVerfG, *PSPP I* (n 1) paras 232, 235.

[15] BVerfG, Case 2 BvR 2728/13 *OMT-Reference* (14 January 2014), English translation, www.bundesverfassungsgericht.de/SharedDocs/Entscheidungen/EN/2014/01/rs20140114_2bvr272813en.htm; BVerfG, Case 2 BvR 2728/13 et al (21 June 2016), English translation, www.bundesverfassungsgericht.de/SharedDocs/Entscheidungen/EN/2016/06/rs20160621_2bvr272813en.htm.

[16] That is the complainants' 'right to democratic self-determination', *cf PSPP I*, paras 100 and 101 ("Anspruch auf demokratische Selbstbestimmung"). In previous decisions, the BVerfG had spoken of a 'right to democracy'.

[17] BVerfG, *PSPP I* (n 1) para 116.

of constitutional law, what both institutions should proactively do in order to stop the alleged ultra vires act on the part of the ECB. The only instruction given by the BVerfG was that the Bundestag and the Bundesregierung should 'take steps seeking to ensure that the ECB conducts a proportionality assessment in relation to the PSPP' and that both institutions had to 'clearly communicate their legal view to the ECB or take other steps to ensure that conformity with the Treaties is restored'.[18]

The operative part and the concrete legal consequences of the PSPP ruling thus demonstrated once again a major conceptual flaw in the BVerfG's approach: it ultimately empowers individuals to judicially demand legally rather indeterminable actions by both parliament and government in the name of democracy, a flaw already criticised by the two dissenting opinions in the preceding OMT saga.[19] In addition, the BVerfG ruled in PSPP that the Bundesbank, after a certain transitional period, could 'no longer participate in the implementation and execution' of PSPP unless the ECB adopted 'a new decision that demonstrates in a comprehensible and substantiated manner that the monetary policy objectives pursued by the ECB are not disproportionate to the economic and fiscal policy effects resulting from the programme'.[20]

The vagueness, especially with regard to the required actions of the Bundestag and the Bundesregierung, immediately raised the question as to what measures could or would have to be taken to sufficiently comply with the ruling. Shortly after the judgment was delivered, the ECB's Governing Council made publicly available certain considerations from the proportionality assessment it had previously conducted.[21] Furthermore, it authorised the Bundesbank to transmit several confidential documents to the Bundesregierung and to the Bundestag.[22] Shortly afterwards, several of these documents were declassified.[23] Against this background, the Federal Parliament, in a resolution[24] adopted after a plenary debate,[25] and the Federal Ministry of Finance[26] expressed the view that the ECB had demonstrated in a comprehensible and substantiated manner that PSPP was proportionate. A comprehensive overview of the measures taken by the Federal Parliament and Federal Government in response to the PSPP ruling can be found in the BVerfG's second PSPP ruling.[27]

[18] BVerfG, *PSPP I* (n 1) para 232.

[19] Dissenting opinions of Judges G Lübbe-Wolff and M Gerhardt to the BVerfG's preliminary reference on OMT (n 15). For the problem in more detail, see M Wendel, 'Exceeding Judicial Competence in the Name of Democracy' (2014) 10 *European Constitutional Law Review* 263.

[20] BVerfG, *PSPP I* (n 1) para 235.

[21] European Central Bank, 'Account of the Monetary Policy Meeting of the Governing Council of the ECB' (3 and 4 June 2020) www.ecb.europa.eu/press/accounts/2020/html/ecb.mg200625~fd97330d5f.en.html.

[22] Decision of 24 June 2020 as referred to by Bundestag, Resolution of 2 July 2020, Doc No 19/20621; BVerfG, *PSPP II* (n 11) para 6.

[23] On 29 June 2020, *cf* BVerfG, *PSPP II* (n 11) para 7.

[24] Doc No 19/20621 (n 22).

[25] Bundestag, Plenary Protocol No 19/170, p 21283.

[26] I.a. in a letter of 16 June 2020.

[27] BVerfG, *PSPP II* (n 11), paras 97–108 and 6–11.

## B. The PSPP II Decision

Why a second PSPP decision? In essence, several of the complainants of the initial PSPP took the view that the (first) PSPP ruling had not been properly implemented and therefore wanted the BVerfG to intervene again. According to them, the measures taken in the wake of the ruling did not comply with the requirements of the BVerfG or were at least not comprehensible, as not all relevant documents were publicly accessible. However, instead of filing a new constitutional complaint against the PSPP follow-up measures, the applicants took a somewhat unusual route and applied for a so-called 'order of execution' (*Vollstreckungsanordnung*). In simplified terms, such an order serves the purpose of enforcing a judgment by the BVerfG. It is of purely ancillary nature, which is why new legislative or executive measures taken after the judgment on the merits has been pronounced cannot be the subject of an order of execution.[28]

Before actually deciding on the applications for an order of execution, the BVerfG's Second Senate excluded its new member, Astrid Wallrabenstein, due to concern of bias.[29] The applicants had questioned Wallrabenstein's impartiality due to an interview she had given after her election and shortly before her appointment as a Federal Constitutional Court judge. Against the background that several members of the Second Senate had previously repeatedly and extensively commented in the media on the Federal Constitutional Court's EU-related jurisprudence, the decision seemed quite astonishing, to say the least.

However, in its PSPP II decision of 29 April 2021 (published on 18 May 2021), the BVerfG finally – and convincingly – declared the applications for an order of execution inadmissible, for they ultimately aimed at a constitutional review of federal measures that were enacted after the pronouncement of the first PSPP ruling and hence could not be subject to a (merely ancillary) order of execution.[30] The BVerfG even went one step further and ruled in an obiter dictum that the applications would have been unfounded even if they had been found admissible.[31] The procedural background to this obiter dictum is that applications for an order of execution are admissible in the exceptional case that the federal legislator,

> despite an obligation to take legislative action imposed on it by the decision on the merits, either fails to take any action at all or only takes measures that so manifestly fall short of satisfying the decision on the merits that they are essentially equivalent to complete inaction.[32]

Or, to frame it differently, while an application for an order of execution cannot, as a general rule, be used to have new measures subjected to constitutional review, it can be a successful remedy if the relevant body, say the Federal Parliament, does

[28] ibid para 78.
[29] BVerfG, Case 2 BvR 2006/15 *Wallrabenstein* (1 January 2021).
[30] BVerfG, *PSPP II* (n 11), paras 82 et seq.
[31] ibid paras 89 et seq.
[32] ibid para 79.

not react to a judgment at all or reacts so obviously inadequately that this amounts to inaction. In PSPP II, the BVerfG held that even if the applications had been declared admissible on the basis of this exception, they would have been unfounded because the PSPP follow-up measures taken by the Federal Government and the Federal Parliament did not, at any rate, fall so obviously short of the PSPP judgment of 5 May 2020 that they essentially amounted to complete inaction.[33]

Despite this specific procedural setting, the obiter dictum is important in at least two respects. First, the BVerfG underlined that, with regard to fulfilling the obligations arising from the PSPP I ruling, both the Federal Government and the Federal Parliament enjoyed 'a broad margin of (political) appreciation, assessment and manoeuvre … which extends to deciding on the best course of action such as the appropriate technical and communicative procedures'.[34] Hence, the vague obligation to 'take action against PSPP'[35] as established by the BVerfG in its PSPP I ruling was complemented by a broadly framed margin of appreciation of the political institutions.[36] Second, the BVerfG highlighted that

> the numerous activities undertaken by the Federal Government and the Bundestag in response to the judgment of 5 May 2020, which were in part carried out via or with the assistance of the Bundesbank, have led to the ECB Governing Council demonstrating … that it conducted a proportionality assessment in accordance with Article 5(1) second sentence and Article 5(4) TEU in conjunction with Article 119 et seq. and Article 127 et seq. TFEU – the lack of which had been objected to by the Second Senate in its judgment. It is not for the Court to decide in the present case whether this proportionality assessment satisfies the substantive requirements deriving from Article 5(1) second sentence and Article 5(4) TFEU in every respect.

Although the scope of constitutional review was quite specific for the reasons outlined above, the PSPP II decision of 29 April 2021 in fact settled the conflict at least with regard to the concrete legal outcome and secured Germany's continued participation in the PSPP. Even if the complainants theoretically still had the possibility to file new constitutional complaints against the PSPP follow-up measures by the Bundestag and the Bundesregierung, the BVerfG's decision effectively took the wind out of the sails of such efforts.

## C. The Infringement Proceeding

### *(i) A Smouldering Conflict*

Although the conflict thus seemed to be settled, the European Commission decided to open an infringement proceeding against Germany only a few

[33] ibid paras 95 et seq.
[34] ibid para 108.
[35] ibid para 96.
[36] For a 'wide political latitude' in terms of how to respond to ultra vires acts in general, see BVerfG, *PSPP I* (n 1) para 109.

weeks later, on 9 June 2021.[37] The letter of formal notice was not published by the Commission, but was made public at a later stage by individuals who had successfully filed 'freedom of information' (FOI) requests with the Commission.[38] The Commission's decision to send a letter of formal notice to Germany was met with sharp criticism by some. In defence of the BVerfG, several scholars held the view that the conflict had in fact already been resolved and pointed to the danger that a European federal state could be introduced 'through the back door' if the national constitutional courts were not permitted to exceptionally control the limits of conferral of competences to the EU, because the lack of such constitutional checks would potentially allow the EU institutions to deprive the Member States of competences against their will.[39]

From the Commission's point of view, however, the deeper legal problems as well as the possible negative role model effect of the PSPP ruling were by no means overcome. Seen from Brussels, the conflict smouldered on. The fact that a national constitutional court claimed the right to declare rulings of the European Court of Justice domestically non-binding was in open contrast to key elements of EU law and hung like a sword of Damocles over the community of law, which was – and still is – threatened by a deep crisis of the rule of law in several Member States. Consequently, the Commission saw in the PSPP I ruling a 'serious precedent' both inside and outside Germany.[40]

### *(ii) Determining the Infringement: A Question of Primacy?*

The European Commission justified its decision to open an infringement proceeding by stating that Germany had violated its obligations under the principles of autonomy, primacy, effectiveness and uniform application of EU law, as well as under Article 267 TFEU, interpreted in the light of the principle of sincere cooperation set out in Article 4(3) TEU.[41] The Commission also explicitly held that the breach of the principle of primacy had not been reversed by the second PSPP decision.[42]

As already stated, the PSPP I judgment of 5 May 2020 was a highly paradoxical ruling. It was an immoderate and unnecessary ruling, too, undermining the autonomy and the equal and effective application of EU law in the Member States

[37] European Commission press release (9 June 2021) www.ec.europa.eu/commission/presscorner/detail/de/inf_21_2743.

[38] i.a. by P Wachowiec, who subsequently made the Commission's letter of formal notice in proceeding INFR/2021/2114 available at www.ruleoflaw.pl/wp-content/uploads/2022/02/doc-1-LFN-to-DE-EN.pdf. Another successful FOI request was filed by J Gallon and subsequently published at https://fragdenstaat.de/anfrage/korrespondenz-zwischen-europaischer-kommission-und-der-bundes republik-deutschland-im-vertragsverletzungsverfahren-az-infr20212114/#nachricht-668051.

[39] See the open letter signed by 29 professors of constitutional law, 'Die Selbstbehauptung Europas!' *Frankfurter Allgemeine Zeitung* (4 July 2021) www.faz.net/einspruch/europaeische-integration-staatsrechtler-kritisieren-eu-kommission-17421926.html?premium.

[40] European Commission press release (n 37).

[41] European Commission letter of formal notice (n 38) and press release (n 37).

[42] ibid.

and openly challenging the CJEU's 'exclusive jurisdiction to provide the definitive interpretation of EU law'.[43] By not having referred a second preliminary reference to the Court of Justice and thus not having continued the dialogue, the BVerfG also failed to comply with Article 267(3) TFEU, interpreted in the light of the principle of sincere cooperation set out in Article 4(3) TEU.[44]

While these infringements appear comparatively clear, it is less trivial to frame the conflict in terms of primacy. This seems counterintuitive at first, as the PSPP conflict is usually presented predominantly as a conflict over primacy and the BVerfG had itself stated in PSPP I that an ultra vires act 'does not partake in the precedence of application of EU law'.[45] However, the principle of primacy is, at its core, a conflict-of-laws principle (*Kollisionsnorm*). It determines which of several potentially applicable but conflicting norms is to be applied to the case at hand. In the famous words of the Spanish Constitutional Court, it is about *primacía* in terms of the application of the norm, not *supremacía* in terms of the validity of the norm.[46] And in the words of the Court of Justice, it resolves a 'conflict between a provision of EU law and a national law' by requiring national bodies and particular courts 'to disregard a national provision or practice which might prevent directly effective EU rules from having full force and effect'.[47] The principle of primacy necessarily presupposes the (direct) applicability of EU law[48] and consequently an existing EU competence.

However, it was precisely the question whether or not the EU was competent, and hence a question that logically precedes the question of primacy, that was at the heart of the PSPP dispute: were the EU institutions acting within the competences conferred on them by the Treaties? And who is empowered to decide, as a final arbiter, on an alleged transgression of competences?[49] Typically, the principle of primacy is violated when a national body refuses to apply (or is prevented from applying) a provision of national law that is in conflict with directly applicable EU law.[50] In the PSPP I ruling, however, the BVerfG ultimately preferred its own interpretation of EU law to that of the CJEU and declared the *Weiß* ruling to be ultra vires. If one were to reformulate this in terms of conflict of laws, the BVerfG would ultimately have violated the principle of primacy by not disapplying the (self-created) constitutional rule that decisions of the CJEU are not to be regarded binding under certain exceptional conditions, thus contravening the relevant rule under EU law, which assigns exclusive jurisdiction to the CJEU for providing the

[43] For this term, see Case C-741/19 *Republic of Moldova* ECLI:EU:C:2021:655, para 45; Case C-430/21 *RS – Effect of judgments of a constitutional court* ECLI:EU:C:2022:99, paras 52 and 72.

[44] This argument is spelt out in more detail in the Commission's letter of formal notice (n 38).

[45] BVerfG, *PSPP I* (n 1) para 234.

[46] See Spanish Tribunal Constitucional, Case DTC 1/2004 *Constitutional Treaty* ECLI:ES:TC:2004:1D, II.4.

[47] Case C-188/10 et al *Melki et al* ECLI:EU:C:2010:363, para 44. See also Case 106/78 *Simmenthal II* [1978] ECR 629 para 23; *RS* (n 43) para 63.

[48] Clearly Case C-573/17 *Popławski II* (2019) ECLI:EU:C:2019:530, paras 60, 62 and 68.

[49] For more detail, see FC Mayer, *Kompetenzüberschreitung und Letztentscheidung* (Munich, Beck, 2000).

[50] For a recent example, see Case C-357/19 et al *Euro Box Promotion et al* ECLI:EU:C:2021:1034, paras 244 et seq.

definitive interpretation of EU law. This almost tautological exercise demonstrates that PSPP was essentially a conflict about competences (vires) and should be predominantly construed as such. In any case, there were more than solid legal grounds for initiating an infringement proceeding against Germany because, in short, a national (constitutional) court must not 'refuse to give effect to a preliminary ruling' from the Court of Justice.[51]

## *(iii) Timing and Tactics*

It certainly came as a surprise that the infringement proceeding was not initiated until 9 June 2021, more than a year after PSPP I. It is likely that the Commission wanted to make its reaction dependent on the outcome of the PSPP II decision. However, due to the specific procedural framework of PSPP II, any expectation that the BVerfG would significantly relativise its judgment on the merits could hardly have been met. Perhaps the late timing was also motivated by tactical considerations. The Commission may have wanted to wait for the BVerfG's decision on Next Generation EU (NGEU) of 15 April 2021, a decision on preliminary injunctions by which the BVerfG effectively paved the way for Germany's participation in NGEU.[52] From the Commission's point of view, there was certainly an interest in not triggering any disagreements in the run-up to this important decision. Be that as it may, the seriousness of the infringements as well as the fact that, in the event of inaction, the Commission would probably have been accused – fairly or not – of applying double standards when it came to violations of core principles of EU law ultimately left the Commission with little choice[53] but to at least initiate the proceeding.[54]

## *(iv) Predicaments*

The problems of the infringement proceeding were obvious from the outset. If the Commission were to bring the case to the CJEU at a later stage, the Court would ultimately have to adjudicate on its own cause, at least to a certain extent. Furthermore, even though the infringement proceeding was directed against Germany as a Member State, Germany was represented by the Federal Government. The Federal Government, however, could by no means interfere with the decision-making powers of the BVerfG without violating the principle of

[51] *RS* (n 43) para 72.

[52] BVerfG, Case 2 BvR 547/21 *NGEU – Preliminary Injunctions* (15 April 2021) www.bundesverfassungsgericht.de/SharedDocs/Entscheidungen/EN/2021/04/rs20210415_2bvr054721en.htm.

[53] Even if the details are disputed, initiating infringement proceedings, and in particular taking the case to the Luxembourg court, falls legally within the Commission's discretionary powers.

[54] In favour of an infringement procedure, see also I Pernice, 'Sollte die EU-Kommission Deutschland wegen des Karlsruher Ultra-Vires-Urteils verklagen? PRO', *Verfassungsblog* (16 May 2020) www.verfassungsblog.de/sollte-die-eu-kommission-deutschland-wegen-des-karlsruher-ultra-vires-urteils-verklagen-pro.

judicial independence, which is protected under both EU and national constitutional law. The Federal Government found itself in a precarious position. Although it was itself firmly opposed to the BVerfG's approach, it had not only to abide by the PSPP ruling at the national level, but also defend it at the European level vis-à-vis the Commission and find a way out of the predicament.

There were many ideas on how to proceed. Putting a complete end to the BVerfG's ultra vires and identity review by way of a constitutional amendment was not an option, since the BVerfG ultimately grounds its approach on the so-called eternity clause of Article 79(3) of the Basic Law, thereby immunising it even from constitutional revision. However, thought was given to amending the statute of the BVerfG and the procedural rules contained therein. One proposal was to introduce the requirement of a qualified majority or even of a decision of the Plenary (both senates of the BVerfG united) for an ultra vires decision.[55] Another proposal was to amend the procedural rules to the effect that a second referral to the CJEU would become mandatory in future cases comparable to PSPP.[56] Admittedly, such modifications would have had the disadvantage of implicitly acknowledging the BVerfG's ultra vires reservation. And the legislator would possibly have exposed itself politically to the accusation of muzzling the BVerfG, which enjoys a strong reputation in the population. Considering the possibility that the Commission might take the case to the CJEU, some even contemplated involving a former constitutional judge as an agent in order to represent the position of the BVerfG authentically, but without involving sitting judges. Admittedly, this solution would have carried the risk that a committed defence of the BVerfG by a former judge could ultimately even increase the tensions with the European institutions.

### *(v) Constructive Misunderstandings and the Closure of the Infringement Proceeding*

In the end, none of these solutions were put into practice. It is no exaggeration to state that it was ultimately constructive misunderstandings that mitigated the conflict. The Federal Government refrained from issuing a legally detailed response to the Commission and instead relied on a strategy of appeasement. It blended out the deeper dimension of the conflict and limited itself to declarative legal statements and general political commitments, thereby attempting, on the one hand, to clearly affirm adherence to core principles of EU law without, on the other hand, openly contradicting the BVerfG.

The task was akin to squaring the circle. As a result, the Federal Government kept its reply of 3 August 2021 brief, declaratory and general. The letter, the wording of which was reportedly coordinated with the BVerfG in advance, only

[55] See U Karpenstein and M Steinbeiß, 'Die Stunde des Gesetzgebers', *Verfassungsblog* (19 July 2021) www.verfassungsblog.de/die-stunde-des-gesetzgebers.
[56] ibid.

became public after the above-mentioned FOI request was made.[57] The text is just four and a half pages long and consists of four parts. In the first part, the Federal Government selectively enlists several EU-friendly elements of the BVerfG's case law,[58] including the more recent case law on the direct application of EU fundamental rights by the BVerfG.[59] In the second part, which is called 'Declaration', the Federal Government refers to the domestic constitutional foundations of Germany's participation in the EU, emphasising, first, that the Basic Law obliges all state bodies to exercise their respective competences in a manner that is friendly towards EU law and in accordance with the Treaties and, second, that Germany 'confirmed' the primacy of EU law by ratifying the Treaty of Lisbon with the declaration No 17 contained therein.[60] The Federal Government declares that, 'in this sense', Germany recognises the principles of autonomy, primacy, effectiveness and uniform application of EU law, as well as the judicial competences of the CJEU.[61] The fact that the Federal Government normatively refers back to the Basic Law and explicitly recognises the fundamental principles of EU law 'in this sense', ie on the basis of the German constitution, illustrates that the Federal Government did not (in fact, could not) openly contradict the approach of the BVerfG, which sets limits to the constitutional foundations of German participation in the EU.[62] Furthermore, the Federal Government stated that Germany was 'expressly committed to a Union which respects the national identities of its Member States and which is deeply rooted in the common values enshrined in Article 2 TEU', values which 'must not be called into question'.[63]

In the third part of the reply, the Federal Government gave the following 'assurance':

> Against this background, the Federal Government will, in accordance with its obligation of loyal cooperation under the Treaties, use all means at its disposal to ensure full compliance with the principles of autonomy, primacy of application, as well as effectiveness and uniform application of Union law, in order to guarantee the judicial competences conferred on the Court of Justice by the Treaties – in particular the competence to provide the binding and definitive interpretation of EU law in accordance with the Treaties and to rule on its validity.[64]

The relationship between the European and the national judiciary was finally addressed in the fourth part. Here, the Federal Government explicitly recognised

[57] Observations of the Federal Government (2 August 2021) www.ruleoflaw.pl/wp-content/uploads/2022/02/doc-2-DE-reply-to-LFN-de.pdf.

[58] ibid.

[59] On that, see M Wendel, 'The Two-Faced Guardian: Or How One Half of the German Federal Constitutional Court Became a European Fundamental Rights Court' (2020) 57 *CML Rev* 1383.

[60] Observations (n 57).

[61] ibid.

[62] These limits are derived from the principle of democracy, as protected in its essence by the eternity clause i.e. Article 79(3) of the German Basic Law.

[63] Observations (n 57).

[64] ibid.

that a national court which considers an act of EU law to be ultra vires or to violate national (constitutional) identity is obliged under Article 267 TFEU to refer the case to the CJEU for a preliminary ruling, if necessary even a second time.[65] Eventually, the Federal Government suggested the establishment of a structured judicial dialogue in the sense of a 'platform of European judges'.[66]

The Commission reacted by closing the infringement proceeding on 2 December 2021.[67] While this outcome is perhaps not surprising as such, given the above-mentioned predicaments that a case before the CJEU would have raised, both the timing and the Commission's reasoning certainly are. As far as timing is concerned, the Commission would still have had the opportunity, after the elections in Germany, to push the matter a bit further and try to get substantial changes on the German side. The Commission could have issued a reasoned opinion to continue to put pressure on the new federal government, for example with regard to a change in procedural law or equivalent measures. From this perspective, the Commission's early concession is certainly somewhat unfortunate and disappointing.

As far as the reasoning is concerned, reading the Commission's press release, one could almost get the impression that the Commission had looked through rose-coloured glasses. At first sight, it might appear astonishing that the Guardian of the Treaties (Article 17 TEU) has interpreted the Federal Government's answer in such an overwhelmingly positive manner. First, the Commission holds the view that Germany 'has provided very strong commitments'.[68] While this is certainly true, it does not alter the fact that the Federal Government did so within the normative framework of the Basic Law, for which the BVerfG has established the notorious red lines and reservations. The Federal Government can express its commitment as 'strong' as it likes. As long as this commitment remains normatively linked to the Basic Law, it remains potentially limited by constitutional boundaries as interpreted by the BVerfG.

Second, the Commission expresses its appreciation that Germany 'explicitly' recognised the authority of the Court of Justice and the fact 'that the legality of acts of Union institutions cannot be made subject to the examination of constitutional complaints before German courts'. As far as 'legality' refers to 'validity', the statement misses the point. Within the framework of ultra vires or identity review, the BVerfG has never claimed to judge on the validity of EU law, but only on its domestic (non-)application. More importantly, the Federal Government only acknowledged the Court's competences 'in accordance with the Treaties'. In view of the BVerfG, however, the Treaties only have binding effect in Germany on the basis of the domestic statute approving their ratification, which is why the exact scope of

[65] ibid.
[66] ibid.
[67] European Commission press release (2 December 2021) www.ec.europa.eu/commission/presscorner/detail/de/inf_21_6201.
[68] ibid.

the conferral of competences on the EU, including judicial competences, is considered to be subject to constitutional review by the BVerfG. In this respect, too, the commitment of the Federal Government cannot resolve the deeper conflict.

Third, the Commission states that the Federal Government had committed 'to use all the means at its disposal to avoid, in the future, a repetition of an ultra vires finding, and take an active role in that regard'.[69] This is a very optimistic reading, because the Federal Government certainly cannot take any 'active role' that would compromise judicial independence, either under EU law or under national constitutional law.

So was it all in vain? Was the Commission's reaction ill-informed, even naïve? The better arguments suggest that it was rather a wise form of constructive misunderstanding. It must have been clear to both the Commission and the Federal Government that the remaining part of the conflict could ultimately not be solved in legal terms. It was legally impossible for the Federal Government to give an answer that would have done full justice to both perspectives, the national and the European, on the question of 'ultimate authority'. Moreover, apart from potential proposals to amend the procedural law, the Federal Government must not influence the BVerfG without compromising judicial independence. The same holds true for the legislator. The Commission's constructive misunderstandings, ie the reading that the specific conflict could be seen as resolved by Germany's 'strong' commitment to core principles and judicial dialogue, made it possible to bring the conflict, which originates in the plurality of independent constitutional claims, out of the impasse and back onto a constructive path: proceduralisation and dialogue. This raises the issue of the pluralist constitutional architecture of the Union.

## III The PSPP Conflict as a Poorly Articulated Expression of Constitutional Pluralism

Did the conflict call into question the pluralist constitutional architecture of the EU? Is it true that the BVerfG's 'real-life attack on supremacy does to legal pluralism theory what the Trump Government's real-life alternative facts and blatant lies in politics did to deconstructionist theory'?[70] Again, the better arguments suggest that this is not the case. On the contrary, the PSPP conflict and its 'real life' resolution, as described in detail above, should not be seen as the destruction, but rather as an expression of the pluralist constitutional architecture of the EU[71] – albeit a poorly articulated and badly tempered expression on the part of the BVerfG.

[69] ibid.
[70] Haltern (n 10) 232 fn 99.
[71] In this sense, see also M Avbelj 'The Right Question about the FCC Ultra Vires Decision' *Verfassungsblog* (6 May 2020) www.verfassungsblog.de/the-right-question-about-the-fcc-ultra-vires-decision.

## A. Constitutional Pluralism and its Critique

It is not the aim of this chapter to provide a detailed description of the elements or variants of constitutional pluralism, or to re-examine all sorts of criticisms that have been raised against it. There can certainly be no doubt that pluralist theories,[72] including multilevel constitutionalism,[73] have strongly influenced the constitutional thinking about EU law in the last two decades.[74] At its core, constitutional pluralism is based on the premise that both national and EU law are autonomous legal orders that raise 'independent constitutional claims' alongside each other.[75] In other words, constitutional pluralism acknowledges (or postulates) that there are multiple, independent and incommensurable claims of constitutional autonomy[76] which relate to each other not hierarchically but heterarchically, while the question of ultimate authority is left open in legal terms.[77] For the relationship between the CJEU and the Bundesverfassungsgericht, this means that the approaches of both courts, while coherent, logical and consistent in themselves, are incommensurable and mutually irreconcilable when it comes to the very constitutional foundations of the EU. The disagreement is principled in nature and may ultimately, albeit highly exceptionally, lead to different results. It is precisely this irreconcilability that the PSPP conflict has brought to the surface.

While constitutional pluralism can be criticised for its basic theoretical premise[78] (which neither stands nor falls with PSPP), the criticism voiced in the course of the OMT and PSPP saga appears to be predominantly utilitarian in nature. According to critics, the 'essential shortcoming' of constitutional pluralism was that it failed to answer the 'question of what should happen when an outright constitutional conflict cannot be avoided and one judicial authority or another has to

[72] For the 'pluralism of pluralisms', see N Krisch, *Beyond Constitutionalism – The Pluralist Structure of Postnational Law* (Oxford, Oxford University Press, 2010) 71.

[73] For the concept of multilevel-constitutionalism, see I Pernice, 'Multilevel Constitutionalism and the Treaty of Amsterdam: European Constitution-Making Revisited?' (1999) 36 *CML Rev* 703; I Pernice, *Der Europäische Verfassungsverbund* (Baden-Baden, Nomos, 2020). If properly understood, there is a significant conceptual intersection of multilevel constitutionalism and constitutional pluralism, *cf* FC Mayer and M Wendel, 'Multivelel Constitutionalism and Constitutional Pluralism' in M Avbelj and J Komárek (eds), *Constitutional Pluralism in the European Union and Beyond* (Oxford, Hart Publishing, 2012) 127, 132 et seq.

[74] For varying concept, see, eg N MacCormick, 'Beyond the Sovereign State' (1993) 56 *MLR* 1; N Walker, 'The Idea of Constitutional Pluralism' (2002) 65 *MLR* 317; M Poiares Maduro, 'Contrapunctual Law: Europe's Constitutional Pluralism in Action' in N Walker (ed), *Sovereignty in Transition* (Oxford, Hart Publishing, 2003) 501, 511 et seq; Avbelj and Komárek (n 73); K Jaklic, *Constitutional Pluralism in the EU* (Oxford, Oxford University Press, 2014).

[75] Walker (n 74) 317, 337.

[76] See in particular A Peters, *Elemente einer Theorie der Verfassung Europas* (Berlin, Duncker & Humblot, 2001) 268 et seq.

[77] Walker (n 74) 337 et seq.

[78] With regard to multilevel constitutionalism, see M Jestaedt, 'Der Europäische Verfassungsverbund – Verfassungstheoretischer Charme und rechtstheoretischer Insuffizienz einer Unschärferelation' in R Krause et al (eds) *Recht der Wirtschaft und der Arbeit in Europa* (2004) 662 et seq; see also A Somek, 'Monism: A Tale of the Undead' in Avbelj and Komárek (n 73) 343, 355 et seq.

have the final say'[79] – or, simply put, that it could not 'provide a practical, ultimate answer to the question at the heart of the *Kompetenz-Kompetenz* conundrum'.[80] Apart from the fact that the alleged failure to provide a 'practical' answer is not a counterargument to the theoretical premise of constitutional pluralism and that there are well-founded (epistemological as well as normative) reasons for scepticism with regard to 'ultimate' answers, claims to the 'last say' and conceptual re-entries of undivided sovereignty,[81] it is important to note that constitutional pluralism, if properly understood, should not be equated with arbitrariness or with the autocratic 'reading', ie the usurpation of constitutional pluralism.[82]

## B. Cooperative Constitutional Pluralism and the BVerfG's Failure

Constitutional pluralism as referred to here is best understood in the sense of a 'cooperative constitutional pluralism'.[83] While recognising that both EU and national constitutional law make independent claims of constitutional autonomy, cooperative constitutional pluralism particularly emphasises that both are closely intertwined, interdependent and based on the same fundamental values.[84] Both legal orders provide for principles of openness, cooperation and mutual adjustment, such as permeability,[85] loyal cooperation and responsiveness.[86] Legally, these principles are not located on a meta-level, but are part of either the European or the national legal order.[87] However, although they are legally part of their respective legal systems – European or national – these principles contribute to both legal systems becoming a functional unit. This functional unit or 'compound' (*Verbund*)[88] is not to be confused with a monist legal order, but emerges out of mutual and coordinated interaction.[89]

[79] RD Kelemen, 'On the Unsustainability of Constitutional Pluralism' (2016) 23 *Maastricht Journal of European and Comparative Law* 136, 146, referring to Somek (n 78), who presents a deeper and more multifaceted critique that goes far beyond the utilitarian aspect.

[80] RD Kelemen et al, 'National Courts Cannot Override CJEU Judgments' *Verfassungsblog* (26 May 2020) www.verfassungsblog.de/national-courts-cannot-override-cjeu-judgments. See also F Fabbrini, 'After the OMT Case: The Supremacy of EU Law as the Guarantee of the Equality of the Member States' (2105) 16 *German Law Journal* 1003.

[81] For the normative claim(s) for constitutional pluralism, see Maduro (n 74) 75 et seq.

[82] In this sense, see also M Avbelj, 'Constitutional Pluralism and Authoritarianism' (2020) 21 *German Law Journal* 1023.

[83] FC Mayer, 'Verfassung im Nationalstaat: Von der Gesamtordnung zur europäischen Teilordnung?' (2016) 75 *Veröffentlichungen der Vereinigung Deutscher Staatsrechtslehrer* 7, 38 et seq ('Kooperativer Verfassungspluralismus').

[84] ibid.

[85] For more detail, see M Wendel, *Permeabilität im europäischen Verfassungsrecht* (Tübingen, Mohr Siebeck, 2011) 5 et seq.

[86] L Viellechner, 'Responsiver Rechtspluralismus' (2012) 51 *Der Staat* 559.

[87] Or both at the same time.

[88] See, again, Pernice (n 73).

[89] Wendel, *Permeabilität im europäischen Verfassungsrecht* (n 85) 34, 43; Mayer and Wendel (n 73) 139.

The problem with the PSPP saga is that said principles – and in particular the conflict-avoidance strategies and dialogical instruments derived from them – were not sufficiently observed by the BVerfG. Or, to frame it differently, the worrying anomaly of the PSPP saga does not relate so much to the fact that a national constitutional court opposed the CJEU in a very exceptional circumstance, but to the way – and, in particular, the legal reasoning on the basis of which – the BVerfG has done so and that it did not even sufficiently adhere to its own standards.[90] The PSPP I ruling was a poorly articulated and badly tempered expression of constitutional pluralism, because the BVerfG did not sufficiently respect core elements of cooperative constitutional pluralism, including principles by which the BVerfG is also bound under German constitutional law.

In this respect, the PSPP I ruling has indeed set a 'serious precedent' across the EU, as the Commission put it. While the BVerfG's long-standing opposition to the CJEU certainly cannot be equated with the systematic dismantling of the rule of law in Poland or Hungary,[91] and avoiding applause from the wrong side should not be a guiding principle for taking counter-majoritarian decisions either, the fact that a national constitutional court violated core principles of EU law on the basis of highly questionable arguments and without sufficient adherence to its own standards certainly poses a serious threat to the community of law.

## C. Lessons Learned?

The PSPP conflict and its political mitigation by the European Commission and the German Federal Government demonstrate that the underlying conflict on the constitutional foundations of the EU cannot, in the current state of the EU and its Member States, be legally resolved by an 'ultimate answer' or by the creation of new institutions, but must be channelled through appropriate procedures and a continuing dialogue instead.[92] If necessary, this requires a national constitutional court to refer a second preliminary reference to the CJEU. This is one of the key lessons that should be learnt from the PSPP saga.

While a return to the status quo was possible in the PSPP saga, this may not always be the case. There are situations in which dialogue alone no longer helps. Such a situation may arise in particular if the common consensus to respect the fundamental values as enshrined in Article 2 TEU and in the constitutions of EU Member States has been revoked. The danger of this basic consensus breaking down exists, for example, in a systemic crisis of the rule of law, as is currently being experienced in Poland,[93] a crisis that is, in substance, considerably different

[90] For more details, see Wendel, 'Paradoxes of Ultra-Vires Review (n 12).

[91] In this sense, see also M Jestaedt, 'Keine Handlangerdienste' *FAZ* (14 May 2020) www.faz.net/einspruch/exklusiv/das-ezb-urteil-ist-kein-handlangerdienst-fuer-populisten-16770506.html.

[92] Similarly on this point, see Haltern (n 10) 238.

[93] W Sadurski, *Poland's Constitutional Breakdown* (Oxford, Oxford University Press, 2019). See, *pars pro toto*, Case C-791/19 *Commission/Poland – Disciplinary regime applicable to judges* ECLI:EU:C:2021:596.

from the PSPP saga when it comes to the case law of constitutional courts.[94] Although such a systemic dismantling of the rule of law may aim particularly at (constitutional) courts, it typically goes far beyond the judiciary and also affects (or emanates from) the other branches of power. Accordingly, the range of responses of the European institutions to such a crisis is different and includes, for example, orders (not) to take certain executive or legislative measures at the national level, or the withholding of financial resources etc. If these and other countermeasures prove ineffective, and should the procedure under Article 7 TEU also fail to have sufficient effect (or not even be applied), sooner or later the question of a withdrawal from the EU will inevitably arise.[95] But even in this gloomy scenario, the dialogue must not break off, because it is a *conditio sine qua non* for finding common ground again.

## IV. Conclusion

The above considerations have traced in detail how the PSPP was (politically) settled and how, in particular, the European Commission's constructive misunderstandings of the German Federal Government's reply helped to bring the conflict back on a constructive path. It became apparent that the deeper-lying conflict – more precisely, the irreconcilable claims about the constitutional foundations of the EU – cannot be resolved by an 'ultimate answer', but must be channelled through the right procedures. It may sound old-fashioned these days, but dialogue is still the way to go.

[94] A crucial difference between the BVerfG and (today's) Polish Constitutional Tribunal is that the latter, due to the direct influence of the government on its decision-making, can no longer be considered an independent court even under the minimum standards of the ECHR (see ECtHR Case No 4907/18 *Xero Flor v Poland* of 7 May 2021) and that the Polish Constitutional Tribunal resists the judicial control of rule-of-law standards by the ECtHR (see Case K 6/21 of 24 November 2021) and by the CJEU (see Case K 3/21 of October 2021), whereas the BVerfG precisely demands a more thorough judicial review by the CJEU, albeit with regard to EU institutions such as the ECB. Consequently, in the infringement procedure launched with regard to the case law of the Polish Constitutional Tribunal, the European Commission also asserts a violation of Art 19(1) TEU, *cf* www.ec.europa.eu/commission/presscorner/detail/e%20n/ip_21_7070.

[95] Both under EU and national constitutional law.

# 6

# Jeffersonian Federalism and Constitutional Conflicts

GIUSEPPE MARTINICO

## I. Is the Compact Theory Alive and Kicking?

The shocking decision of the German Constitutional Court (Bundesverfassungsgericht, BVerfG) on the Public Sector Purchase Programme (PSPP)[1] shows that nullification strikes back. On that occasion, the German Constitutional Court declared that the CJEU had acted ultra vires because of the way in which the Luxembourg Court had exercised the proportionality review. Many have seen in that decision the moment of rupture of the integration process, but I believe that it can be better understood as a confirmation of the federal nature of the EU. However, rather than analysing the content of the German decision, this chapter will argue that decisions like this appear far less shocking when viewed in the light of the compact theory[2] supported by Calhoun and other scholars of pre-Civil War America.[3] Indeed, the conclusion reached by the German Court and the application of the ultra vires doctrine, with its nullification effects, reminds me of what Boom wrote in 1995 about Germany being the Virginia of Europe.[4] Federal systems properly

[1] Case *Weiss* 2 BvR 859/15, 5 May 2020.

[2] See LM Bassani, 'Stati e Costituzione: il federalismo autentico di John C. Calhoun (1782–1850)' (2015) *Eunomia. Rivista semestrale di Storia e Politica Internazionali* 291; LM Bassani, 'John C. Calhoun: Nullification, Secession, Constitution' (2014) www.abbevilleinstitute.org/review/john-c-calhoun-nullification-secession-constitution/.

[3] Fabbrini and Kelemen briefly mention the nullification crisis in their short comment on the German decision: F Fabbrini and RD Kelemen, 'With One Court Decision, Germany May Be Plunging Europe into a Constitutional Crisis' (2020) www.washingtonpost.com/politics/2020/05/07/germany-may-be-plungingeurope-into-constitutional-crisis/.

[4] SJ Boom, 'The European Union after the *Maastricht* Decision: Will Germany be the Virginia of Europe' (1995) *American Journal of Comparative Law* 177. See also T Dumbrovsky, 'Federal Solution to the EU Internal Sovereignty Conundrum: The European Doctrine of the Czech Constitutional Court and the U.S. Compact Theory' in L Tichy and T Dumbrovsky (eds), *Sovereignty and Competences of the European Union* (Prague, Charles University, 2010) 80; R Schütze, 'Federalism as Constitutional Pluralism: "Letter from America"' in M Avbelj and J Komárek (eds), *Constitutional Pluralism in the European Union and Beyond* (Oxford, Hart Publishing, 2012) 185.

understood have been no stranger to constitutional conflicts[5] of this sort.[6] To demonstrate this, in what follows, I will analyse the viewpoint of Thomas Jefferson, the first great theorist of nullification. Thomas Jefferson is one of those figures who are 'veiled in fable'[7] and who strongly marked the experience of revolutionary constitutionalism.[8] He died on the anniversary of American independence – 4 July 1826 – just like his comrade in arms and later political rival, John Adams.

The aim of this chapter is to provide a broad reflection on Thomas Jefferson's contribution to the history of federalism, a contribution that I will trace back to a central point: the relationship between Jefferson and what one could call the 'vanquished federalists'[9] (a deliberately ambiguous concept, which includes both anti-federalists and supporters of the compact theory, such as John Calhoun). In this, although their idea of federalism does not coincide with what emerged in the aftermath of the American Civil War, the anti-federalists are understood here as the 'vanquished' simply because they were the supporters of a vision of federalism that has remained a minority view since the Civil War and appears different from what has gone down in history as 'American federalism'. By American federalism, I am referring to a dual federalism characterised by a pioneering and diffuse system for the judicial review of legislation that is accompanied by a certain cultural homogeneity and a certain strength in federal government.

However, all of that was, of course, not present in the early years of the American experience. On the contrary, it was a matter of building a strong centre that would resist the centrifugal forces coming from states that were in some cases already endowed with a constitution. Moreover, at that time there was no real American nation. Until the so-called post-war (secession) amendments and the passing of the Fourteenth Amendment,[10] the Bill of Rights was also not seen as applying to the states. This was also somewhat confirmed by the letter of the First Amendment, which states that 'Congress shall make no law', and thus seems to limit the application of the document only to the federal legislature (the Congress). This can be explained because, at that stage in history, the place of rights was thought to lie in the state constitutions, which were seen as more mature. Jefferson himself had

[5] I have elsewhere explained why constitutional conflicts can play a systemic function in EU constitutional law: G Martinico, 'The "Polemical" Spirit of European Constitutional Law: On the Importance of Conflicts in EU Law' [2019] *German Law Journal* 1343.

[6] S Levinson (ed), *Nullification and Secession in Modern Constitutional Thought* (Kansas, University Press of Kansas, 2016).

[7] Adapting a quote from Jefferson's great friend James Madison: 'The infant periods of most nations are buried in silence or veiled in fable; and the world perhaps has lost but little which it needs regret. The origin and outset of the American Republic contain lessons of which posterity ought not to be deprived: and happily there never was a case in which every interesting incident could be so accurately preserved', 'From James Madison to William Eustis, 6 July 1819', https://founders.archives.gov/documents/Madison/04-01-02-0432.

[8] B Ackerman, *We the People: Foundations: 1* (Cambridge, Belknap Press, 1991).

[9] G Martinico, 'Il federalismo dei vinti. Appunti sul pensiero di John Calhoun' [2017] *Studi parlamentari e di politica costituzionale* 99.

[10] On reconstruction as a second founding moment, see E Foner, *The Second Founding. How the Civil War and Reconstruction Remade the Constitution* (New York, WW Norton & Company, 2019).

written this, stating that 'the true barriers of our liberty in this country are our state-governments'.[11]

Thomas Jefferson therefore took a position similar to those of the anti-federalists, and influenced the debate on the ratification of the Constitution from France (as he did not participate directly in the work of the Philadelphia Convention),[12] arguing, for example, for the need for a Bill of Rights. At the same time, however, Jefferson's viewpoint presents traits of autonomy from that of the anti-federalists and, not by chance, it is for this reason that Jefferson was able to enter into a dialogue with such a prominent federalist as Madison. Although the relationship between Madison and Calhoun has been analysed in some interesting studies,[13] the one between Calhoun and Jefferson has been less well studied,[14] even if Jefferson was the author of the Kentucky resolutions, in which the concept of nullification, as we will see, played an essential role.

## II. The 'Anti-federalists' and Jefferson

It is important to clarify that the so-called anti-federalists were not opposed to federalism as such. Indeed, in some ways they were the forerunners of, and many of their battles made important contributions to the history of, American federalism. Not surprisingly, scholars have addressed a 'persistence of Anti-federalism' after 1789.[15] The anti-federalists were a large group of people, including George Mason, Patrick Henry and Melancton Smith, among others. As Bassani points out, they 'did not advocate a specific project of government'[16] and were a very heterogeneous group. However, it is possible to find some common traits, starting with their harsh criticism of the product of the Philadelphia Convention. Other common elements consisted of a liberal vision of the state–individual relationship, a conviction of the virtue and adequacy of the Articles of Confederation (which did not exclude the need for their reform), and a fear of an overly robust federal level. Finally, they believed that democracy worked only for small political units and not for large states.[17]

[11] T Jefferson, 'Thomas Jefferson to Destutt de Tracy, 26 January 1811', https://founders.archives.gov/documents/Jefferson/03-03-02-0258.

[12] Defined as 'an assembly of demigods' by Jefferson: 'Thomas Jefferson to John Adams, 30 August 1787' https://teachingamericanhistory.org/library/document/thomas-jefferson-to-john-adams/.

[13] On the relationship between Madison and Calhoun, see W Bolt, 'Founding Father and Rebellious Son: James Madison, John C. Calhoun, and the Use of Precedents' [2004] *American Nineteenth Century History* 1.

[14] With some notable exceptions, including, for instance, in Italy, LM Bassani, *Thomas Jefferson. Un profilo intellettuale* (Naples, Guida, 2002) 164.

[15] RE Ellis, 'The Persistence of Antifederalism after 1789' in R Beeman et al (eds), *Beyond Confederation: Origins of the Constitution and American National Identity* (Chapel Hill, University of North Carolina Press, 1987).

[16] LM Bassani, 'Gli avversari della Costituzione americana: "antifederalisti" o "federalisti autentici"?' in *Gli Antifederalisti. I nemici della centralizzazione in America (1787–1788)* (Milan, IBL Libri, 2011) 49.

[17] ibid.

In this respect, as has been argued,[18] the anti-federalists were, above all, enemies of centralisation. It is no coincidence that they did not call themselves 'anti-federalists' – a label they rejected and that was given to them by their rivals.[19] As Bassani argued, they were in some ways the 'authentic federalists',[20] and, in fact, were rediscovered by historians and jurists as early as in the aftermath of the American Civil War.[21] The anti-federalists also shared something with the supporters of the compact theory. Amongst these common elements we find, for example, an aversion to the 'invention'[22] of 'We the People of the United States', the formula that opens the preamble to the federal Constitution and that was contested in the following terms by Patrick Henry:

> I have the highest veneration for those gentlemen; but, sir, give me leave to demand, What right had they to say, We, the people? My political curiosity, exclusive of my anxious solicitude for the public welfare, leads me to ask, Who authorized them to speak the language of, We, the people, instead of, We, the states? States are the characteristics and the soul of a confederation. If the states be not the agents of this compact, it must be one great, consolidated, national government, of the people of all the states. I have the highest respect for those gentlemen who formed the Convention, and, were some of them not here, I would express some testimonial of esteem for them. America had, on a former occasion, put the utmost confidence in them – a confidence which was well placed; and I am sure, sir, I would give up anything to them; I would cheerfully confide in them as my representatives. But, sir, on this great occasion, I would demand the cause of their conduct. Even from that illustrious man who saved us by his valor [George Washington], I would have a reason for his conduct: that liberty which he has given us by his valor, tells me to ask this reason; and sure I am, were he here, he would give us that reason. But there are other gentlemen here, who can give us this information. The people gave them no power to use their name. That they exceeded their power is perfectly clear. It is not mere curiosity that actuates me.[23]

In fact, the decision to include the formula 'We the People' in the preamble was made by the Committee of Style to avoid inserting the names of the states before they ratified the Constitution.[24]

Years later, a similar aversion to the popular and unitary reconstruction of the American constitutional subject can be discerned, especially in the words of John Calhoun. He is one of the most controversial figures in American history. Salvadori defined him as an 'embarrassing genius',[25] a definition that captures many aspects

[18] ibid 9.

[19] HJ Storing, *What the Anti-Federalists Were for. The Political Thought of the Opponents of the Constitution* (Chicago, University of Chicago Press, 1981) 9; Bassani, 'Gli avversari' (n 16) 46.

[20] Bassani, 'Gli avversari' (n 16) 9.

[21] ibid 60.

[22] E Morgan, *Inventing the People: The Rise of Popular Sovereignty in England and America* (New York, WW Norton & Company, 1988) 15.

[23] P Henry, 'We the People? or We the States?', 4 June 1788, www.redhill.org/speech/we-people-or-we-states.

[24] Bassani, 'Gli avversari' (n 16) 48.

[25] ML Salvadori, *Potere e libertà nel mondo moderno. John C. Calhoun: un genio imbarazzante* (Bari, Laterza, 1996).

of his complex personality and thoughts. Calhoun was Secretary of War under James Monroe's presidency, Secretary of State under John Tyler and Vice President of the United States twice (from 1825 to 1832), under John Quincy Adams and Andrew Jackson. He was also one of only two Vice Presidents (the other being Spiro Theodore Agnew under Nixon) who have resigned before the end of their mandate. A fierce defender of the states' rights and someone who studied the right to secession, he was a man of his times. Born in Abbeville, South Carolina, he was a Jeffersonian Republican, a member of South Carolina's legislature in 1808 and then of the House of Representatives of the United States in 1811.[26] He was a champion of the agrarian south against the industrialised north of the country, even during his vice presidency, when he assumed a clear position and wrote (anonymously) the 'South Carolina Exposition and Protest',[27] a document that then inspired the nullification crisis in 1832 after the approval of the Tariff of Abominations.

The story of John Calhoun is that of a man rooted in the culture of a country that was quickly moving from the end of the Revolution to the start of the Civil War.[28] He defended slavery and, although he passed away in 1850, Calhoun has always been seen as 'the man who started the Civil War'.[29] However he was also one of the most brilliant champions of the so-called compact theory.[30] Nevertheless, the result of the Civil War marginalised him and his theories, and confined secession as a 'taboo' in constitutional theory, as Mancini powerfully wrote:

> A paramount consideration in any secession-related discussion is that, irrespective of the nature of secessionists claims, secessions are not prima facie desirable, because they jeopardize world stability. However, demonizing secession, turning it into a constitutional taboo, often adds fuel to secessionist claims.[31]

This explains why Calhoun's intellectual legacy has frequently been neglected, as the following two very different but significant examples show. In 1965, Freehling defined Calhoun as 'one of the more confused political philosophers in the American tradition',[32] and in a very important monograph on secession published in 2014, Calhoun's name is not even present in the bibliographical references.[33] Despite this marginalisation, Calhoun has nevertheless had an incredible influence

[26] For further bibliographical details, see the entry published on the US Senate's website: United States Senate, 'John C Calhoun, 7th Vice President (1825–1832)', www.senate.gov/artandhistory/history/common/generic/VP_John_Calhoun.htm.

[27] JC Calhoun, 'South Carolina Exposition and Protest' (1828) https://clockworkconservative.wordpress.com/freedom/primary-documents/south-carolina-exposition-and-protest/.

[28] LM Bassani, *Dalla Rivoluzione alla Guerra Civile. Federalismo e Stato moderno in America (1776–1865)* (Soveria Mannelli, Rubbettino, 2009).

[29] To cite the emblematical title of an article by ES Rafuse, 'John C. Calhoun: He Started the Civil War' (2002) www.historynet.com/john-c-calhoun-he-started-the-civil-war.htm.

[30] A La Pergola, *Residui contrattualistici e struttura federale nell'ordinamento degli Stati Uniti* (Milan, Giuffrè, 1969).

[31] S Mancini, 'Secession and Self-Determination' in M Rosenfeld and A Sajò (eds), *The Oxford Handbook of Comparative Constitutional Law* (Oxford, Oxford University Press, 2012) 482.

[32] WW Freehling, 'Spoilsmen and Interests in the Thought and Career of John C. Calhoun' [1965] *Journal of American History* 42.

[33] D Haljan, *Constitutionalising Secession* (Oxford, Hart Publishing, 2014).

on a number of important legal scholars and political theorists, such as Jellinek, Schmitt and Seydel (who, not by coincidence, is called 'the Bavarian Calhoun').[34] In his Constitutional Theory, Carl Schmitt recognises the importance of both Calhoun's and Seydel's theories, 'the scholarly value of which persists even if their creators stood on the defeated side'.[35]

Calhoun's reflections are part of a series of ambiguities that characterised the constitutional design of 1787, relating, for example, to concepts such as 'the people' and 'the supremacy of federal law', and arising from the absence of a clear indication of who was the arbiter in charge of resolving conflicts between the different levels of government[36] As is well known, the Supreme Court of the United States contributed to resolving this ambiguity with its rulings. The case of *Martin v Hunter's Lessee*,[37] decided in 1816, has been called by Warren 'the keystone of the whole arch of the federal judicial power'.[38] In that case, the Supreme Court reaffirmed its jurisdiction, starting from the premise that 'the Constitution of the United States was ordained and established not by the States in their sovereign capacities, but emphatically, as the preamble of the Constitution declares, by "the people of the United States"'.[39] This consideration led to the conclusion that

> there can be no doubt, that it was competent to the people to invest the general government with all the powers which they might deem proper and necessary; to extend or restrain these powers according to their own good pleasure, and to give them a paramount and supreme authority.[40]

Two key provisions of the Constitution, Article III, section 2 and the Supremacy Clause (Article VI, section 2), were referred to, and the Supreme Court's jurisdiction to review the decisions of state courts was inferred from them. As noted by Boom, Justice Story's reference to the existence of the American people and their unity also implied the need to ensure the uniformity of law for Americans. Judge Story formulated the core of his reasoning in the following terms:

> If there were no revising authority to control these jarring and discordant judgments and harmonize them into uniformity, the laws, the treaties, and the Constitution of the United States would be different in different States, and might perhaps never have precisely the same construction, obligation, or efficacy in any two States. The public mischiefs that would attend such a state of things would be truly deplorable, and it cannot be believed that they could have escaped the enlightened convention which formed the Constitution.[41]

[34] As recalled by M Forsyth, 'The Political Theory of Federalism' in JJ Hesse and V Wright (eds), *Federalizing Europe? The Costs, Benefits, and Preconditions of Federal Political Systems* (Oxford, Oxford University Press, 1996) 36.

[35] C Schmitt, *Constitutional Theory* (Durham, Duke University Press, 2008) 391.

[36] Schütze (n 4) 185–86.

[37] 14 US 304 (1816), https://supreme.justia.com/cases/federal/us/14/304/case.html.

[38] C Warren, *The Supreme Court in United States History* (Boston, Little Brown & Company, 1926).

[39] *Martin v Hunter's Lessee* (n 37), as quoted by Warren (n 38) 449.

[40] *Martin v Hunter's Lessee* (n 37); Warren (n 38) 449.

[41] *Martin v Hunter's Lessee* (n 37).

In other words, the need for uniformity of interpretation was explained in the light of the unity of the American people, and this inevitably ended up justifying the role of the federal Supreme Court as the apex and final decision maker. Boom strongly questioned Judge Story's reconstruction, pointing out the problematic definition as 'historical facts' of many passages that are far from unambiguous in their interpretation,[42] such as the claim that the Virginia Court of Appeals was the first ever case of disobedience of a state court.[43] First of all, many state courts – in spite of what Judge Story said – had opposed the Supreme Court as early as 1798, as reported by Boom: 'when the Supreme Court of Pennsylvania stated that the Constitution did not provide for a particular tribunal to decide the limits of federal power'.[44] In the following years, as is well known, there was no lack of contested decisions of the Supreme Court, from *McCulloch v Maryland*[45] to *Cohens v Virginia*,[46] which were opposed by various forms of resistance from the states, and this resistance of course intensified as the Civil War approached.

However, if the contestation of the existence of a unitary entity called 'the American people' represented an element of contact between the anti-federalists and the proponents of the compact theory, Jefferson's position was more elusive. While Calhoun and others located the origin of the constitutional compact in the sovereignty of states (understood as something different from the government exercised by the federal level), Jefferson advocated for the 'sovereignty of the living generation',[47] built upon a theory of constituent power and the idea of the generation of the living as the driving force of the concrete order.

While having points in common with both anti-federalists and proponents of compact theory, Jefferson's viewpoint stands out for its originality. With the anti-federalists, Jefferson shared a 'veneration' for the old Constitution and for the Confederation, defining it as a 'wonderfully perfect instrument, considering the

[42] 'Story bolstered his uniformity analysis with assertions of "historical fact". Unfortunately, the historical accuracy of these facts is debatable. For example, according to Story, the Supreme Court's authority to draw the lines of federal power was specifically contemplated at the Constitutional Convention and during the deliberations of the first Congress. This proposition, if true, adds a degree of legitimacy to the outcome. However, it simply ignores the fact that Patrick Henry and James Madison were among of the most virulent opponents of the Supreme Court at this time', Boom (n 4) 190.

[43] 'Another of Story's "historical facts" was that "the supreme court of the United States has, from time to time, sustained this appellate jurisdiction in a great variety of cases, brought from the tribunals of many of the most important states in the union, and that no state tribunal has ever breathed a judicial doubt on the subject, or declined to obey the mandate of the supreme court, until the present occasion". Even if true, this does little to legitimate the legal basis of Story's position: the mere fact that state courts had not previously disobeyed a Supreme Court mandate, though giving rise to de facto authority, does not create de jure authority for the exercise of that power. At any rate, it is untrue. Although state courts had not offered serious resistance in cases which reached the Supreme Court, there were cases which did not reach the Supreme Court, in which state courts had, in fact, specifically rejected the Supreme Court's authority', Boom (n 4) 191.

[44] ibid 196.

[45] 17 US (4 Wheat) 316 (1819).

[46] 19 US 264 (1821).

[47] MD Peterson, 'Mr. Jefferson's "Sovereignty of the Living Generation"' [1976] *Virginia Quarterly Review* 437.

circumstances under which it was formed'[48] (with a partial exception for the role reserved to Congress, for example), a liberal vision of society and an aversion to a dirigiste approach to the State. The common premise of their view of the relationship between civil society and the State was that of anthropological optimism, which was combined by the anti-federalists with the myth of the 'good and simple life'.[49] In this, at first sight, Jefferson and Madison (but also Hamilton) seem to be at opposite ends of the spectrum. This is evident from Federalist 51, in which it was argued that 'if men were angels, no government would be necessary. If angels were to govern men, neither external nor internal controls on government would be necessary.'[50] It is true that Jefferson's vision was balanced by an awareness of the importance of the 'chains of the constitution',[51] but undoubtedly the common positive vision of human nature represented the glue that tied Jefferson to the anti-federalists.

## III. Jefferson, the Compact Theory and the Question of Secession

Thomas Jefferson's vision of federalism is one piece in the wider mosaic of his political and constitutional theory. For confirmation of this, it is enough to think of the origins of the Kentucky resolutions, which were drafted by Jefferson, and even of the Declaration of Independence, which, after all, has been defined by some as a real case of secession from the British empire.[52] To reduce the relationship between Jefferson and the supporters of the compact theory to a theoretical problem seems very ungenerous. This is so not only because the 'seeds of secession'[53] are to be found in the principles inspiring the Kentucky and Virginia Resolutions adopted in 1798 (Principles of 1798), to which Jefferson (and Madison) had contributed, but also because, as historians have discovered, in Jefferson's immense epistolary we can find ambiguous statements that have been used both by the supporters of

[48] T Jefferson, 'I. Answers to DéMeunier's First Queries, 24 January 1786', https://founders.archives.gov/documents/Jefferson/01-10-02-0001-0002.

[49] Bassani, 'Gli avversari' (n 16) 57.

[50] Federalist Papers No 51 (1788) https://billofrightsinstitute.org/primary-sources/federalist-no-51.

[51] See the text of the Kentucky resolutions: https://jeffersonpapers.princeton.edu/selected-documents/resolutions-adopted-kentucky-general-assembly. See also the draft of the Kentucky resolutions of 1798: https://jeffersonpapers.princeton.edu/selected-documents/jefferson%E2%80%99s-draft.

[52] 'After all, the United States began as what well might be conceived as a secessionist movement from the British Empire', S Levinson, 'Perpetual Union, Free Love, and Secession: On the Limits to the Consent of the Governed' [2013] *Tulsa Law Review* 457, 460; S Levinson, 'Secession versus Revolution' (2020) https://balkin.blogspot.com/2020/08/secession-versus-revolution.html; D McCarthy, 'Was the American Revolution Secessionist?' (2014) www.theamericanconservative.com/mccarthy/was-the-american-revolution-secessionist/.

[53] P Smith, *Sowing the Seeds of Secession: The Virginia and Kentucky Resolutions 1798, the Hartford Convention 1814 and the South Carolina Nullification Crisis 1830–32* (CreateSpace Independent Publishing Platform, 2019).

Jefferson's secessionist reading and the supporters of Jefferson's unionist vision. Without claiming to exhaust the debate in a brief contribution like this one, I will try to reconstruct that discussion.

The first manifestation of the compact theory can be found at least 10 years before the Principles of 1798, in the declaration of the delegates of Virginia concerning the ratification of the Constitution. However, the words used on that occasion refer to the 'people of the United States', and clarify that

> the powers granted under the Constitution being derived from the People of the United States may be resumed by them whensoever the same shall be perverted to their injury or oppression and that every power not granted thereby remains with them and at their will.[54]

This declaration by the Virginia delegates also contained an essential element that would, in fact, trigger the Virginia and Kentucky resolutions 10 years later. It stated that 'among other essential rights the liberty of Conscience and of the Press cannot be cancelled abridged restrained or modified by any authority of the United States'.[55]

In this sense, it is worth remembering that the genesis of the Kentucky resolutions confirmed the unitary nature of Jeffersonian thought, because the resolutions were triggered by the violation of the liberal premise par excellence: freedom of thought.[56] It was in reaction to the Alien and Sedition Acts, a set of laws approved by the federal Congress in fear of an imminent war with France, that Jefferson's greatest contribution to the theory of the rights of the states was made, with particular reference to the concept of nullification, a powerful instrument through which the states recognised the possibility of declaring certain federal acts to be invalid.

The resolutions were presented in Kentucky by John Breckinridge, through his intermediary Wilson Cary Nicholas. It is probably to John Breckinridge that we also owe the formal changes between Jefferson's draft and the approved one, and, in particular, the disappearance of the term 'nullification' from the final version.[57] Almost certainly, however, Jefferson did not write the draft resolutions with Kentucky[58] in mind. It has been argued that he was concerned with North Carolina,[59] but some textual passages suggest that Jefferson was actually thinking of Virginia. In particular, the reference to 'this commonwealth'[60] and, above

[54] 'Ratification of the Constitution by the State of Virginia; June 26, 1788', https://avalon.law.yale.edu/18th_century/ratva.asp.

[55] ibid.

[56] Bassani, *Thomas Jefferson* (n 14) 146–48.

[57] The different versions and Jefferson's notes can be viewed at https://jeffersonpapers.princeton.edu/selected-documents/kentucky-resolutions-1798.

[58] Bassani, *Thomas Jefferson* (n 14) 149.

[59] KRC Gutzman, 'The Virginia and Kentucky Resolutions Reconsidered: "An Appeal to the Real Laws of Our Country"' [2000] *Journal of Southern History* 473.

[60] 'Resolutions Adopted by the Kentucky General Assembly, 1798–1799' in *The Papers of Thomas Jefferson, Volume 30: 1 January 1798 to 31 January 1799* (Princeton, Princeton University Press, 2003) 550–56, https://jeffersonpapers.princeton.edu/selected-documents/resolutions-adopted-kentucky-general-assembly.

all, the reference to a law passed by 'this state' are suspicious.[61] In fact, at that time there was no trace of such a law in either North Carolina or Kentucky, while in Virginia, in 1785, the Statute for Establishing Religious Freedom,[62] drafted by Jefferson himself, had been approved.

To cut a long story short, it is worth briefly recalling the common premise of nullification and interposition, understood as 'states' rights' (although sometimes referred to more properly as constitutional remedies[63]), in the compact theory.[64] 'Interpose' was the term used in the Virginia resolutions – the mind of which was Madison's – to describe the line to be taken in the event of the federal government acting ultra vires, using a terminology which is much in vogue today:

> Assembly doth explicitly and peremptorily declare, that it views the powers of the federal government, as resulting from the compact, to which the states are parties; as limited by the plain sense and intention of the instrument constituting the compact; as no further valid than they are authorized by the grants enumerated in that compact; and that in case of a deliberate, palpable, and dangerous exercise of other powers, not granted by the said compact, the states who are parties thereto, have the right, and are in duty bound, to interpose for arresting the progress of the evil, and for maintaining within their respective limits, the authorities, rights and liberties appertaining to them. That the General Assembly doth particularly protest against the palpable and alarming infractions of the Constitution, in the two late cases of the 'Alien and Sedition Acts' passed at the last session of Congress … that the acts aforesaid, are unconstitutional; and that the necessary and proper measures will be taken by each, for co-operating with this state, in maintaining the Authorities, Rights, and Liberties, referred to the States respectively, or to the people.[65]

Nullification, on the other hand, was the term used in the Kentucky resolutions of 1798, drafted, as is well known, by Jefferson:

> In cases of an abuse of the delegated powers, the members of the general government, being chosen by the people, a change by the people would be the constitutional remedy;

[61] ibid: 'As this state by a Law passed on the general demand of its Citizens, had already protected them from all human restraint or interference.'

[62] 'After Wilson Cary Nicholas informed Jefferson on 4 Oct. 1798 that John Breckinridge could furnish a means of introducing the resolutions in the Kentucky legislature, Jefferson replied that "I had imagined it better those resolutions should have originated with N. Carolina. But perhaps the late changes in their representation may indicate some doubt whether they would have passed" (TJ to Nicholas, 5 Oct. 1798). It seems unlikely, however, that Jefferson had North Carolina in mind when he penned the resolutions. In the resolves he almost exclusively characterised the state that would pass them as "this commonwealth", a term that had no particular reference to North Carolina. Moreover, in his third resolution Jefferson, discussing encroachments on religious freedom, noted that "this state, by a law passed on the general demand of its citizens, had already protected" religious exercise and opinion "from all human restraint or interference". No North Carolina statute of the time, and for that matter none passed by Kentucky, matched that description. The reference actually seems to point to the Statute for Establishing Religious Freedom drafted by Jefferson and passed into law in Virginia in 1785. If that is the case, then Virginia was the "commonwealth" Jefferson had in mind as he drafted the resolutions', BB Oberg, 'Editorial Note' in *The Papers of Thomas Jefferson, Volume 30* (n 60) 529, https://jeffersonpapers.princeton.edu/selected-documents/kentucky-resolutions-1798.

[63] Schütze (n 4) 186.

[64] La Pergola (n 30) 58.

[65] Virginia resolutions, 1798, https://founders.archives.gov/documents/Madison/01-17-02-0128.

> but, where powers are assumed which have not been delegated, a nullification of the act is the rightful remedy: that every State has a natural right in cases not within the compact, (*casus non fœderis*) to nullify of their own authority all assumptions of power by others within their limits.[66]

In this, the great characteristic that makes Jefferson's federalism different from Calhoun's was linked, once again, to the doctrine of natural rights that inspired all aspects of his thought. As we have seen, in fact, even nullification, in the words of the Kentucky resolutions, was a 'natural right', as was even more clearly evident in the draft drawn up by Jefferson. This element was absent from Calhoun's theory.[67]

The term 'nullification' did not appear in the final text of the Kentucky resolutions of 1798, which did, however, retain the passage in which an ultra vires federal act was conceived as 'unauthoritative, void, and of no force'. In that text, it was also argued that 'the Government created by this compact was not made the exclusive or final judge of the extent of the powers delegated to itself'. Finally, in the Kentucky resolutions, it was stated that, because of the absence of a 'common Judge', 'each party has an equal right to judge for itself, as well of infractions as of the mode and measure of redress'.[68] Incidentally, the word 'nullification' would later be used in the Kentucky resolutions of 1799,[69] although it is not clear whether the author of this text was also Jefferson.[70] Like Calhoun years later, Jefferson kept the authorship of the Kentucky resolutions of 1798 a secret[71] because he was Vice President of the United States at the time. Taylor was reportedly the first to mention Jefferson as the 'mastermind' behind the resolutions.[72]

A comparison of the Virginia and Kentucky texts reveals another important difference: whereas nullification seems to have been conceived as a unilateral right of each state, interposition seems to have been a kind of 'collective' right of the states.

[66] Kentucky resolutions, 1798: 'Jefferson's Draft' in *The Papers of Thomas Jefferson, Volume 30* (n 60) 536–43, https://jeffersonpapers.princeton.edu/selected-documents/jefferson%E2%80%99s-draft.

[67] Bassani, *Thomas Jefferson* (n 14) 165.

[68] 'Resolutions Adopted by the Kentucky General Assembly' (n 60).

[69] 'Kentucky Resolution – Alien and Sedition Acts' (1799) https://avalon.law.yale.edu/18th_century/kenres.asp.

[70] 'The Kentucky Resolutions of 1799 are of uncertain authorship, but revived Jefferson's nullification language, asserting that "the several states who formed [the Constitution] … have the unquestionable right to judge of its infraction; and, That a nullification … of all unauthorized acts … is the rightful remedy"', N Verell and J Ragosta, 'Kentucky and Virginia Resolutions' (The Jefferson Monticello, 2018) www.monticello.org/site/research-and-collections/kentucky-and-virginia-resolutions.

[71] 'The ethics of secrecy may be questioned but in this case the necessity for the real authors to conceal their identity was plain. The war fever which permitted the bitterly anti-French Congress of 1798 to initiate and pass the Alien and Sedition Acts could have been relied on for explosive retaliations had the principal author of the Kentucky Resolutions been publicly identified as Thomas Jefferson, then Vice President in the John Adams administration', A Koch and H Ammon, 'Virginia and Kentucky Resolutions: An Episode in Jefferson's and Madison's Defense of Civil Liberties' [1948] *William and Mary Quarterly* 145, 147.

[72] 'Taylor was also the first person to reveal Jefferson's connection with the Kentucky Resolutions. He explicitly named Jefferson in a footnote to his An Inquiry into the Principles and Policy of the Government of the United States which was published in 1814. But general notice was not attracted to Jefferson's authorship until the same information appeared in the Enquirer in 1821', ibid 148. On the relationship between Taylor and Jefferson, see B McClanahan, 'Taylor and Jefferson on Secession' (*Abbeville Institute blog*, 2019) www.abbevilleinstitute.org/blog/taylor-and-jefferson-on-secession/.

The Kentucky resolutions were harshly criticised by Madison himself in the Report of 1800, precisely because of the unilateral nature of the concept of nullification.[73] It is worth quoting the (long) passage in full:

> The constitution of the United States was formed by the sanction of the states, given by each in its sovereign capacity. It adds to the stability and dignity, as well as to the authority of the constitution, that it rests on this legitimate and solid foundation. The states then being the parties to the constitutional compact, and in their sovereign capacity, it follows of necessity, that there can be no tribunal above their authority, to decide in the last resort, whether the compact made by them be violated; and consequently that as the parties to it, they must themselves decide in the last resort, such questions as may be of sufficient magnitude to require their interposition. It does not follow, however, that because the states as sovereign parties to their constitutional compact, must ultimately decide whether it has been violated, that such a decision ought to be interposed either in a hasty manner, or on doubtful and inferior occasions. Even in the case of ordinary conventions between different nations, where, by the strict rule of interpretation, a breach of a part may be deemed a breach of the whole; every part being deemed a condition of every other part, and of the whole, it is always laid down that the breach must be both wilful and material to justify an application of the rule. But in the case of an intimate and constitutional union, like that of the United States, it is evident that the interposition of the parties, in their sovereign capacity, can be called for by occasions only, deeply and essentially affecting the vital principles of their political system.[74]

Moreover, in criticising South Carolina's decision at the time of the nullification crisis, Madison also defended the memory of his friend Jefferson against the exploitations made years earlier by the supporters of the South Carolina action, writing that 'it is remarkable how closely the nullifiers who make the name of Mr. Jefferson the pedestal for their colossal heresy, shut their eyes and lips, whenever his authority is ever so clearly and emphatically against them'.[75] Madison probably thought that the words used in the draft Kentucky resolutions arose from his friend's fiery temper,[76] but he was certainly also trying to defend his own position as expressed in the Virginia resolutions; these were more moderate than the Kentucky resolutions, and he added that the latter had been 'more easily perverted'.[77]

Furthermore, the usefulness of the distinction between interposition and nullification has been contested in scholarship. For example, La Pergola wrote, in an unmistakable style, that 'it seems to us, however, that any distinction between

[73] As recalled by Schütze (n 4) 190. See also HJ Powell, 'The Principles of' 98: An Essay in Historical Retrieval' [1994] *Virginia Law Review* 689, 718, in which it is said that the resolutions of Virginia 'did not in fact license any legally significant action by an individual state. The authority of the states over the Constitution and its interpretation was collective and could be exercised only in concert through the electoral process or by a quasi-revolutionary act of the people themselves'.

[74] 'The Report of 1800, [7 January] 1800', https://founders.archives.gov/documents/Madison/01-17-02-0202.

[75] J Madison, 'Letter to Nicholas Trist, 23 December 1832', https://teachingamericanhistory.org/library/document/letter-to-nicholas-trist/.

[76] Bolt (n 13).

[77] Madison, 'Letter to Nicholas Trist' (n 75).

these figures of the *Hoheitsrechte* is, perhaps, more subtle than productive'.[78] For Schütze, however, it was possible to distinguish between these instruments in the light of the concept of sovereignty. While the idea of interposition did not contradict Madison's well-known position in Federalist 51[79] on the existence of a shared sovereignty, the idea of nullification would have been irreconcilable with such an approach (in fact, the concept of nullification for Calhoun went along with the refusal to conceive of a shared sovereignty). Moreover, as seen above, the idea of nullification seemed to refer to a right exercisable unilaterally by each state, while that of interposition appeared as a remedy exercisable collectively.[80]

In this regard, it is worth recalling how Calhoun used the two concepts in a fungible manner. In his words, in fact, 'This right of interposition, thus solemnly asserted by the State of Virginia, be it called what it may – State-right, veto, nullification, or by any other name – I conceive to be the fundamental principle of our system'.[81]

In 1832, John Calhoun wrote a very long letter to General James Hamilton, Governor of the State of South Carolina, in which he clarified some of the fundamental points of his thought on the so-called states' rights.[82] The text of that letter cannot be isolated from what the same author had argued a few years earlier in another fundamental document of American constitutional history.

It was, in fact, in 1828 that Calhoun, as Vice President of the United States, had anonymously published the 'South Carolina Exposition and Protest',[83] which contained a very harsh attack on the choices made by the federal government:

> Previously to the adoption of the Tariff system, such was the unanimous feeling of this State; but in speaking of its operation, it will be impossible to avoid the discussion of sectional interest, and the use of sectional language. On its authors, and not on us, who are compelled to adopt this course in self-defence, by injustice and oppression, be the censure. So partial are the effects of the system, that its burdens are exclusively on one side and its benefits on the other. It imposes on the agricultural interest of the

[78] La Pergola (n 30) 62.

[79] 'In the compound republic of America, the power surrendered by the people is first divided between two distinct governments, and then the portion allotted to each subdivided among distinct and separate departments. Hence a double security arises to the rights of the people. The different governments will control each other, at the same time that each will be controlled by itself', J Madison, 'The Structure of the Government Must Furnish the Proper Checks and Balances Between the Different Departments' in 'Federalist No 51, [6 February 1788]', www.constitution.org/fed/federa51.htm.

[80] 'Madison's constitutional "contractualism" thus did not acknowledge unilateral rights to the States. States' rights were collective rights: only the States – in the collective plural – were masters of the Constitution. By contrast, interposition was a constitutional remedy that belonged to the State governments. The State governments could place themselves "between" their people and the national government. They would signal a (potential) breach of the federal contract by means of – to borrow a constitutional concept from European constitutionalism – a yellow card mechanism', Schütze (n 4) 190–91.

[81] JC Calhoun, 'Fort Hill Address, 26 July 1831', http://teachingamericanhistory.org/library/document/fort-hill-address/.

[82] JC Calhoun, 'To General Hamilton on the Subject of State Interposition, 28 August 1832', https://archive.org/stream/correspondenceof00calhrich/correspondenceof00calhrich_djvu.txt.

[83] Bassani, *Stati e Costituzione* (n 2) 301.

> South, including the Southwest, and that portion of the country particularly engaged in commerce and navigation, the burden not only of sustaining the system itself, but that also of the Government. In stating the case thus strongly, it is not the intention of the committee to exaggerate. If exaggeration were not unworthy of the gravity of the subject, the reality is such as to make it unnecessary.[84]

The problem of customs tariffs was not new; indeed, it was a raw nerve that led to the famous nullification crisis, when a special South Carolina state convention, putting into practice what Calhoun had said in the 'South Carolina Exposition and Protest', declared federal acts 'null, void, and no law, nor binding upon this State, its officers or citizens' with the well-known ordinance of nullification of 1832.[85] This, in turn, led to an escalation of events, culminating in Congress passing the Force Bill of 1833, which authorised President Jackson to use the army, if necessary, to collect taxes. However, the Force Bill was declared 'null and void' by the South Carolina Convention.[86] In the 'South Carolina Exposition and Protest' and in his letter to General James Hamilton, Calhoun took up and developed elements already present in the so-called Principles of' 98,[87] which were proclaimed in response to the passing of the Alien and Sedition Acts. Reference was made to the famous Kentucky and Virginia resolutions and to the concepts of nullification and interposition,[88] based on the premise that the interpreters of the states' rights were the states themselves. This, according to Calhoun, was an interpretation that could be inferred from the letter of Article VII of the US Constitution: 'The ratification of the conventions of nine states shall be sufficient for the establishment of this Constitution between the states so ratifying the same.'

It was precisely this 'between' that gave the idea of the Constitution as a pact 'between' the states; or, in Calhoun's words:

> They established it as a compact between them, and not as a constitution over them; and that, as a compact, they are parties to it, in the same character. I have thus established, conclusively, that these States, in ratifying the constitution, did not lose the confederated character which they possessed when they ratified it, as well as in all the preceding stages of their existence; but, on the contrary, still retained it to the full.[89]

As historians of political doctrine have pointed out, the 'South Carolina Exposition and Protest' represented a turning point in American constitutional history, since 'this document divides American political history into a before and an after'.[90]

It is worth remembering that interposition and nullification, concepts linked to a 'contractual' reading that saw the federation as the 'agent' and the product

[84] JC Calhoun, 'South Carolina Exposition and Protest' (n 27).

[85] The text can be found at http://avalon.law.yale.edu/19th_century/ordnull.asp.

[86] On conventions in American law, see GS Wood, *The Creation of the American Republic, 1776–1787* (University of North Carolina Press, 1998) ch 8.

[87] On the importance of the Virginia and Kentucky resolutions, see Gutzman (n 59) 473.

[88] La Pergola (n 30) 58.

[89] JC Calhoun, 'A Discourse on the Government and Constitution of the United States' (1851) www.constitution.org/jcc/dcgus.htm.

[90] Bassani, *Stati e Costituzione* (n 2) 301.

of the compact, were discussed in a context that did not know the turning point represented by *Marbury v Madison*.[91] Criticism of the idea of the Supreme Court as an impartial arbiter was therefore an important element in Calhoun's thinking. If Jefferson was one of the fathers of compact theory, his ambiguity on the question of secession has been the subject of a long debate,[92] itself meriting a separate article. In short, in Jefferson's immense epistolary there are various passages[93] that have been put forward to justify his presumed adhesion to the vision of secession as a free choice of a state.[94] However, historians have recalled his reactions to New England's (unsuccessful) attempt to secede and, indeed, the New England events were harshly criticised in a letter to Lafayette in 1815.[95] Since the history of the compact theory cannot be reduced to the theory of secession, it is indeed possible to say that Jefferson sowed the seeds of the compact theory, but this does not automatically make him an advocate of secession as a right of states.

## IV. Conclusion

In conclusion, with reference to the theme of secession, although the relationship between Madison and Calhoun has been widely studied over the years, much less has been written about the relationship between Jefferson and Calhoun. Although Jefferson had been theoretically tolerant in his correspondence on possible secessionist claims, and although he had undoubtedly been a proponent of nullification, these considerations did not automatically make him a supporter of secession in practice.

Finally, for those interested in American federal dynamics, Jefferson's viewpoint still remains an inexhaustible source of insights and ideas, typical of a man rooted in his time, but also capable of explaining the intimate contradictions that have always nourished the spirit of American constitutionalism.[96] Moreover, rediscovering Jefferson's viewpoint is also helpful when trying to read the current developments of comparative federalism,[97] as we saw at the beginning of this chapter.

[91] 5 US 137 (1803).

[92] B Steele, 'Thomas Jefferson, Coercion, and the Limits of Harmonious Union' [2008] *Journal of Southern History* 823, 853.

[93] T Jefferson, 'From Thomas Jefferson to Joseph Priestley, 29 January 1804', https://founders.archives.gov/documents/Jefferson/01-42-02-0322; T Jefferson, 'From Thomas Jefferson to John Breckinridge, 12 August 1803', https://founders.archives.gov/documents/Jefferson/01-41-02-0139.

[94] A Stephens, *A Constitutional View of the Late War Between the States*, vols I and II (Philadelphia, National Publishing Company, 1868).

[95] T Jefferson, 'From Thomas Jefferson to Lafayette, 14 February 1815', https://founders.archives.gov/documents/Jefferson/03-08-02-0210.

[96] G Bognetti, *Lo spirito del costituzionalismo americano. Breve profilo del diritto costituzionale degli Stati* (Turin, Giappichelli 2000).

[97] P Hay, *Federalism and Supranational Organizations. Patterns for New Legal Structures* (Champaign, University of Illinois Press, 1966).

The historical itinerary carried out in this chapter confirms that the concept of nullification is part of the history and the present of federalism. It would be a mistake to see it only as a pathological element confined to the past. Indeed, as Hirschl argued, 'from recalcitrant states in the U.S. to member states of the EU, the notion of an issue-based withdrawal from the overarching "federal" pact – what is often referred to in American constitutional thought as nullification – is commonly invoked'.[98] Conflicts, after all, do happen even in mature federal systems. 'Nullification is considered an antebellum relic. But recently several state legislatures have passed or introduced bills asserting a state's right to judge federal laws unconstitutional and block implementation within the state.'[99] In short, while many have recently written about a 'Hamiltonian moment' for the European Union, in the light of what we have seen in this chapter, it might be better to say that the EU is experiencing a Jeffersonian moment, full of contradictions, but also deeply federal, in which states still play a major role.

After all, there are interesting similarities between the pre-Civil War United States and the European Union today: the existence of a federal bill of rights with a limited scope, the absence of a common nation and the belief that states are the main defenders of the rights of their citizens. What does this imply? Should we despair? Should we think that a future civil war in Europe is inevitable? I would not be so pessimistic. The architecture of EU federalism is based on the constitutionalisation of cooperative instruments[100] and is not based on the dualist fiction of American tradition. At the same time, the position of the Court of Justice is certainly stronger today than that of the Federal Supreme Court in those years. This is not a negligible detail, but an important difference. There are also remedies to test compliance with the principle of loyal cooperation and to protect the rights guaranteed by European rules: from infringement proceedings to the *Köbler* doctrine.[101] The principle of loyal cooperation also allows us to distinguish the position of the German Constitutional Court from that of the other Constitutional Courts that have used the ultra vires argument. The German court declared the *Weiss* judgment ultra vires only after having used the preliminary ruling procedure, thus respecting the pattern given in *Honeywell*.[102] The same cannot be said for the other courts.[103] In conclusion, while the German court's judgment may appear problematic, it does not represent the end of the process of European integration, but is a sign of the existence of federal dynamics that may pave the way for clearer relations between constitutional courts and the Court of Justice.

[98] R Hirschl, 'Opting Out of "Global Constitutionalism"' (2018) https://papers.ssrn.com/sol3/papers.cfm?abstract_id=3201564.

[99] JH Read and N Allen, 'Living, Dead, and Undead: Nullification Past and Present' [2012] *American Political Thought* 263, 263.

[100] R Schütze, *From Dual to Cooperative Federalism: The Changing Structure of European Law* (Oxford, Oxford University Press, 2009).

[101] Case C-224/01 *Köbler* ECLI:EU:C:2003:513, [2003] ECR I-10239.

[102] Case *Honeywell*, 2 BvR 2661/06, 6 July 2010.

[103] G Martinico, 'Taming National Identity: A Systematic Understanding of Article 4.2 TEU' [2021] *European Public Law* 447, 462.

# 7

# The European Union and its Three Constitutional Problems

SACHA GARBEN

## I. Introduction

This book is concerned with the constitutional future of the European Union and asks whether the latter is likely to remain a tacit, 'small c' constitutional order or whether there is a 'real' future of EU constitutionalism.[1] This chapter argues that if we consider that the central function of a constitution is the establishment, operationalisation and regulation of democratically derived authority, then EU primary law is currently suffering from three profound constitutional problems.

Firstly, and most fundamentally, while the EU, on the basis of the CJEU's landmark rulings in *Van Gend*, *Costa*, *Internationale* and *ERTA*,[2] makes a claim to the establishment of final and autonomous authority, this claim has not been explicitly deliberated and endorsed by the only legitimate source of that authority: the peoples of Europe (Problem 1, section IIA). This lack of popular sovereignty causes a deep legitimacy deficit, although it is buffered to some extent by the achievements towards a constitutionalisation of EU law in terms of the operationalisation and regulation of democratically derived authority: the EU's ordinary legislative process possesses triple-tracked democratic legitimacy (deriving from the European Parliament, the national governments and the national parliaments),[3] and the EU's actions are now explicitly embedded and conditioned by reference to the fundamental values and rights as laid down in Articles 2 and 3 TEU and the EU Charter of Fundamental Rights. This means that much of the actual,

[1] See ch 1 of this volume.

[2] Case 26-62 *NV Algemene Transport- en Expeditie Onderneming van Gend & Loos v Netherlands Inland Revenue Administration* ECLI:EU:C:1963:1, [1963] ECR 1; Case 6-64 *Flaminio Costa v ENEL* ECLI:EU:C:1964:66, [1964] ECR 585; Case 11-70, *Internationale Handelsgesellschaft mbH v Einfuhr- und Vorratsstelle für Getreide und Futtermittel* ECLI:EU:C:1970:114, [1979] ECR 1125; Case 22-70, *Commission of the European Communities v Council of the European Communities (European Agreement on Road Transport)* ECLI:EU:C:1971:32, [1971] ECR 263 (*ERTA*).

[3] National parliaments participate directly in the legislative process through the Early Warning Mechanisms in areas that are not in the EU's exclusive competence.

hard-felt authority exercised by the EU on a daily basis has been democratically operationalised and constitutionally regulated. Yet, two fundamental problems remain in this regard. The regulation of EU authority by reference to fundamental rights and principles suffers from a crucial flaw: it has 'over-constitutionalised' the economic freedoms (Problem 2, section IIB). Furthermore, any achievements in the constitutionalisation of the EU's exercise of authority are undermined by the 'legitimacy-leak' that results from authority being exercised at EU level (*sensu largo*) not through the legislative process but though the under-constitutionalised 'Union method' (Problem 3, section IIC).

The stakes are high. These three problems will need to be resolved, as the status quo based on a tacit constitution is untenable in legitimacy terms. If, however, the EU manages to address these issues, it can successfully develop into a constitutional democracy.

## II. Three Constitutional Problems

### A. Problem 1: The Lack of Popular Sovereignty, as the Peoples of Europe have not Endorsed the EU's Core Constitutional Claim to Final, Autonomous and Expansive Authority

#### *(i) The EU's Core Constitutional Claim*

When the Court of Justice of the European Union (CJEU, the Court) held in *Van Gend en Loos*[4] that Community law imposes obligations on individuals as well as confers rights upon them that become part of their legal heritage, that the Treaty of Rome had established institutions 'endowed with sovereign rights the exercise of which affects Member States and their citizens', and – especially – that the Community constituted a 'new legal order' comprising the Member States and their nationals, and that for the benefit of that new legal order the Member States limited their sovereign rights, the Court was making a profound constitutional claim. While it also stated that the new legal order thus created was one 'of international law', and that the sovereign rights limited thereby were 'in limited fields', the Court posited that the Treaty of Rome established a degree of sovereign authority.[5] More specifically, the Court claimed the jurisdictional *Kompetenz-Kompetenz* to determine, on the basis of Community law, what effect that law was to have in the

[4] Above (n 2).

[5] To an extent contra are Chalmers and Barroso where they argue that *Van Gend* lays down the 'claim that EU law limits national sovereign rights, while claiming no sovereignty of its own': D Chalmers and L Barroso, 'What Van Gend en Loos Stands For' (2014) 12 *International Journal of Constitutional Law* 105. While the Court does not say that the new legal order itself possesses sovereignty, it does consider that the institutions of that new legal order have been endowed 'with sovereign rights the exercise of which affects Member States and their citizens'.

national legal orders regardless of the latter's constitutional stipulations. While the phenomenon of direct effect of international norms, as well as their precedence over national norms, was not new,[6] the claim that this followed autonomously from *a new and (partially) sovereign European legal order as interpreted by the CJEU* constitutes the inner core of the EU's constitutional claim and – with subsequent cases shedding the 'partial' part – remains one of the most important, if not the most important, proposition of the European integration process.[7] So, while direct effect and primacy are very powerful constitutional(ising) elements, the most fundamental character of the constitutional claim by the CJEU resides in the autonomy claim that precedes and supersedes the doctrines of direct effect and primacy. For it proclaims independence of the national constitutions which were to that point understood to provide the constitutional framework, the legality and the legitimacy of the Community's authority.

That independence[8] of the Community from national constitutions is rendered from a largely theoretical notion in *Van Gend* and *Costa* to a more concrete one in *Internationale Handelsgesellschaft*,[9] where the CJEU unequivocally confirms that Community law takes precedence over national constitutions. In exchange for the attendant disapplication of the human rights guarantees enshrined in national constitutions, the CJEU in the same ruling creates Community-level protection of fundamental rights through the general principles of law, under the exclusive purview of the CJEU. The comprehensive jurisdictional *Kompetenz-Kompetenz* that results from these three foundational rulings, moreover, makes possible the dynamic expansion of the Community's sovereign material territory through the cross-cutting approach to EU powers that was launched by the Court in the fourth case of the constitutional quartet: *ERTA*.[10] In *ERTA*, the Court considers that Community competence can be derived implicitly from a purposive reading of the legal bases. Together with the direct application of Treaty provisions as laid down in *Van Gend* (and then sweepingly applied to the internal market provisions in *Dassonville*[11] and *Cassis*[12]), this 'implied powers' approach – subsequently replicated in different contexts but to the same effect[13] – parts with the notion

[6] B de Witte, 'Direct Effect, Primacy and the Nature of the Legal Order' in P Craig and G de Búrca (eds), *The Evolution of EU Law* (Oxford, Oxford University Press, 2011).

[7] Indeed, the Court itself, on the occasion of *Van Gend*'s 50th anniversary, stated that it was to be regarded as the 'source of and a framework for the principles which have shaped the constitutional structure of the European Union'. See CJEU, 'The Court Marks the 50th Anniversary of the Judgment in *Van Gend en Loos*', http://curia.europa.eu/jcms/jcms/P_95693/.

[8] National constitutional traditions are considered a source of inspiration by the Court especially in its development of the EU fundamental rights *acquis* and its general principles of law.

[9] Above (n 2).

[10] ibid.

[11] Case 8-74 *Procureur du Roi v Benoît and Gustave Dassonville* ECLI:EU:C:1974:82, [1974] ECR 837.

[12] Case 120/78 *Rewe-Zentral AG v Bundesmonopolverwaltung für Branntwein* ECLI:EU:C:1979:42, [1979] ECR 649.

[13] See, eg *Casagrande*, where the Court held that even though the EU did not possess a direct competence as regards education, this did not preclude legislation adopted on other legal bases from affecting education: Case 9-74 *Donato Casagrande v Landeshauptstadt München* ECLI:EU:C:1974:74, [1974]

of a priori limited, partial 'sovereignty' conditioned on the principle of conferral (and thus the idea of 'limited fields' of Community authority, and ultimate *Kompetenz-Kompetenz* for the Member States), and instead (re)conceptualises the Community project as an intrinsically open-ended, dynamically integrative one. This amounts to a material *Kompetenz-Kompetenz* for the Community, deriving from and feeding into its autonomy.

### *(ii) Lack of Endorsement of the Core Constitutional Claim*

The cumulative constitutional implication of the above-mentioned quartet is 'revolutionary'.[14] As authoritatively described by Weiler in 'The Transformation of Europe', these rulings in the EU's 'Foundational Period' 'created a strong constitutional integrative process that in radical mutation of the Treaty linked the legal order of the Community with that of the Member States in a federal-like relationship'.[15] However, although this claim has helped transform the EEC into the EU that it is today, and thus certainly has produced significant effects, it should be emphasised that this claim has not yet been accepted. Neither national (constitutional) courts nor the population have acquiesced to the full extent of the constitutional claim. National courts have sought to accommodate, within their own constitutional frameworks and the limits on international transfer of authority that these impose, the practical content of the Court's constitutional quartet to the greatest possible extent. This means they accept, largely without contestation,[16] the precedence of EU law over national law, the direct effect of EU provisions and the CJEU's interpretation of EU law – including, in nearly all concrete cases, whether the EU provisions fall within the EU's competence and comply with fundamental rights. But the 'higher law-making'[17] core of the constitutional quartet, ie the

ECR 00773, para 12. This cross-cutting approach was confirmed in *Tobacco Advertisement* even as regards areas where the direct legal basis features a prohibition of harmonisation, such as public health. As long as the conditions for recourse to a legal basis (such as Art 114 TFEU on the internal market) are fulfilled, the measure may have a profound impact on other policy areas where no direct legislative competence is given. Case C-376/98 *Federal Republic of Germany v European Parliament and Council of the European Union* ECLI:EU:C:2000:544, [2000] ECR I-08419, para 88.

[14] JHH Weiler, 'The Transformation of Europe' (1991) 100 *The Yale Law Journal* 2403, 2429.

[15] ibid 2428.

[16] The instances where national courts have refused to apply EU law in open defiance of the CJEU's doctrines remain very rare: the Czech Constitutional Court has refused to apply a CJEU ruling concerning Slovak pensions, deeming it ultra vires; the Danish Supreme Court in *Ajos* refused to apply the direct effect of the general principle of EU law of non-discrimination on grounds of age in a case against a private employer; in *PSPP* the German Constitutional Court condemned as ultra vires and disapplied the CJEU's *Weiss* ruling on the validity of the ECB's programme for the purchase of government bonds on secondary markets; and the Polish Constitutional Tribunal has considered the CJEU's case law concerning the organisation and operation of the Polish judiciary as ultra vires and disapplied it. As regards Polish ruling, which was widely reported in global newspapers as a high-profile rejection of the primacy of EU law altogether, it could be argued not to constitute a judgment altogether, since – as the ECHR has held – it lacks judicial independence, and thus arguably no longer constitutes a credible 'court'.

[17] In the sense of Bruce Ackerman's notion of the 'constitutional moment': B Ackerman, *We the People, Volume 1: Foundations* (Cambridge, MA, Harvard University Press, 1993); B Ackerman, *We the People, Volume 2: Transformations* (Cambridge, MA, Harvard University Press, 2000); B Ackerman, *We the People, Volume 3: The Civil Rights Revolution* (Cambridge, MA, Harvard University Press, 2018).

central constitutional claim about the authority for EU law, through the Court of Justice, to autonomously define its own content and limits, independent from national constitutions and without a final say by the national constitutional courts, has either been rejected or is being deliberated by all but one[18] of the Member States' constitutional orders.[19] EU constitutional scholars have rightly spent much time theorising the extent, degree, legitimacy and practicability of national courts' refusal to fully apply the CJEU's case law.[20] But it could be argued that it is, in fact, neither for the national courts nor for the CJEU to 'finally' decide over this issue of constitutional authority, but instead for the peoples of Europe, both separately as people of their country and collectively as the composite people of Europe, as only they can be the legitimate source of authority in a constitutional democracy.

To what extent has the CJEU's constitutional claim as set out in *Van Gend*, *Costa*, *Internationale* and *ERTA*, rendered as an interpretation of the original Rome Treaty, been codified by the subsequent Treaties? For a period of about 30 years, the Single European Act and the Maastricht, Amsterdam and Nice Treaties remained silent on the core constitutional claim set out by the Court in its constitutional quartet in the 1960s and early 1970s. There was not a word about the autonomy of the Community/EU legal order nor its supremacy, or the direct effect of Treaty provisions. As regards fundamental rights, the Nice Treaty launched the EU Charter of Fundamental Rights (now binding since Lisbon), but EU law's absolute primacy over national fundamental rights was not codified. And concerning the EU's jurisdictional/material *Kompetenz-Kompetenz* following from the constitutional quartet, while the Rome Treaty contained a reference in the preamble to 'ever closer Union' as well as some open-ended legal bases (such as the flexibility clause) – which have been kept[21] – the subsequent Treaties have made a point of making the conferral principle ever-more explicit over time, reaching a pinnacle in Lisbon.

On the one hand, it is, of course, notable that the Treaty revisions did not explicitly overturn the revolutionary doctrines proclaimed by the Court. On the other hand, this evasion – whatever the reasons for it – lies at the heart of the EU's constitutional legitimacy predicament. Even if we could go so far as to construe this lack of resistance to the Court's constitutional quartet – this 'collective inaction'[22] – as some kind of passive consent by the political powers of the Member States (which would be a stretch),[23] it clearly lacks the necessary degree of active deliberation and validation – the active consent – of the European people(s) to draw

[18] The Netherlands.

[19] de Witte (n 6).

[20] With reference to the jurisprudence of the German Federal Constitutional Court, see in particular ch 5 of this volume.

[21] The UK settlement agreement would, in case of a remain vote, have meant a disapplication of the notion of ever-closer Union to the UK (the concrete legal value thereof being unclear). The open-ended nature of the flexibility clause (now Art 352 TFEU) was critically reviewed following the Laeken Declaration, but while it has been amended somewhat by the Lisbon Treaty in terms of procedure, the essentially open-ended nature of it has only been confirmed (with Lisbon removing the prior reference to the common market).

[22] M Kumm and VF Comella, 'The Primacy Clause of the Constitutional Treaty and the Future of Constitutional Conflict in the European Union' (2008) 3 *International Journal of Constitutional Law* 477.

[23] ibid.

convincing legitimacy conclusions therefrom. Here it is useful to reflect on the 'extra-legal'[24] dimension of the constitutional change initiated by the Court. Most national political powers are not actually authorised to (consent to) 'transfer' final, supreme and open-ended authority outside their national constitutional framework. For such constitutive constitutional decision-making,[25] only a significant mobilisation of the European *demoi*[26] would do.

The Constitutional Treaty could have made a difference, but not a decisive one. It contained in its proposed Article I-6 a primacy clause: 'The Constitution and law adopted by the institutions of the Union in exercising competences conferred on it shall have primacy over the law of the Member States.' This, together with the word 'Constitution' in the title of the Treaty, was the first step towards the political signalling of profound constitutional change. Yet, it still did not express the full extent of the Court's constitutional claim: primacy is made conditional on the principle of conferral, and nothing is said about where the jurisdictional final authority lies in this regard. This means the EU legal order is not explicitly conceptualised as original and autonomous, or open-ended. Article I-6, groundbreaking as it was, did not convey the tectonic shift in authority that the Court's constitutional quartet implies; it did not signal the creation of an original, final, direct and open-ended power. If it had been successfully adopted, the Constitutional Treaty and its Article I-6 would overall have amounted to a constitutionalisation of the EU, though not a full political and democratic validation of the most important elements of the Court's constitutional claim. And although it failed to be ratified,[27] I would argue that the rejections in the Dutch and French referendums of the Constitutional Treaty overall cannot be taken as a rejection of the Court's constitutional claim outright and as such by sufficiently mobilised European peoples.[28]

[24] In the sense of Ackerman's work (n 17).

[25] See S Choudhry, 'Ackerman's Higher Lawmaking in Comparative Constitutional Perspective: Constitutional Moments as Constitutional Failures?' (2008) 6 *International Journal of Constitutional Law* 193.

[26] On demoïcracy, see K Nicolaïdis, 'The Idea of European Demoicracy' in J Dickson and P Eleftheriadis (eds), *Philosophical Foundations of European Union Law* (Oxford, Oxford University Press, 2012).

[27] The Lisbon Treaty eventually relegated the primacy provision to a non-binding Declaration (17). It is however noteworthy that the wording has changed, and the text now seems to accept the full extent of the Court's case law. For further discussion, see S Garben, 'The Constitutionalisation of European Integration as a Single, Protracted 'Constitutional Moment' Towards the Establishment of Autonomous, Expansive and Final Authority' in M Dani, M Goldoni and A Menendez (eds), *The Legitimacy of European Constitutional Orders* (Edward Elgar 2023) forthcoming.

[28] Not only has the exact content of the constitutional proposal not been sufficiently clearly proposed and deliberated, the referendum votes did not express a clear conviction of the French or Dutch public against EU authority (even if some strands of the 'no' vote may have pertained to that) – for that, the margins were too narrow and the scope of the discussion too broad and vague. Furthermore, the French and Dutch rejection cannot be taken as a rejection on behalf of all the European people(s). This latter point is reinforced by the Spanish and Luxembourgish pro-Constitutional Treaty votes.

## *(iii) Towards Resolving the Problem?*

Thus, the core constitutional claim still needs to be put front and centre of the political debate. This is a somewhat daunting idea for those who are partial to a positive outcome for the EU. Yet, this problem definition also implies an empowering opportunity: instead of casting the EU and the Member States as (now for decades) adrift on the stormy waves of unpredictable cross-currents, with all hands on deck simply trying to survive by weathering crisis after crisis without a compass or even a destination, it provides focus and purpose to the turmoil of the increasingly emotional public engagement with, political electioneering in and constitutional contestation of the EU (and the national) project.

Interestingly, a certain momentum seems to be building, with political forces in France and Germany openly prepared to consider a new constitutional settlement for the EU and their countries within it, while at the same time constituting a highly divisive issue. Brexit could be posited as having played a crucial role in that development. The issue of sovereignty was central in the UK Brexit debate and will have played at least some role in the vote. Despite what some may argue, from the analytical angle taken in this chapter, putting a finger on the sovereignty issue means putting it on the right spot. While the withdrawal has disconnected the UK from the EU's ongoing constitutional project, it has forced political actors in the remaining EU Member States to take a clearer stance on EU membership and what it means for their country, and has invited the peoples of Europe to do the same. Similarly, the German PSPP ruling, and the rule-of-law crisis in Poland and its outright rejection of EU law's primacy, while (deeply) troublesome developments from the perspective of a stable and well-functioning EU legal order, are putting the issue of the EU's constitutional identity more and more clearly into the spotlight. And that is, in itself, a necessary thing, for it is not enough to have either a 'permissive consensus' or continue to live in a 'constraining dissensus'[29] on EU membership in the face of the constitutional magnitude of the EU's core constitutional claim to an autonomous and open-ended authority. Nor is it a legitimate way forward to (re-)depoliticise the EU project, trying to (re-)establish an elite pathway towards a new European Constitution.

With this in mind, after the Conference on the Future of Europe, a new reform movement should take the form of an explicitly constitutional project once again – but this time with the EU's core constitutional authority claim at the core of the public deliberations.

[29] L Hooghe and G Marks, 'A Postfunctionalist Theory of European Integration: From Permissive Consensus to Constraining Dissensus' (2009) 39 *British Journal of Political Science* 1.

## B. Problem 2: An Inappropriate Normative Hierarchy, where the Fundamental Market Freedoms are 'Over-constitutionalised'

### *(i) Fundamental Rights in the EU Legal Order*

To carry its constitutional claim, the EU has to regulate the authority it (purports to) establish(es) in the sense that it ensures that this authority respects a number of fundamental values and rights. As mentioned above, ensuring the respect of fundamental rights at EU level was a necessary precondition for the CJEU's claim of independence of national constitutions in *Internationale*. This goes to the root of a problem with the way that the normative structure of the EU legal order has developed: it has not been built towards orienting ideals of democracy, self-determination, representation, constituent power, separation of powers and fundamental rights, both as legitimating foundations and as outcomes to be achieved,[30] but instead these primordial concepts of legitimate authority have been attached to the project instrumentally, incidentally and ornamentally. Fundamental rights have come into play as a side effect of economic integration on the basis of the free movement provisions, and it is the latter that have been the analytical starting point and driving source of the EU's authority. Even if we now have a binding Charter, as well as an explicit embedding of EU policies – including the internal market – in higher fundamental values (Articles 2 and 3 TEU), as Chalmers and Trotter argue:

> A series of discrete doctrines govern methods of interpreting the Charter, the standard of protection secured by it, its relationship to other instruments and its scope of review. These are spliced together to form EU fundamental rights law. Such splicing is thin on how different aspects of EU fundamental rights law relate to each other or to EU law as a whole. Without this, however, fundamental rights do not have the coherence to set out an imaginary of what is good and right, something central to both their moral status and their iconographic appeal.[31]

In general, the current case-by-case, right-by-right assessment, without a sensible hierarchical structure of EU law's plethora of constitutional values and norms, results in a high measure of unpredictability in the adjudication on the various EU Charter rights, their direct/horizontal applicability and their interaction or mutual 'balancing',[32] and thus presents a constitutional challenge. But most problematic in

[30] See M Cahill, 'European Integration and European Constitutionalism: Consonances and Dissonances' in D Augenstein (ed), *'Integration Through Law' Revisited – The Making of the European Polity* (Surrey, Ashgate, 2012) 28.

[31] ibid.

[32] As Jonathan Griffiths argues, 'despite (its) pedigree, the concept of the "fair balance" is, without further elucidation, vacuous and unhelpful'. See J Griffiths, 'Constitutionalising or Harmonising? The Court of Justice, the Right to Property and European Copyright Law' (2013) 38 *EL Rev* 65, 74.

this fundamental disorder is, in my view, the current (largely implicit) approach to the question to what extent the free movement provisions are considered part of EU fundamental rights law, and what hierarchical status should be accorded to them.

### *(ii) The 'Over-constitutionalisation' of the 'Fundamental Freedoms'*

I would argue that the free movement provisions (in particular, the free movement of goods, services, capital and companies) have been 'over-constitutionalised' in two ways: firstly, they are insulated from democratic decision-making to an extent that cannot be defended on the basis of constitutional and democratic reasons; and secondly, they are given undue weight in relation to (other) fundamental rights where they clash. Elsewhere, I have argued in more detail[33] that, to a limited extent, a constitutionalisation of the free movement provisions can reasonably be defended by transnational democratic and individual justice (dignity) arguments: they allow certain interests that are excluded from domestic decision-making to be included,[34] they expand 'individual agency beyond the parameters of permissive behaviour in the citizens' own Member State, and as such provides a trampoline for the attainment of the individual's aspirations'[35] on an equal basis throughout the EU territory, and they protect individual economic autonomy in a cross-border setting.[36] The individual justice and dignity arguments provide a strong normative justification for treating free movement provisions as fundamental rights, but only when it comes to the actual movement of individuals in their capacity as citizen, worker or self-employed – which is the dimension of the 'fundamental freedoms' that is already captured in the EU Charter in Article 15(2). The transnational democracy argument may serve to justify a limited constitutional protection for economic actors to challenge protectionist (directly discriminatory) measures, as this arguably cannot be satisfactorily addressed by national actors that share the same economic interest[37] or by the EU legislative process.[38] However, the direct application of the goods, capital and services provisions against indistinctly applicable national measures, and their conditioning of norms adopted

[33] S Garben, 'The "Fundamental Freedoms" and (Other) Fundamental Rights: Towards an Integrated Democratic Interpretation Framework' in S Garben and I Govaere, *The Internal Market 2.0* (Oxford, Hart Publishing, 2021).

[34] M Maduro, 'Article 30 and the European Economic Constitution: Reforming the Market or the State?' in M Maduro, *We The Court: The European Court of Justice and The European Economic Constitution* (Oxford, Hart Publishing, 1998) 167–68: 'the representation of the interests of nationals of other Member States within national political processes' argues in favour of a 'fundamental rights conception of the free movement rules'.

[35] F de Witte, 'Sex, Drugs & EU Law: The Recognition of Moral and Ethical Diversity in EU Law' (2013) 50 *CML Rev* 1545, 1552.

[36] See generally R Babayev, 'Private Autonomy at Union Level: On Article 16 CFREU and Free Movement Rights' (2016) 53 *CML Rev* 979.

[37] A Somek, 'The Argument from Transnational Effects I: Representing Outsiders through Freedom of Movement' (2010) 16 *European Law Journal* 315.

[38] Garben (n 33).

in the EU legislative process, goes beyond this legitimate degree of 'fundamentalisation'. Thus, it is to this extent that the fundamental freedoms have been 'over-constitutionalised' in the first sense: these politically salient socio-economic issues are excessively insulated from democratic decision-making at national and EU level.

This constitutes a constitutional problem *in se*, but it especially manifests itself in conjunction with the second way in which the fundamental freedoms have been over-constitutionalised: namely, how they are weighed against (other) fundamental rights. The Court's official line is that all are equal.[39] Some, it turns out, are just more equal than others. Of course, in the CJEU's analytical framework, indistinctly applicable restrictions of the free movement provisions can be justified by reference to the protection of fundamental rights.[40] Former CJEU President Skouris considers, citing *Omega*[41] and *Schmidberger*,[42] that 'the order in which the Court of Justice looks at fundamental freedoms and fundamental rights is not indicative of a hierarchy between the two'.[43] While it is of course true that a prima facie restriction of the free movement provisions has to be established first, it does not mean that the Court has to follow the analytical framework that it imposes in terms of justification. The Court could, after establishing that there has been a prima facie restriction, consider that we are in the scope of EU law for the purposes of *both* the free movement provisions *and* the fundamental right in question as protected by the EU Charter, and conduct a 'bidirectional' assessment:[44] considering both the justification of the infringement entailed by the fundamental right on the free movement provision and the justification of the (potential) infringement entailed by the free movement provision on the fundamental right. In that bidirectional

[39] V Skouris, 'Fundamental Rights and Fundamental Freedoms: The Challenge of Striking a Delicate Balance' (2006) *European Business Law Review* 234; K Lenaerts, 'Exploring the Limits of the EU Charter of Fundamental Rights' (2012) 8 *European Constitutional Law Review* 375. Trstenjak and Beysen consider that fundamental rights and free movement provisions should be on a par with an exception with regard to Title I of the EU Charter, but that the CJEU has not respected that with regard to the judgments in *Viking* and *Laval:* V Trstenjak and E Beysen, 'The Growing Overlap of Fundamental Freedoms and Fundamental Rights in the Case-Law of the CJEU' (2013) 38(3) *EL Rev* 293. That view is shared by S Weatherill, 'From Economic Rights to Fundamental Rights' in S de Vries, U Bernitz and S Weatherill (eds), *The Protection of Fundamental Rights in the EU After Lisbon* (Oxford, Hart Publishing, 2013) 27–28. The approach has also been condemned internationally as in breach of fundamental rights by the ILO and Council of Europe's European Social Committee.

[40] It is not yet clear whether, apart from indistinctly applicable restrictions, directly discriminatory restrictions can be justified by reference to fundamental rights. On the basis of the Court's general approach, one has reason to expect that the Court will be highly reluctant to allow the justification of directly discriminatory measures on this basis, but that would contradict the assertions that the fundamental freedoms and fundamental rights rank 'equal'. See Trstenjak and Beysen (n 39) 312.

[41] Case C-36/02 *Omega Spielhallen v Oberbürgermeisterin der Bundesstadt Bonn* EU:C:2004:614, [2004] ECR I-9609.

[42] Case C-112/00 *Eugen Schmidberger, Internationale Transporte und Planzüge v Republik Österreich* EU:C:2003:333, [2003] ECR I-5659.

[43] Skouris (n 39).

[44] D Schiek, 'Towards More Resilience for a Social EU – the Constitutionally Conditioned Internal Market' (2017) 13 *European Constitutional Law Review* 611, 629.

assessment, the Court could assume the equivalence of all fundamental rights and freedoms, it could determine the 'essence' of each fundamental right and freedom in isolation or it could come to an integrated and hierarchical understanding of the meaning of fundamental rights and freedoms in the EU legal order which would inform the interpretation of the substance of each right and their relationships. Alternatively, or in conjunction, it could consider that in the case of fundamental rights, the Member State should benefit from a wide margin of appreciation, and thus conduct a deferential proportionality test.

The Court does not really do any of these things. While it arguably carried out a deferential proportionality test in *Omega*, it clearly did not in other landmark cases such as *Viking* and *Laval*.[45] *Schmidberger*[46] is an interesting example because it is often held up as good practice of the Court in relation to the fair balancing of fundamental freedoms and rights.[47] While the Court did say that the 'Member States enjoy a wide margin of discretion',[48] it continued by saying that 'nevertheless, it is necessary to determine whether the restrictions placed upon intra-Community trade are proportionate in the light of the legitimate objective pursued'[49] and proceeded to do the exact opposite with a very detailed assessment of all the extenuating elements that could eventually serve to justify this infringement of what for the Court is clearly a particularly fundamental right: the free movement of goods. Despite appearances, the assessment is unidirectional, and thus inherently *not* 'fair'.[50] When it comes down to it, the Court applies the free movement provisions as the rule and fundamental rights as the exception. In determining whether there should be a margin of discretion for national authorities, the approach is not one that looks at the fundamental nature of the right in question and its purpose, but instead, as Weatherill says,

> the more sensitive and the more remote from commercial considerations the matters advanced in the context of justification of trade barriers are, the more generous the Court is to the available scope for justification and also to the breadth of the margin of appreciation enjoyed by the regulator.[51]

Davies has argued against this framework in relation to all sorts of public interest justifications, considering that the Court's approach to restrictions and justification is 'substantively nonsense', for when national laws conflict with free movement there is substantive legitimacy on both sides and one can equally argue that respect

[45] Case C-438/05 *International Transport Workers' Federation and Finnish Seamen's Union v Viking Line ABP and OÜ Viking Line Eesti* ECLI:EU:C:2007:772, [2007] ECR I-10779; Case C-341/05 *Laval un Partneri Ltd v Svenska Byggnadsarbetareförbundet, Svenska Byggnadsarbetareförbundets avdelning 1, Byggettan and Svenska Elektrikerförbundet* ECLI:EU:C:2007:809, [2007] ECR I-11767.

[46] *Schmidberger* (n 42).

[47] See Trstenjak and Beysen (n 39) 312.

[48] Para 82 of the judgment.

[49] ibid.

[50] Para 81 of the judgment.

[51] Weatherill (n 39) 25.

for national constitutional orders, for substantive subsidiarity and for democracy entails that free movement must in such a situation be interpreted restrictively.[52] This would apply with all the more force when it concerns fundamental rights that are to be weighed against free movement.

### *(iii) The EU Charter of Fundamental Rights: Towards Resolving the Problem or Making it Worse?*

Due to the particular way in which the EU legal order has developed, the fundamental status of the free movement provisions in traditional EU law goes unquestioned, and it is rather the authority of fundamental rights that is up for discussion. In that context, the EU Charter is held up as a celebratory moment as, post-Lisbon, it received formal recognition of having the 'same legal value as the Treaties'.[53] In fact, in accordance with Article 2 TEU, 'The Union is *founded on* the values of respect for human dignity, freedom, democracy, equality, the rule of law and respect for human rights' (emphasis added), which argues for priority of fundamental rights over free movement provisions.[54] Regardless, there is more than a single judgment available to support the argument that instead the free movement provisions are given a more forceful protection and higher status in EU law than certain fundamental rights, especially collective rights[55] such as the freedom of assembly and the right to strike,[56] the right to collective bargaining[57] and the right to protection in case of collective dismissal.[58] As many fundamental social rights are collective rights, this creates a hierarchy of fundamental rights that generally favours the economic over the social, thereby deepening the asymmetry of European integration caused by the constitutionalisation of the free movement provisions vis-à-vis public interest regulation and legislation at national and EU level, as described by Scharpf and others.[59]

[52] G Davies, 'The Competence to Create an Internal Market: Conceptual Poverty and Unbalanced Interests' in Garben and Govaere (n 33).

[53] Art 6(1) TEU.

[54] NN Shuibhne, 'Fundamental Rights and the Framework of Internal Market Adjudication: Is the Charter Making a Difference?' in P Koutrakos and J Snell (eds), *Research Handbook on the Law of the EU's, Research Handbooks in European Law* (Cheltenhem, Edward Elgar Publishing, 2017).

[55] A Lo Faro, 'Toward a De-fundamentalisation of Collective Labour Rights in European Social Law?' in M-A Moreau (ed), *Before and After the Economic Crisis, What Implications for the European Social Model?* (Cheltenhem, Edward Elgar Publishing, 2011) 203.

[56] *Viking Line* (n 45); *Laval* (n 45).

[57] Case C-426/11 *Mark Alemo-Herron and Others v Parkwood Leisure Ltd* EU:C:2013:521, [2013] ECR I-000.

[58] Case C-201/15 *Anonymi Geniki Etairia Tsimenton Iraklis (AGET Iraklis) v Ypourgos Ergasias, Koinonikis Asfalisis kai Koinonikis Allilengyis* EU:C:2016:972, [2016] ECR I-00.

[59] F Scharpf, 'The Asymmetry of European Integration, or Why the EU Cannot Be a "Social Market Economy"' (2010) 8 *Socio-Economic Review* 211; D Grimm, *The Constitution of European Democracy* (Oxford, Oxford University Press, 2017); S Schmidt, *The European Court of Justice and the Policy Process – The Shadow of Case Law* (Oxford, Oxford University Press, 2018).

This applies both to the pre- and post-Charter case law.[60] In fact, it appears that in some respects, the coming into force of the Charter has aggravated the problem. In particular, the Court has given a very forceful interpretation of Article 16 EU Charter on the freedom to conduct a business. In *Alemo-Herron*,[61] the Court used Article 16 to read a minimum harmonisation Directive adopted on an internal market basis but intended to protect the interests of workers in the event of a transfer of undertakings in a way that it precluded a Member State from providing, in the event of a transfer of an undertaking, that dynamic clauses referring to collective agreements negotiated and adopted after the date of transfer are enforceable against the transferee. The judgment has been widely criticised on a variety of grounds.[62] What is interesting for our purposes is that Article 16 was given an interpretation that allows it to be used as an instrument for further economic integration and liberalisation even in purely internal situations, and that the Court does not even mention, let alone fairly balance, the various fundamental social rights that would be relevant to the case, and that should at least have been used to balance Article 16 EU Charter, such as those in Article 28 EU Charter on collective bargaining and those in Article 31 EU Charter on fair and just working conditions. Similarly, in *AGET Iraklis*,[63] the Court practically ignores[64] the fundamental social right in Article 30 EU Charter on protection against unjustified dismissal while somewhat forcedly drawing Article 16 EU Charter into its assessment of a restriction of the freedom of establishment. The Court in that judgment deploys a language that seems more cognisant of the need for public interest restrictions of Article 16 EU Charter, but the asymmetry in the treatment of economic fundamental rights and fundamental social rights is striking, as is the conflation of the freedom of establishment and the freedom to conduct a business. Taken together, these developments suggest that the CJEU's interpretation of the Charter is leading to an even more forceful application of the free movement provisions in conjunction with Article 16 EU Charter, moving towards a general 'economic freedom' approach, while it is instead a bit of a 'damp squib'[65] for the fundamental social rights contained therein.

[60] Shuibhne (n 54).

[61] *Alemo-Herron* (n 57).

[62] ibid; X Groussot et al, 'Weak Right, Strong Court – The Freedom to Conduct Business and the EU Charter of Fundamental Rights' (2014) Lund University Legal Research Paper 01/201; J Prassl, 'Freedom of Contract as a General Principle of EU Law? Transfers of Undertakings and the Protection of Employer Rights in EU Labour Law' (2013) 42 *Industrial Law Journal* 434; P Syrpis and T Novitz, 'The EU Internal Market and Domestic Labour Law: Looking Beyond Autonomy' in A Bogg et al (eds), *The Autonomy of Labour Law* (Oxford, Hart Publishing, 2015); M Bartl and C Leone, 'Minimum Harmonisation after Alemo-Herron: The Janus Face of EU Fundamental Rights Review' (2015) 11/1 *European Constitutional Law Review* 140.

[63] Above (n 58).

[64] Art 30 is mentioned once, almost as an afterthought, to indicate that Art 16 may be limited, but is not made an integral, let alone equal, part of any 'balancing'. See para 89 of the judgment.

[65] C Barnard, 'EU Employment Law and the European Social Model: The Past, the Present and the Future' (2014) 67 *Current Legal Problems* 199, 207.

## C. Problem 3: Under-constitutionalisation of European Integration Through the 'Union Method'

### *(i) The Constitutionalisation of EU Law and the De-constitutionalisation of European Integration*

It is problematic that the accomplishments as regards the constitutional and democratic legitimacy of EU decision-making in the context of the ordinary legislative procedure (OLP) are accompanied, and thus diminished, by a simultaneous rise[66] in European decision-making through intergovernmental 'modes of governance' outside the Community method and sometimes even outside the EU framework altogether (despite of an overlap of actors, instruments and/or responsibilities).[67] Former German Chancellor Angela Merkel, in her 'Bruges speech', described this as the new 'Union method': a pragmatic approach geared towards the achievement of 'common positions', departing from the 'entrenched' thinking of the Community method and instead applying 'the intergovernmental method'.[68] It amounts to a 'bits-and-pieces'[69] approach, where highly salient policies – such as notably in the area of economic policy[70] and migration[71] – comprise a variety of legal and non-legal, EU and non-EU, norms and instruments. Some justify this modus operandi by reference to output legitimacy and (existential) crisis governance. The idea that this approach ultimately serves the higher goal of European integration may explain the CJEU's permissive – and surprisingly unconstitutional – approach to the matter. It has held that parallel intergovernmental action, in areas of EU policies and even with the use of EU institutions, is in conformity with EU law when the EU does not possess a 'specific competence' to undertake the same action within the EU's legal framework. Notably, in *Pringle*,[72] the Court validated the conclusion of the ESM Treaty outside the EU framework. Although the

[66] Of course, intergovernmentalism has been present in the functioning of the European Community since its very early days, and as such does not constitute a new phenomenon. However, with the 'Union method' in recent years being used so deliberately in high-profile policy areas such as EMU and migration, I would contend that the problem has increased. But even if that (quantitative) argument would be rejected, the legitimacy concern posed by European decision-making outside the Community method but within or on the border of its institutional framework, remains.

[67] On this generally, see S Garben, 'From Sneaking to Striding: Combatting Competence Creep and Consolidating the EU Legislative Process' [2022] *European Law Journal* 429.

[68] Speech by Federal Chancellor Angela Merkel at the opening ceremony of the 61st academic year of the College of Europe in Bruges on 2 November 2010: www.coleurope.eu/sites/default/files/speech-files/europakolleg_brugge_mitschrift_englisch_0.pdf.

[69] D Curtin, 'The Constitutional Structure of the Union: A Europe of Bits and Pieces' (1993) 30 *CML Rev* 17.

[70] For instance, a number of important pieces of euro crisis legislation have been enacted by intergovernmental agreements between Member States: the ESM Treaty, the Fiscal Compact and the Agreement on the Single Resolution Fund for banks. The EU's yearly framework of economic policy coordination, the European Semester, similarly operates in an executive-dominated intergovernmental fashion.

[71] The EU–Turkey Statement.

[72] Case C-370/12 *Thomas Pringle v Government of Ireland and Others* ECLI:EU:C:2012:756, [2012] ECR I-756.

Member States had considered it necessary to amend Article 136 TFEU to allow the establishment of such a mechanism outside the Treaty, the Court held that the parallel action was legal with or without such formal authorisation.

Some read *Pringle* as a step forward in the defence of the autonomy of the EU competence order, in that whenever there would be specific EU competence to act the Member States would be obliged to use this *inter se* rather than acting internationally, as opposed to the *Bangladesh* doctrine, which considered such an obligation only to exist when EU internal competence is exclusive.[73] Moreover, the CJEU in *Ledra* partially redressed the constitutional deficit arising from the fact that the Charter would not apply to such non-EU agreements: it considered that when EU institutions participate in such constructions they remain liable to comply with fundamental rights.[74] Regrettably, however, the Court confirmed its permissive, hands-off approach to these Member State twilight dealings more recently in *NF*, concerning the EU–Turkey Statement,[75] where inter alia it adopted a curiously narrow reading of the Council as an EU institution and allowed it to escape democratic and constitutional scrutiny altogether. While perhaps best understood in the context of the political crises that both *Pringle* and *NF* were rendered in, what remains is a deep stain on the EU's overall democratic and constitutional credentials.

Indeed, such intergovernmental law-making on the borders of the EU legal and institutional framework raises fundamental democratic concerns. It is especially national executives that are empowered in these intergovernmental settings. As Moravcsik has argued, 'international cooperation redistributes domestic power in favour of national executives by permitting them to loosen domestic constraints imposed by legislatures, interest groups, and other societal actors'.[76] Although all EU or European action empowers national governments vis-à-vis all other national actors, EU legislative procedures at least offer checks and balances that are largely absent in intergovernmental processes. In the words of Chalmers et al:

> Indeed, it is positively perverse for those who criticise the European Union because it is executive-oriented or does not sufficiently involve national parliaments to hark back nostalgically to [the] intergovernmental model. It leads to an even higher executive dominance and even greater parliamentary exclusion.[77]

But it is not *all* national executives that are empowered: in this setting of intergovernmental decision-making, powers shift to a small group of more powerful Member

[73] C Timmermans, 'The Competence Divide of the Lisbon Treaty Six Years After' in S Garben and I Govaere (eds) *The Division of Competences between the EU and the Member States Reflections on the Past, the Present and the Future* (Oxford, Hart Publishing, 2017).

[74] Joined Cases C-8/15 P to C-10/15 P *Ledra Advertising Ltd and Others v European Commission and European Central Bank (ECB)* ECLI:EU:C:2016:701.

[75] Joined Cases C-208/17 P to C-210/17 P, *NF and Others v European Council*, ECLI:EU:C:2018:705, [2018] ECR I-1

[76] A Moravcsik, 'Why the European Union Strengthens the State: Domestic Politics and International Cooperation' (1994) 52 *Harvard University Centre for European Studies WPS* 1.

[77] D Chalmers et al, *European Union Law* (Cambridge, Cambridge University Press, 2010) 132.

States (due to size, economic strength or more intangible standing/prestige), leaving other Member States and thus entire national democracies disempowered. As Scharpf notes in the context of the Memorandums of Understanding concluded in the euro crisis by which countries received financial assistance, 'these conditionalities were not defined by European legislation under the Community method or through consensus-oriented voting in the Council but through extremely asymmetric bargaining between creditor and debtor governments that resembled conditions of an unconditional surrender'.[78] Its power to displace an entire national democratic process was for the whole EU to witness in the 2015 Greek 'bailout', where a newly elected national government with an explicit mandate concerning the euro crisis was unable to change anything about the measures that would fundamentally impact its national law and policy.

### *(ii) Ex Post Integration into the EU Constitutional Framework: Resolving the Problem or Making it Worse?*

Some of the most prominent examples of such parallelism and intergovernmentalism, such as the Dublin and Schengen Conventions, have subsequently been integrated into the EU framework. Furthermore, where, in the Maastricht Treaty, two entire intergovernmental 'pillars' were added to the increasingly constitutionalising community, these have now, with the Lisbon Treaty, been 'collapsed' into the EU's single overarching 'constitutional' structure, and while the Common Foreign and Security Policy continues to operate rather differently, the area of freedom, security and justice has been 'normalised' and now operates under the Community method (to the extent that this is not undermined by further parallel dealings, such as in the case of the EU–Turkey agreement, discussed above). Does such integration serve to ex post legitimise the democratic and constitutional deficits of their intergovernmental origins? And could it be argued that, as such, these alternative methods of integration are to be welcomed as transition phases, where the legitimacy problem is ultimately only temporary and perhaps a worthy price to pay for a subsequent communitarisation and thus constitutionalisation of these policy areas that the Member States would otherwise be unwilling to relinquish?

In my view, the answer to both questions is in the negative. The Community method should not be (ab)used to whitewash laws that have been derived from such decidedly undemocratic parallel and intergovernmental decision-making. Even where these instruments are readopted or revised formally using the OLP, such as, for instance, in the Dublin Regulation, there remains a profound undemocratic legacy effect as the bargaining position of especially the European Parliament is drastically affected by the existing piece of legislation. The undemocratically derived status quo 'occupies the field' and dampens the possibility of

[78] F Scharpf, 'After the Crash: A Perspective on Multilevel European Democracy' (2015) 21 *European Law Journal* 384, 389.

achieving the high consensus levels required for ambitious reforms. Only if such instruments had been abolished, and renegotiated on a clean slate, would there have been a genuine legitimacy gain from the absorption of these areas into the 'community' framework.

Precisely two of the acts that have caused most controversy with scholars, civil society actors and national judiciaries as regards their respect for fundamental rights in recent years, to wit the European Arrest Warrant and the Dublin Regulation, are instances of such (un)constitutional whitewashing. In clear contravention of the legality principle that laws limiting fundamental rights can only be adopted by parliamentary legislation, these acts that deeply affect the legal position of (vulnerable) individuals have been adopted without meaningful parliamentary involvement at EU or national level. These acts continue to be challenged precisely with regard to their respect for fundamental rights, and even though they are now fully within the CJEU's jurisdiction, it has not been eager to adopt a critical human rights-oriented approach. It has, instead, developed a principle of 'mutual trust', to ward off a strong fundamental rights review (either by itself or allowing this to be done by national courts),[79] even elevating this controversial principle to the core of the EU's autonomy and constitutional identity in Opinion 2/13.[80] While more recently the Court's approach has somewhat evolved,[81] the knee-jerk reaction remains rather defensive of these instruments.[82] Such leeway may be understandable when it concerns legislation adopted following the Community method, but it cannot hold in the case of ex-Third Pillar acts, which do not benefit from any presumption of compliance with core constitutional standards.

It is a tragic thought that it may be precisely the legitimacy and authority-gain that is connected to the constitutionalisation of 'Community' law that is being used to increase the authority of all other sorts of EU (*sensu largo*) decision-making: would there be a successful Union method without the achievements of the Community method? The constitutionalisation of EU law is, on that take, complicit in the de-constitutionalisation of (and by) European integration, the latter riding on the former's coat-tails. And where the spoils of intergovernmentalism are later formally integrated into the constitutionalised *acquis*, this does not serve to genuinely legitimate these instruments, but rather serves to smuggle undemocratically derived products into the 'community' framework and attaching to them the full force of its legal authority – without their having earned it. The corrosion of the constitutionalisation of EU law by the Union method is perhaps

[79] Joined Cases C-411/10 and C-493/10 *NS and ME v Refugee Applications Commissioner and Minister for Justice, Equality and Law Reform* ECLI:EU:C:2011:865, [2011] ECR-I-0000; Case C-399/11 *Stefano Melloni v Ministerio Fiscal* ECLI:EU:C:2013:107, [2013] ECR.

[80] Opinion 2/13, ECLI:EU:C:2014:2454.

[81] Case C-578/16 PPU *CK and Others v Republika Slovenija* ECLI:EU:C:2017:127; Case C-42/17 *Criminal proceedings against MAS and MB* ECLI:EU:C:2017:936; Case C-216/18 PPU *LM* ECLI:EU:C:2018:586.

[82] Joined Cases C-297/17, C-318/17, C-319/17 and C-438/17 *Ibrahim* ECLI:EU:C:2019:219.

most poignantly displayed where it has led to the creation of 'mutual trust' as a 'constitutional' principle in order to ward off a genuine constitutional fundamental rights review of decidedly undemocratically adopted legal acts. In any event, as long as such bypassing of the Community method by parallel integration or differentiation is allowed by EU law, any achievements in solving the first two problems outlined above will to a large extent be hollow.

## III. Conclusion

The EU cannot indefinitely retain this current quasi-constitutional operation. All three of the problems described above need to be resolved, and preferably at the same time. Not only would I consider it unlikely that the peoples of Europe would endorse the EU's full authority claim without the current normative asymmetry between market freedom and other rights and values being resolved, but any success in solving the first two problems would be nullified if the legitimate Constitution thus created could be circumvented by the exercise of authority parallel to that Constitution. And while it may be tempting to only resolve Problems 2 and 3, as they are more 'easily' addressed (it would basically take a handful of Court rulings, rectifying *Bangladesh/Pringle*, revisiting *Dassonville* along the lines of an upgraded *Keck* and expanding the approach in *CK* and *LM*) and would in themselves already drastically improve the EU's constitutional and democratic legitimacy, it should be stressed that if we do not face the most fundamental first (order) problem head on, any EU constitution will be a castle built on quicksand. Thus, the present chapter argues that in order to pass from its current functional, 'small c' constitution to a real, fully fledged Constitutional Democracy, the EU will have to: (i) obtain the peoples' agreement on the EU's core constitutional claim to final, autonomous and expansive authority; (ii) recalibrate the normative hierarchy as regards fundamental rights and fundamental freedoms; and (iii) fix the problem of parallelism and intergovernmentalism that are currently thriving in the shadow of EU constitutionalism. The only other legitimate option is to fundamentally scale back the EU's authority, shedding its constitutional claims and ambitions – which would be a real pity.

# 8

# The EU Economic Constitution after COVID-19 and 'Next Generation EU'

FEDERICO FABBRINI

## I. Introduction

The outburst of COVID-19 has profoundly challenged and changed the world we live in. As the former President of the European Central Bank (ECB) and Prime Minister of Italy Mario Draghi put it, COVID-19 immediately appeared to be 'a human tragedy of potentially biblical proportions'.[1] Since the explosion of the pandemic in spring 2020, the institutions and Member States of the European Union have taken unprecedented steps to tackle this dramatic health crisis and its devastating socio-economic consequences. The quick spread of the virus starting in late February 2020 forced governments and public authorities worldwide to adopt unprecedented measures, including lockdowns, border closures and requisition of essential properties, to contain contagions and prevent hospitalisations and deaths. At the same time, though public authorities in the early days of the pandemic focused on the adoption of sanitary measures to address the dramatic health costs of COVID-19, they quickly had to shift their attention to the devastating socio-economic implications of the pandemic.

The purpose of this chapter is to outline from an EU law and policy perspective the key economic policy responses adopted by the EU to address the COVID-19 pandemic and to assess their implications on Europe's Economic and Monetary Union (EMU).[2] As such, the chapter focuses specifically on the economic-related aspects of the response to the pandemic, with the aim of assessing their impact on the European architecture of economic governance. As is well known, EMU represents a pillar of the EU and is one of the most tangible achievements of European

[1] M Draghi, 'Interview "We Face a War Against Coronavirus and Must Mobilize Accordingly"' *Financial Times* (25 March 2020) www.ft.com/content/c6d2de3a-6ec5-11ea-89df-41bea055720b.

[2] This chapter builds on F Fabbrini, 'The Legal Architecture of the Economic Responses to COVID-19' (2022) 60 *Journal of Common Market Studies* 186; and F Fabbrini, 'Europe's Economic & Monetary Union beyond COVID-19', report commissioned by the Presidency of the Eurogroup/Department of Finance of Ireland, June 2021.

integration. Nevertheless, the constitutional architecture of EMU has been afflicted since its creation by a significant imbalance between the monetary policy, which was centralised in a new federal institution – the ECB – and the economic policy, which instead remained decentralised at state level. In fact, while EMU was transformed significantly in the aftermath of the euro crisis, the legal and institutional reforms adopted in this period did not alter this original asymmetry, with the EU still lacking a fiscal capacity at the dawn of the COVID-19 pandemic.

The argument of this chapter is that the measures adopted by the EU institutions and Member States to address the devastating economic damages of COVID-19 have had important implications for Europe's EMU, leading towards a major rebalancing between its economic and monetary elements. Indeed, the chapter suggests that the extraordinary measures prompted by the COVID-19 pandemic constitute a watershed in the process of European integration. In particular, besides the early emergency support measures deployed by the European Commission,[3] the ECB[4] and the Eurogroup,[5] the real game changer emerged with the EU recovery plan known as 'Next Generation EU' (NGEU). This initiative, sponsored by several Member States[6] and proposed by the European Commission in May 2020,[7] was approved by the European Council in July 2020,[8] and eventually entered into force in spring 2021. NGEU consists in the creation of a new €750bn EU Recovery Fund. This is resourced by raising common debt on the financial markets; it is being disbursed to the Member States (between 2021 and 2026) in the form of both grants and loans; and it will be repaid (after 2028) by raising new EU own resources. As such, by endowing the European Commission, for the first time, with significant borrowing, spending and taxing powers, NGEU represents a paradigm change in the functioning of EMU, pushing the EU architecture of economic governance towards an arrangement akin to that of federal regimes.

This chapter surveys the various EU legal and policy measures adopted to contain the economic effects of COVID-19, and considers their implications for the EU constitutional architecture of economic governance. In particular, the chapter outlines how, by strengthening the so-far underdeveloped economic leg of EMU, NGEU constitutes a turning point in the process of European integration which profoundly changes the constitutional outlook of EMU, and in turn raises important questions about the future of the EU. By embracing a chronological perspective, the chapter highlights the difficulties in establishing NGEU: to this

[3] European Commission press release, 'Coronavirus: Commission Proposes to Activate Fiscal Framework's General Escape Clause to Respond to Pandemic' (20 March 2020) IP/20/499.

[4] Decision (EU) 2020/440 of the European Central Bank of 24 March 2020 on a temporary pandemic emergency purchase programme (ECB/2020/17) [2020] OJ L91/1.

[5] Council of the EU Report on the Comprehensive Economic Policy Responses to the COVID-19 Pandemic, 9 April 2020.

[6] French–German Initiative for a European Recovery from the Coronavirus Crisis, 18 May 2020.

[7] European Commission, 'Europe's Moment: Repair and Prepare for the Next Generation' (Communication) COM (2020) 456 final.

[8] European Council Conclusions, 17–21 July 2020, EUCO 10/20.

end, the chapter traces both the initial political opposition to this initiative and the subsequent challenges to its entry into force, due to interplay between NGEU and the rule-of-law crisis. As the chapter underlines, in fact, NGEU risked becoming a casualty of the rule-of-law crisis – with a threat by Hungary and Poland to block the entry into force of this innovative instrument in an attempt to avoid the entry into force of a regulation conditioning disbursement of EU funding on respect for the rule of law.

This chapter is structured as follows. Section II analyses the initial EU policy measures adopted to tackle the economic damages of the COVID-19 pandemic, focusing in particular on the action taken by the European Commission, the ECB and the Eurogroup. Section III considers the NGEU Recovery Fund, put forward by the Commission in May 2020 and endorsed by the European Council in July 2020, as well as its difficult entry into force in December 2020, after the European Council overcame the vetoes against it by Hungary and Poland. Section IV then discusses how the pandemic-related economic policy measures adopted during COVID-19, most notably NGEU, represent a paradigm change for the EU architecture of economic governance by rebalancing the monetary and economic legs of EMU. Section V concludes.

## II. Early Responses to COVID-19

The explosion of COVID-19 constituted a major challenge for the EU, and EMU specifically. While, in an earliest phase of the pandemic, EU Member States focused mainly on containing the spread of contagions, attention rapidly shifted to the devastating socio-economic consequences of the pandemic.[9] At the same time, while Member States quickly deployed domestic measures to tackle the sudden freezing of the economy – including the postponement of tax deadlines, the injection of cash to support firms and workers, and guarantees on bank loans – the nature of the crises forced EU Member States to promptly coordinate action at supranational level too.

### A. The Suspension of the Stability & Growth Pact

With the pandemic, and the health measures to contain it, bringing to a sudden halt the global economy, on 20 March 2020 the European Commission for the first time ever triggered the general escape clause of the Stability & Growth Pact (SGP),[10] temporarily putting on hold the application of EMU fiscal rules. This decision, which suspended the key deficit and debt rule governing Member States'

[9] European Parliament Resolution of 17 April 2020 on EU coordinated action to combat the COVID-19 pandemic and its consequences, P9 TA(2020)0054.

[10] European Commission press release (n 3).

fiscal policy, was immediately accepted by the Council on 23 March 2020,[11] hence creating a greater margin of manoeuvre for the Member States to inject financial resources into the economy to deal with the supply and demand shocks caused by the pandemic. Also on 20 March 2020, the Commission suspended the application of state aid rules,[12] giving greater leeway to Member States in supporting ailing firms. At the same time, the Commission activated the EU Solidarity Fund, to provide some cash aid to Member States,[13] and also put together a coronavirus response investment initiative, which redirects up to €37bn of the cash reserves available in the EU Structural and Investment Funds towards COVID-19-related expenses.[14]

Moreover, the European Commission also proposed the establishment of a European instrument for temporary support to mitigate unemployment risks in an emergency (SURE)[15] – a secondary insurance system designed to support the heavily under-pressure national unemployment insurance regimes through loans backed up by Member States' guarantees.[16] In particular, the Commission proposal – which was based on Article 122 TFEU – envisaged establishing an instrument, worth €100bn, which would provide financial assistance in the form of loans to those Member States whose public expenditures had suddenly and severely increased as of February 2020 due to the adoption of national measures directly related to short-time work schemes and similar measures to address the unemployment caused by the pandemic. From a financing point of view, the Commission proposed to establish SURE on the basis of irrevocable guarantees by the Member States, worth €25bn, which allowed the EU to contract borrowing on the financial markets in line with the EU budget constraints.

## B. The Pandemic Emergency Purchase Programme

Nevertheless, the most significant initial effort to support the EU Member States' response to the economic consequences of COVID-19 came from EU financial

[11] Council of the EU Statement, 23 March 2020.

[12] European Commission, 'Temporary Framework for State Aid Measures to Support the Economy in the Current COVID-19 Outbreak' (Communication) 2020/C 91 I/01.

[13] Regulation (EU) 2020/461 of the European Parliament and of the Council of 30 March 2020 amending Council Regulation (EC) No 2012/2002 in order to provide financial assistance to Member States and to countries negotiating their accession to the Union that are seriously affected by a major public health emergence [2020] OJ L99/9.

[14] Regulation (EU) 2020/460 of the European Parliament and of the Council of 30 March 2020 amending Regulations (EU) No 1301/2013, (EU) No 1303/2013 and (EU) No 508/2014 as regards specific measures to mobilise investments in the healthcare systems of Member States and in other sectors of their economies in response to the COVID-19 outbreak (Coronavirus Response Investment Initiative) [2020] OJ L99/5.

[15] European Commission, 'Proposal for a Council Regulation on the establishment of a European instrument for temporary support to mitigate unemployment risks in an emergency (SURE) following the COVID-19 outbreak' COM (2020) 139 final.

[16] See also C Dias and A Zoppè, 'The SURE: Main Features', European Parliament Research Service in-depth analysis, 28 May 2020.

institutions. While the European Investment Bank (EIB) developed a special COVID-19 investment scheme of €40bn to support small- and medium-sized enterprises,[17] the most powerful response to the economic uncertainties caused by the COVID-19 pandemic came from the ECB. Thanks to its federal-like features, the ECB had already played a key role in responding to the euro crisis. In fact, it was the statement by then ECB President Mario Draghi in July 2012 that the ECB would do 'whatever it takes' to save the euro[18] that was perceived to be crucial in stabilising the single currency. Moreover, to respond to the euro crisis, the ECB had deployed a number of groundbreaking unconventional monetary policies, including in 2010 the Securities Market Programme to purchase government bonds on the secondary market;[19] in 2012 the Outright Monetary Transactions (OMT) programme to buy state securities of countries which agreed to enter into a European Stability Mechanism (ESM)-financed support programme;[20] and in 2015 a quantitative easing programme – known as the Public Sector Purchase Programme (PSPP),[21] which significantly contributed to supporting growth policies in the EMU states.

The initial ECB response to COVID-19 proved once again its centrality in EMU. In fact, on 24 March 2020, the ECB launched the Pandemic Emergency Purchase Programme (PEPP),[22] in which it committed to buy public bonds and commercial papers in the financial markets up to €750bn, which subsequently almost doubled in size to €1350bn,[23] then increased still further to €1850bn.[24] The PEPP presented features similar to the PSPP, which the ECB had established in 2015 to fight deflation. However, it also differed from it in allowing the ECB to buy government bonds without having to adhere to the Member States' capital key allocation, so as to maximise its impact in supporting those eurozone Member States most affected by the pandemic and its consequences.[25] The PEPP greatly contributed to stabilising the financial markets, essentially securing all the necessary funding for Member States, which were issuing debt to pay for the massive pandemic-related recovery measures adopted at the national level.

Nevertheless, despite the importance of the ECB action, its role was called into question as a result of legal challenges before Germany's Constitutional Court,

[17] European Investment Bank press release, 'EIB Group Will Rapidly Mobilize up to $40 Billion to Fight Crisis Caused by COVID-19', 16 March 2020.

[18] ECB President Mario Draghi, speech at the Global Investment Conference, London, 26 July 2012.

[19] See Decision of the European Central Bank of 14 May 2010 establishing a securities market programme (ECB/2010/5) [2010] OJ L124/8.

[20] European Central Bank press release, 'Technical Features of Outright Monetary Transactions', 6 September 2012.

[21] See Decision (EU) 2015/774 of the European Central Bank of 4 March 2015 on a secondary markets public sector asset purchase programme (ECB/2015/10) [2015] OJ L121/20, amended several times.

[22] European Central Bank Decision (n 4).

[23] European Central Bank press release, Monetary policy decisions, 4 June 2020.

[24] European Central Bank press release, Monetary policy decisions, 10 December 2020.

[25] A Mooij, 'The Legality of the European Central Bank's Pandemic Emergency Purchase Programme' (2020) BRIDGE Working Paper No 5.

the Bundesverfassungsgericht (BVerfG), which coincidentally occurred during the early phases of the COVID-19 pandemic. In fact, on 5 May 2020, the BVerfG took the unprecedented step of declaring the ECB's PSPP programme illegal, while simultaneously declaring a judgment of the European Court of Justice (ECJ) inapplicable in Germany.[26] Whereas in 2014 the BVerfG has raised concerns about the ECB's monetary policy[27] but eventually retracted its views,[28] abiding by an ECJ judgment which had upheld the OMT programme,[29] in its recent judgment the BVerfG crossed the Rubicon and for the first time ever declared EU action ultra vires.[30] In its ruling, the BVerfG refused to follow the judgment of the ECJ in *Weiss*[31] – which had already declared the PSPP compatible with the EU Treaties – and imposed a three-month time frame on the ECB to better explain the proportionality of its programme. The ruling of the BVerfG drew a strong response from the EU institutions.[32] In fact, there is no doubt that the BVerfG ruling threatens the EU legal order,[33] and constitutes an illegal breach of the principle of the supremacy of EU law, which is designed to guarantee the equality of the Member States under the Treaties.[34] However, the judgment also posed a potential threat to further ECB action because, even though it explicitly declared that it was considering the PSPP and not the PEPP, it still endeavoured to set limits on the ability of the ECB to pursue its mandate.

## C. The Eurogroup Package

The actions of the Commission and the ECB were eventually also backed up by the intervention of the intergovernmental institutions. This was not an easy process and the European Council initially struggled to reach an agreed-upon course of action. In fact, the Member States were heavily split on what new measures to put in place to sustain the economy during the pandemic and relaunch it afterwards.[35] In particular, on 25 March 2020, a group of nine euro area states – Belgium, France, Greece, Ireland, Italy, Luxembourg, Portugal, Slovenia and Spain – requested in a letter to the European Council President that the EU start 'working on a common

[26] See BVerfG, 2 BvR 859/15, 2 BvR 980/16, 2 BvR 2006/15, 2 BvR 1651/15, judgment of 5 May 2020.
[27] See BVerfG 2 BvR 2728/13 et al, order of 7 February 2014.
[28] See BVerfG 2 BvR 2728/13 et al, judgment of 21 June 2016.
[29] See Case C-62/14 *Gauweiler* ECLI:EU:C:2015:400.
[30] S Baroncelli, 'Monetary Policy and Judicial Review' in F Fabbrini and M Ventoruzzo (eds), *Research Handbook on European Economic Law* (Cheltenham, Edward Elgar Publishing, 2019) 199.
[31] See Case C-493/17 *Weiss* ECLI:EU:C:2019:1046.
[32] See European Commission President Ursula Von der Leyen, Statement, 10 May 2020, 20/846.
[33] See also F Fabbrini and D Kelemen, 'With One Court Decision, Germany May be Plunging Europe into a Constitutional Crisis', *Washington Post* (7 May 2020).
[34] See F Fabbrini, 'After the OMT Case: The Supremacy of EU Law as the Guarantee of the Equality Between the Member States' (2015) 16 *German Law Journal* 1003.
[35] See also S Grund et al, 'Sharing the Fiscal Burden of the Crisis' Hertie School Jacques Delors Centre policy paper, 7 April 2020.

debt instrument issued by a European institution to raise funds on the market on the same basis and to the benefit of all Member States'.[36] Yet Germany and the Netherlands fiercely rejected this proposal as an unacceptable effort of debt mutualisation and rather called for the ESM to be used as a crisis response tool.[37] In this context, the European Council, meeting by videoconference three times in two weeks in March 2020, failed to reach a deal[38] – and pushed the file to the Eurogroup.

Eventually, on 9 April 2020, the Eurogroup, meeting in an inclusive format (open to Member States from outside the eurozone) came up with a package of measures to respond to the economic consequences of COVID-19, potentially worth €540bn.[39] First, the Eurogroup decided to create a pan-European guarantee fund of €25bn for the EIB, thus expanding its ability to deploy up to €200bn of financing for companies.[40] Second, the Eurogroup decided to open the possibility of using the ESM to support domestic financing of direct and indirect healthcare-, cure- and prevention-related costs due to the COVID-19 crisis. Specifically, in their role as members of the Governing Board of the ESM, eurozone Ministers of Finance decided to establish a Pandemic Crisis Support Line, which would be available to all euro area Member States during these times of crisis, with standardised terms and a value of up to 2% of a Member State's GDP at end-of-2019 terms.[41] Third, the Eurogroup also approved the Commission's proposal for the establishment of SURE on the basis of Article 122 TFEU and committed €25bn national guarantees, allowing the Commission to raise up to €100bn of capital on the financial market.[42]

Moreover, the Eurogroup also agreed to work on 'a Recovery Fund to prepare and support the recovery, providing funding through the EU budget to programmes designed to kick-start the economy in line with European priorities and ensuring EU solidarity with the most affected Member States'.[43] Due to divisions among Member States, details on the latter were scant. Nevertheless, the gravity of the pandemic prompted in subsequent weeks a highly salient change of position by Germany, which abandoned its traditional opposition to common debt, and opened itself up towards innovative solutions to deal with COVID-19 on the understanding that the euro area financial crisis-related instruments, and

[36] Joint letter from Belgium, France, Greece, Ireland, Italy, Luxembourg, Portugal, Slovenia and Spain to the European Council President Charles Michel, 25 March 2020.

[37] Statement from Dutch Finance Minister Wopke Hoekstra at the Twedde Kammer, 7 April 2020.

[38] See Joint Statement of the Members of the European Council, 26 March 2020.

[39] Council of the EU Report (n 5).

[40] European Investment Bank press release, 'EIB Board Approves $25 Billion Pan-European Guarantee Fund in Response to COVID-19 Crisis', 26 May 2020.

[41] G Zaccaroni, 'The Future of the ESM within a Hybrid EMU Law' (2020) BRIDGE Working Paper No 6.

[42] Council Regulation (EU) 2020/672 of 19 May 2020 on the establishment of a European instrument for temporary support to mitigate unemployment risks in an emergency (SURE) following the COVID-19 outbreak [2020] OJ L159/1.

[43] Council of the EU Report (n 5) para 16.

especially the ESM, were not fit for this new purpose.[44] In fact, on 18 May 2020, France and Germany jointly put forward an initiative for a European Recovery Fund, proposing to establish a temporary and targeted facility connected to the new EU budget and worth €500bn, to be funded by borrowing on the markets and disbursed through grants (rather than loans) to the Member States worst hit by the crisis.[45]

# III. The Recovery Fund NGEU

The Franco-German initiative opened the way to the European Commission, and ultimately shaped the response to COVID-19 that was embraced by the European Council. However, the entry into force of the Recovery Fund remained subject to additional unforeseen challenges – connected to the rule-of-law crisis rather than to the pandemic – which threatened the whole initiative and were eventually resolved only in December 2020.

## A. Proposal

On 27 May 2020, the European Commission presented an ambitious proposal for an EU recovery plan to repair the economic damage of the health crisis and to prepare the EU for the next generation. Specifically, the Commission proposed a major increase in EU resources, revamping the size of the next multi-annual financial framework (MFF), for 2021–27,[46] and creating a new €750bn Recovery Fund, called NGEU, connected to the MFF and designed to support Member States and businesses affected by COVID-19.[47] From a policy viewpoint, the European Commission[48] proposed that NGEU would provide resources, two-thirds of which would be disbursed as grants and one-third as loans, to fund the reconstitution of the EU economy along the Commission priorities of a green deal, digitalisation and social inclusion. Moreover, in a major break with the past, the Commission proposed that the recovery instrument would be financed by the issuance of new EU debt on the financial markets (rather than states' transfers), to be repaid after 2028 but before 2058 through an increase in the headroom of

[44] German Finance Minister Olaf Scholz, 'Interview "Jemand muss vorangehen"' *Die Zeit* (19 May 2020) www.zeit.de/zustimmung?url=https%3A%2F%2Fwww.zeit.de%2F2020%2F22%2Folaf-scholz-europaeische-union-reform-vereinigte-staaten.

[45] French–German Initiative (n 6).

[46] European Commission, 'On the EU Budget Powering the Recovery plan For Europe' (Communication) COM (2020) 442 final.

[47] European Commission, 'Europe's Moment' (n 7).

[48] European Commission, 'Proposal for a Council Regulation establishing a European Union Recovery Instrument to support the recovery in the aftermath of the COVID-19 pandemic' COM (2020) 441 final.

the EU's own resource ceilings,[49] and prospectively the introduction of new EU taxes.

From a legal viewpoint, the European Commission based NGEU on a multi-faceted legal constellation. On the one hand, the Commission proposed an EU Recovery Instrument (EURI),[50] to be adopted as a Council regulation based on Article 122 TFEU – which allows the adoption of measures appropriate to the economic situation in a spirit of solidarity between Member States – indicating the size of NGEU and the allocation of the funds. The EURI was then complemented by a Recovery and Resilience Facility (RFF)[51] – a regulation to be jointly adopted by the European Parliament (EP) and the Council, on the basis of Article 175 TFEU, on economic, social and territorial cohesion – regulating the objectives and the governance of NGEU. On the other hand, the Commission proposed to revise the EU Own Resources Decision (ORD)[52] – the Council's legal act, adopted on the basis of Article 311 TFEU, that authorises the raising of EU revenues – increasing the EU expenditures ceilings and empowering the EU to issue debt. At the same time, the Commission connected NGEU to the MFF – the multi-annual expenditure bill, to be approved by the Council ex Article 312 TFEU – as well as to the regulation on a general regime of conditionality for the protection of the EU budget against the continuing phenomenon of rule-of-law backsliding.[53]

The Commission recovery plan built on prior proposals by Spain[54] and by France and Germany[55] jointly, and tracked the strategy endorsed by the EP.[56] Nevertheless, by proposing to endow the EU with new fiscal powers, the Commission proposal was met with initial pushbacks. In fact, on 20 May 2020, a coalition of northern countries – the Netherlands, Austria, Denmark and Sweden – responded to the Franco-German initiative with a joint non-paper which instead proposed the creation of an emergency fund disbursing loans to states, de facto along the model of the ESM.[57] Moreover, criticism against the Recovery Fund was articulated by the Visegrád countries – Poland, Hungary, Czechia and Slovakia – which complained that the instrument did not set aside sufficient funding for lower-income Member States and introduced against their wishes a rule-of-law conditionality in the

[49] European Commission, 'Amended Proposal for a Council Decision on the system of Own Resources of the European Union' COM (2020) 445 final.

[50] COM (2020) 441 final (n 48).

[51] European Commission, 'Proposal for a Regulation of the European Parliament and the Council establishing a Recovery and Resilience Facility' COM (2020) 408 final.

[52] COM (2020) 445 final (n 49).

[53] European Commission, 'Proposal for a Regulation of the European Parliament and the Council on the protection of the Union's budget in case of generalised deficiencies as regards the rule of law in the Member States' COM (2018) 324 final.

[54] Spain, 'Non-paper on a European Recovery Strategy', 19 April 2020.

[55] French–German Initiative (n 6).

[56] European Parliament Resolution of 15 May 2020 on the new multiannual financial framework, own resources and the recovery plan, P9 TA(2020)0124.

[57] Austria, Denmark, the Netherlands and Sweden, 'Non-paper EU Support for Efficient and Sustainable COVID-19 Recovery', 20 May 2020.

disbursement of EU funds.[58] As a result, a first European Council meeting to discuss the Commission proposal, scheduled on 19 June 2020, was unable to find an agreement,[59] prompting the organisation of a new summit just a few days later.[60]

## B. Approval

Eventually, after five days of meeting on 17–21 July 2020, the European Council managed to find a deal on the EU recovery plan and, relatedly, on the next MFF.[61] In the longest European Council since the 2001 Nice Summit, EU heads of state and government approved the new MFF for a value of €1074bn. At the same time, they approved the establishment of NGEU, worth €750bn, thus authorising the Commission to issue debt on behalf of the EU and envisioning a roadmap for the introduction of new taxes aimed at repaying the capital and interest on the money borrowed. To muster the necessary unanimity, the European Council amended the Commission's plan, reducing the overall size of grants from €500bn to €390bn and increasing the loans component from €250bn to €360bn.[62] Moreover, as requested by northern Member States, the European Council agreed to cap the size of the next MFF[63] and maintain their rebates.[64] Furthermore, to obtain the crucial support of central and eastern Member States, it avoided giving any details on the obligation to respect the rule of law as a condition to receive EU funding.[65] At the same time, the European Council somehow left unsettled the governance of NGEU – entrusting the management to the Commission, but subject to control of the Economic and Financial Committee, and with a back-up role for itself in extraordinary cases.[66]

Crucially, however, the European Council gave its blessing to the establishment of a highly innovative Recovery Fund. On the one hand, it authorised the Commission for the first time to act as a quasi-EU treasury and borrow substantive amounts of funds, totalling €750bn 'on behalf of the Union on the capital markets'.[67] The European Council clarified that such funding was due to be used to secure the European recovery from the pandemic, as well as to strengthen the EU economic resilience. On the other hand, the EU also agreed on a roadmap to repay this common debt through new, genuine EU taxes. While the European Council

[58] Czech Republic Government press release, 'V4 Common Lines Regarding the Multiannual Financial Framework/Next Generation EU', 11 June 2020.
[59] European Council President Charles Michel Remarks, 19 June 2020.
[60] European Council President Charles Michel Remarks, 10 July 2020.
[61] European Council Conclusions (n 8).
[62] ibid para A6.
[63] ibid para A23.
[64] ibid para A30.
[65] ibid para A24.
[66] ibid para A19.
[67] ibid para A3.

agreed to increase the EU spending ceiling during the next MFF,[68] it also committed to 'work towards reforming the own resources system and introduce new own resources',[69] with a new plastic tax,[70] a carbon border adjustment tax, a digital tax[71] and potentially a financial transaction tax.[72]

## C. Implementation

Some of the details in the European Council agreement were met with scepticism by the European Parliament,[73] which, according to Article 312 TFEU, has a veto right to the approval of the MFF. The European Parliament, therefore, leveraged its budgetary powers, and in subsequent negotiations with the Council of the EU managed to secure a slight increase in the MFF, as well as to strengthen the rule-of-law conditionality applicable to the disbursement of EU funds, under both the MFF and NGEU. Yet, while a political agreement between the European Parliament and the Council was achieved on this revised package deal,[74] in November 2020 Hungary and Poland put their veto to the MFF and NGEU as a way to block the entry into force of the EU rule-of-law conditionality regulation.[75] As is well known, Hungary and Poland are two Member States which in the last decade have experienced a dramatic backsliding in respect for the rule of law and democracy.[76] In fact, the EU had responded to the increasing threats to the independence of the national judiciary, freedom of the media and respect for human rights by activating Article 7 TEU.[77] The action by Hungary and Poland action nevertheless threatened NGEU.[78]

Ultimately, in December 2020, Member States in the European Council managed to overcome the Polish and Hungarian veto,[79] albeit in a way which

[68] ibid para A9.
[69] ibid para 145.
[70] ibid para 146.
[71] ibid para 147.
[72] ibid para 149.
[73] European Parliament Resolution of 23 July 2020 on the conclusions of the extraordinary European Council meeting of 17–21 July 2020, P9 TA(2020)0206.
[74] Council of the EU press release, 'MFF and Recovery Package: Council Presidency Reaches Political Agreement with European Parliament', 10 November 2020, PRESS 763/20.
[75] Joint Declaration of the Prime Minister of Poland and the Prime Minister of Hungary, 26 November 2020.
[76] See, inter alia, B Bugaric, 'Central Europe's Descent into Autocracy: A Constitutional Analysis of Authoritarian Populism' (2019) 17 *International Journal of Constitutional Law* 597; R Uitz, 'The Perils of Defending Rule of Law through Dialogue' (2019) 15 *European Constitutional Law Review* 1.
[77] See in particular European Commission, 'Reasoned proposal in accordance with Article 7(1) Treaty on European Union for a Council Decision on the determination of a clear risk of a serious breach by the Republic of Poland of the rule of law' COM (2017) 835 final; European Parliament Resolution of 12 September 2018 on a proposal calling on the Council to determine, pursuant to Article 7(1) of the Treaty on European Union, the existence of a clear risk of a serious breach by Hungary of the values on which the Union is founded, P8 TA(2018)0340.
[78] R Uitz, 'Funding Illiberal Democracy' (2020) BRIDGE Working Paper No 7.
[79] European Council Conclusions, 10–11 December 2020, EUCO 22/20.

diluted the impact of the rule-of-law regulation. In its conclusions the European Council adopted a political declaration on the rule-of-law conditionality regulation which dictated action for all the other EU institutions. In particular, to soothe Hungary and Poland, the European Council determined that the regulation ought to be interpreted in such a way that 'the mere finding that a breach of the rule of law has taken place does not suffice to trigger the mechanism'.[80] Moreover, the European Council mandated the Commission to adopt guidelines on the application of the regulation.[81] At the same time, it ruled that these were to be finalised only after a forthcoming action of annulment to be brought by Hungary and Poland against the regulation.[82] As the EP immediately pointed out in a highly critical resolution,[83] the European Council had clearly overstepped its powers, and 'the content of [its] conclusions on the Regulation on a general regime of conditionality for the protection of the Union budget [were] superfluous'.[84] First, they did not change the text of the regulation, which had already been approved by the EP and the Council. Secondly, 'any political declaration of the European Council cannot be deemed to represent an interpretation of legislation as interpretation is vested within the [ECJ]'.[85] Thirdly, 'the conclusions of the European Council cannot be made binding on the Commission in applying legal acts'.[86]

Albeit at a high moral price, the European Council compromise led to the formal legal approval, just in time before the end of 2020, of the ORD,[87] the new MFF 2021–27[88] and the EURI.[89] This was accompanied by the rule-of-law conditionality regulation[90] and an inter-institutional agreement on a roadmap to introduce new taxes,[91] and was later followed by the RFF in February 2021.[92]

[80] ibid para 2.e).

[81] ibid para 2.c).

[82] ibid. See now also Case C-156/21 *Hungary v European Parliament and Council* ECLI:EU:C:2022:97; Case C-157/21 *Poland v European Parliament and Council* ECLI:EU:C:2022:98.

[83] See European Parliament Resolution of 17 December 2020 on the Multiannual Financial Framework 2021–2027, the Inter-Institutional Agreement, the EU Recovery Instrument and the Rule of Law Regulation, P9 TA(2020)0360.

[84] ibid para 4.

[85] ibid para 5.

[86] ibid para 8.

[87] Council Regulation (EU, Euratom) 2020/2053 of 14 December 2020 on the system of own resources of the European Union [2020] OJ L424/1.

[88] Council Regulation (EU) 2020/2093 of 17 December 2020 laying down the multiannual financial framework for the years 2021 to 2027 [2020] OJ L433I/11.

[89] Council Regulation (EU) 2020/2094 of 14 December 2020 establishing a European Recovery Instrument to support the recovery in the aftermath of the COVID-19 crisis [2020] OJ L 433I/23.

[90] Regulation (EU, Euratom) 2020/2092 of the European Parliament and of the Council of 16 December 2020 on a general regime of conditionality for the protection of the Union budget [2020] OJ L433I/1.

[91] Interinstitutional Agreement between the European Parliament, the Council of the European Union and the European Commission on budgetary discipline, on cooperation in budgetary matters and on sound financial management, as well as on new own resources, including a roadmap towards the introduction of new own resources [2020] OJ L433I/28.

[92] Regulation (EU) 2021/241 of the European Parliament and of the Council of 12 February 2021 establishing the Recovery and Resilience Facility [2021] OJ L57/17.

In spring 2021, therefore, EU Member States were asked to approve the ORD, as required by Article 311(3) TFEU, as this conditioned the financing of the MFF and the issuance of EU bonds under NGEU. During the ratification process, NGEU was thus put on hold for almost a month in April 2021, when the BVerfG temporarily suspended Germany's ratification of the ORD.[93] The BVerfG however then rejected in preliminary terms the constitutional challenge raised against NGEU by anti-EU applicants.[94] Therefore, since the end of May 2021, following the approval by all national parliaments of the ORD,[95] the EU has been endowed with a powerful Recovery Fund, supporting Member States to rebuild their economies and social structures ravaged by the COVID-19 pandemic. In particular, in June 2021, the European Commission has started issuing bonds on the financial markets,[96] and since July 2021 it has begun pre-financing the national recovery and resilience plans that Member States have presented to receive NGEU funds.[97]

## IV. The Implications of the Responses to COVID-19 for EMU

The multiplicity of legal and institutional measures adopted to address the economic consequences of COVID-19 profoundly affected the architecture of EU economic governance. In fact, as a result of the pandemic-response initiatives, the constitutional outlook of EMU has significantly changed, with the EU now enjoying fiscal powers that were, until recently, seen as impossible to achieve.[98] According to some, this is a dividend of Brexit, as the UK withdrawal from the EU removed a veto player who would most certainly have opposed such a dramatic transfer of borrowing, spending and taxing power from the national to the supranational level.[99] Be that as it may, the EU responses to COVID-19 proved the resilience of the European project, and significantly differed from the responses to the euro crisis. NGEU, in particular, rebalanced the economic and monetary legs of EMU, and effectively endowed the EU with the fiscal capacity that it had hitherto lacked.

[93] See 2 BvR 547/21, order of 26 March 2021.

[94] See 2 BvR 547/21, order of 15 April 2021.

[95] See also A D'Alessandro, 'National Ratification of the Own Resources Decision' European Parliament Research Service Briefing, June 2021.

[96] See European Commission press release, 'NextGenerationEU: European Commission raises €20 Billion in First Transaction to Support Europe's Recovery' (15 June 2021) IP/21/2982.

[97] See, eg European Commission press release, 'NextGenerationEU: European Commission Endorses Italy's €19.5 Billion Recovery and Resilience Plan' (22 June 2021) IP/21/3126.

[98] European Commissioner Tierry Breton, 'La fin de la naiveté' *Les Echos* (10 August 2020) www.lesechos.fr/idees-debats/cercle/la-fin-de-la-naivete-1229485.

[99] See 'The EU's Recovery Fund Is a Benefit of Brexit' *The Economist* (30 May 2020).

## A. The Responses to the COVID-19 Crisis Compared to the Responses to the Euro Crisis

The developments that have occurred in EMU in response to COVID-19 go well beyond what occurred in response to the euro crisis. While there is still extensive debate among political scientists whether the legal and institutional measures adopted to tackle the euro crisis strengthened more the EU intergovernmental institutions[100] or the EU supranational ones,[101] there is little doubt that in legal terms the new powers acquired by the European Commission were purely coordinating powers, as evident in the framework of the European Semester, or surveillance power, as shown in the Excessive Deficit Procedure. Instead, departing from a 'surveillance model' of fiscal federalism,[102] NGEU shifts to the EU a significant degree of new, *real* fiscal powers – including the ability for the Commission to raise and mobilise resources, and to run a supranational economic policy, investing in transnational political priorities like the Green Deal and digitalisation.[103]

In fact, thanks to NGEU, the EU now presents features which are similar to those of mature federal systems, all of which are endowed with a centralised countercyclical fiscal tool to support the economic policy of component units, also via grants.[104] From a legal point of view, this EMU development occurred without any amendment of the EU Treaties. The existing legal bases – including Article 122 TFEU (on financial solidarity) jointly with Articles 311 and 312 TFEU (the provisions on the ORD and the MFF), as well as Article 175 TFEU (on social and territorial cohesion) – provided a constitutional grounding to increase the EU fiscal power to tackle COVID-19. Interestingly, this resembles the expansion of federal fiscal powers in the USA, which occurred during the New Deal in the 1930s without any formal amendment of the US Constitution.[105] Nevertheless, the constitutional significance of these changes for the architecture of European economic governance did not go unnoticed at the national level. In fact, challenges to the legality of NGEU have been raised, for example, in Germany and Finland, notably in the context of the domestic ratification of the ORD. These challenges have so far proved unsuccessful, confirming that the EU Treaties can dynamically adapt in light of changing circumstances.[106] They do,

[100] U Puetter, *The European Council and the Council: New Intergovernmentalism and Institutional Change* (Oxford, Oxford University Press, 2014).

[101] JD Savage and A Verdun, 'Strengthening the European Commission's Budgetary and Economic Surveillance Capacity since Greece and the Euro Area Crisis: A Study of Five Directorates' [2016] *Journal of European Public Policy* 101.

[102] A Hinarejos, 'Fiscal Federalism in the European Union' (2013) 50 *CML Rev* 1621.

[103] B de Witte, 'The European Union's COVID-19 Recovery Plan: The Legal Engineering of an Economic Policy Shift' (2021) 58 *CML Rev* 635.

[104] S Ylmaz and F Zahir (eds), *Intergovernmental Transfers in Federations* (Cheltenham, Edward Elgar Publishing, 2020).

[105] D Super, 'Rethinking Fiscal Federalism' [2005] *Harvard Law Review* 2546.

[106] J-C Piris, 'Why the German Constitutional Court Will (Probably) Not Kill the €750bn Recovery Fund', European Policy Centre, 7 April 2021 https://epc.eu/en/publications/Why-the-German-Constitutional-Court-will-probably-not-kill-the-750~3d5ef0.

however, reveal the paradigm change brought about by NGEU compared to the euro crisis.

How can we explain the difference in the responses to the euro crisis and the pandemic? Several explanations can be put forward. First, the euro crisis had had asymmetrical effects, hitting the northern European economies differently to the southern European ones. In contrast, the pandemic hit all EU Member States indiscriminately – even though the health measures adopted by countries were not identical, and the socio-economic costs of the pandemic varied from one country to another. Second, the euro crisis was blamed on the irresponsible behaviour of several EU Member States – namely, the spendthrift countries of the south. In contrast, no Member State could be blamed for causing the pandemic, which was an exogenous shock, entirely outside the control of any public authority. Also, the risks that the economic consequences of the pandemic – deepening the legacy of the euro crisis – would cause an unbridgeable economic divergence in the eurozone, leading potentially to its disintegration, pushed particularly Germany to change its stance and opened the door towards greater financial solidarity. Finally, the humanitarian drama caused by COVID-19 – with shocking images of piles of graves in Bergamo, Italy – mobilised public opinion also in the fiscally rigorous northern European states, convincing them of the need to develop new instruments of mutual aid to face the pandemic. And thanks to that, in 2020, the EU managed to make a major leap forward with the institution of NGEU.

## B. The Rebalancing of EMU

From this point of view, therefore, NGEU constitutes a paradigm change for EMU, and goes a long way towards rebalancing its original asymmetry. Through NGEU, in fact, the European Commission has acquired borrowing, spending and taxing powers that it hitherto lacked. This contributes to strengthening the economic policy leg of EMU, by making the Commission a quasi-EU treasury office.[107] Certainly, the whole approval process of NGEU confirmed the intergovernmental drift at play in the EU, and the leading role of the European Council as the supreme decision-making institution. At the same time, NGEU maintains important intergovernmental features which are visible in the need to have the approval of the ORD by each Member State in accordance with its national constitutional requirements as foreseen in Article 311 TFEU. Nevertheless, NGEU contributes in important ways to empowering the Commission with economic policy powers. Moreover, by strengthening the EU political branches, NGEU improves the collaboration between the EU monetary and fiscal institutions. Admittedly, the ECB had previously acted in concert with the EU intergovernmental institutions: for instance, the launch of the OMT in 2012 followed the approval of the banking union by the European Council. Nevertheless, the ECB had lamented the lack of a

[107] See also European Commission, 'A European Minister of Economy and Finance' (Communication) COM (2017) 823 final.

treasury office at the EU level.[108] As such, the reforms brought about in response to COVID-19 go a long way towards meeting the calls made during the last decade to complete EMU.

## C. The Establishment of a Fiscal Capacity

NGEU endows the EU with a fiscal capacity – a budgetary instrument, funded by genuine own resources – to support its spending programmes. As I have explained elsewhere, the EU lacked a fiscal capacity even after the euro crisis.[109] In fact, despite multiple proposals – including by High Level Groups, the European Commission, the European Parliament and several Member States jointly – the political cleavage between northern and southern EU Member States which emerged during the euro crisis had made progress on this issue impossible. Certainly, the EU had the MFF. However, the general EU budget did not include much discretionary spending, as its funding is mostly pre-committed for key policy programmes, including agriculture and cohesion. Moreover, notwithstanding the spirit and the letter of the EU Treaties, which require the EU budget to be funded by the EU's own resources, the MFF is for the most part today financed by contributions from the Member States.[110] As a result, EU countries consider the contributions they make to the EU budget as *their* money, and aggressively measure the difference between their contributions to, and their receipts from, the EU budget. This created an embarrassing spectacle, visible at all new MFF negotiations, revealing the unsustainability of a system where Member States quarrel about how much they pay into, and get from, the EU budget.[111] From this standpoint, therefore, NGEU constitutes a game-changer: by allowing the EU to run a large budget, funded by resources raised on the capital markets and to be paid for over the long term by raising new EU taxes, NGEU effectively endows the EU with a fiscal capacity independent from state transfers, and suitable to invest in EU programmes to promote EU public goods, akin to those of federal regimes.[112]

Nevertheless, it remains to be seen whether NGEU constitutes a 'Hamiltonian moment', permanently transforming European integration, or is an exceptional initiative to be discontinued as the pandemic abates.[113] In fact, the extraordinary

[108] M Chang, 'The (Ever) Incomplete Story of Economic and Monetary Union' [2016] *Journal of Contemporary European Research* 486.

[109] F Fabbrini, 'A Fiscal Capacity for the Eurozone', study commissioned by the European Parliament Constitutional Affairs Committee, February 2019.

[110] U Villani-Lubelli and L Zamparini (eds), *Features and Challenges of the EU Budget* (Cheltenham, Edward Elgar Publishing, 2019).

[111] M Maduro, 'A New Governance for the European Union and the Euro', study commissioned by the European Parliament Constitutional Affairs Committee, September 2012.

[112] See also B Gordon, *The Constitutional Boundaries of European Fiscal Federalism* (Cambridge, Cambridge University Press, 2022).

[113] S Disegni (ed), *Europe at a Crossroads after the Shock* (Milan, Monographs of RESET with Fondazione Corriere della Sera, 2020).

measures deployed by the EU institutions and the Member States to tackle the COVID-19 emergency are mostly crafted as temporary responses, which raises the question whether it is conceivable after the pandemic to return to a pre-COVID-19 normal. The suspension of EU state aid rules and the SGP are meant to be provisional, with the aim of gradually reintroducing the application of these rules as soon as the health situation improves.[114] Moreover, the SURE unemployment insurance scheme has a sunset clause, which foresees that the availability of the instrument shall end on 31 December 2022[115] – even though the Council, on a proposal of the Commission, may decide to extend the instrument's operation for a period of six months at a time. Most crucially, NGEU is conceived as an exceptional, one-off initiative. As the July 2020 European Council conclusions state, 'the powers granted to the Commission to borrow are clearly limited in size, duration and scope'[116] – a point restated in the EURI Regulation, which is defined as 'an exceptional response to temporary but extreme circumstances'.[117]

Certainly, by the EU institutions' and Member States' own admission, the return to normal in EMU rules and governance will not occur until a number of years have passed. In fact, with continuing uncertainty on when the pandemic will be fully contained, and new challenges on the horizon due to the Russian invasion of Ukraine, it cannot be excluded that the emergency measures adopted to tackle the socio-economic consequences of COVID-19 will need to be continued, or even expanded, in the time ahead. Nevertheless, there will be important pressures to time-limit the experience of NGEU, including from specific national parliaments or courts. The April 2021 decision by the BVerfG on a legal challenge brought against the German act ratifying the ORD demonstrates this.[118] In this case, the BVerfG rejected the request for an injunction and ruled that, while proceedings on the merit of the case would continue, Germany could ratify the ORD, and thus authorise NGEU. At the same time, however, the BVerfG underlined that NGEU funds can be used exclusively to address the COVID-19 crisis and that this initiative is time-limited, and as such cannot lead to the creation of a permanent instrument.

Yet, because the adoption of NGEU constitutes a crisis-driven paradigm change for EMU, it may leave a legacy in EMU – particularly if it turns out to be a successful economic policy measure.[119] In fact, political scientists have emphasised that institutions generally follow a logic of path-dependency, in that once an economic

[114] European Commissioner Valdis Dombrovskis, 'Dombrovskis: "Le regole europee di bilancio? Dopo la recessione torneranno. Il Mes è come chiesto dall'Italia"' *Corriere della Sera* (4 July 2020) www.corriere.it/economia/finanza/20_luglio_04/dombrovskis-le-regole-europee-bilancio-la-recessione-torneranno-mes-come-chiesto-dall-itali-b93236fa-bd61-11ea-9366-e0fed13f309c.shtml.

[115] Regulation (EU) 2020/672 (n 42), Art 12(3).

[116] European Council Conclusions (n 8) para A4.

[117] Regulation (EU) 2020/2094 (n 89) recital 6.

[118] BVerfG, 1 BvR 547/21, order of 15 April 2021.

[119] European Commissioner Paolo Gentiloni, speech at the Conference 'Progettiamo il Rilancio', 13 June 2020.

process or a governance arrangement is in place over time, it becomes locked in and it will be difficult to change it, as institutional actors become accustomed to the status quo.[120] At the same time, legal scholars have also pointed out that measures adopted in times of emergency tend to sediment and become normalised as the emergency ends.[121] From this viewpoint, therefore, one cannot exclude that the policy measures put in place in response to COVID-19 will become a part of the new normal for the EU, even after COVID-19. Otherwise, it should be borne in mind that several of the measures deployed to address COVID-19 reflected policy proposals that had long been sought after by several institutional actors. For instance, SURE tracks earlier proposals for a permanent EU unemployment insurance system[122] – and, as such, its success in the COVID-19 context may pave the way for its institutionalisation on a broader scale. In fact, the literature on fiscal federalism shows that when the central level of government in multilevel systems acquires new fiscal competences and the ability to mobilise resources, this tends to remain a lasting feature of the system – a pattern particularly visible in the USA after the New Deal.[123]

## V. Conclusion

COVID-19 represented a watershed moment – not just for the lives of millions of Europeans, but also for the life of the EU itself. In response to a dramatic health crisis, and with the aim of containing its devastating socio-economic consequences, the EU institutions and Member States took unprecedented steps in 2020, with important implications for European integration in the field of economic governance. In fact, while COVID-19 has had significant negative effects on several other areas of European integration, such as Schengen and free movement, action taken to respond to the socio-economic effects of the pandemic have boosted integration in EMU. In particular, besides the initial legal and policy measures adopted by the ECB, Commission and Eurogroup, the approval of NGEU constitutes a paradigm change for the EU architecture of economic governance, completing EMU and rebalancing the monetary and economic pillars of EU fiscal integration in ways that are reminiscent of federal regimes.

EMU had been originally established by the Maastricht Treaty as an asymmetric architecture, with a full centralisation of monetary policy but without an equivalent federalisation of economic policy. Even though the responses to the

[120] K Dopfer, 'Toward a Theory of Economic Institutions: Synergies and Path Dependency' (1991) 25 *Journal of Economic Issues* 535.

[121] F Ní Aoláin and O Gross, *Law in Times of Crises: Emergency Powers in Theory and Practice* (Cambridge, Cambridge University Press, 2006).

[122] European Commission Roadmap for a European Unemployment Benefit Scheme, 27 January 2017.

[123] R Henning and M Kessler, 'Fiscal Federalism: US History for Architects of Europe's Fiscal Union' (2012) Peterson Institute for International Economics Working Paper No 2012-1.

euro crisis had prompted a number of important transformations, EMU remained incomplete. Since the explosion of the COVID-19 pandemic, however, the EU institutions and the Member States have adopted a multiplicity of measures, pushing integration in fiscal affairs beyond what could ever have been imagined before. In particular, the NGEU has been a game-changer. This innovative instrument empowers the Commission to borrow money on the financial markets and to transfer those resources to the Member States as both grants and loans to support an inclusive recovery and the realignment of the EU economies towards shared EU priorities.

As this chapter has argued from an EU law and policy perspective, the transformations brought about in the architecture of EU economic governance during COVID-19 constitute a paradigm change for EMU, significantly altering its constitutional outlook. However, important questions remain about the future of NGEU, including the opportunities and obstacles to make it a permanent feature of EMU after COVID-19. In fact, while most pandemic-related measures are designed to be temporary, political science theories of historical institutionalism and legal theories of emergency legislation suggest that it is uncertain whether it would be feasible for the EU to return to a pre-COVID-19 normal, or whether this is the new normal for the EU. These changes have gone a long way to addressing some of EMU's ongoing weaknesses – namely, the absence of a fiscal capacity. With NGEU, the EU has now been endowed with proper fiscal powers which match its monetary powers, thus rebalancing the relation between the 'economic' and 'monetary' legs of EMU. Nevertheless, such changes also require constitutional adjustments to enhance the EU's legitimacy and effectiveness, and it remains to be seen whether they can be rolled back, or if they will consolidate as the new normal for EMU.

# 9

# *Eppur Esiste!*: Legitimacy and Longevity in the EU's Long Decade of Crisis

CORMAC MAC AMHLAIGH

## I. Introduction

Based on Lincoln's famous account of democracy in his Gettysburg address and refracted through the lens of systems theory,[1] the traditional story of legitimacy in the EU famously posits three typologies of legitimacy: input, throughput and output legitimacy.[2] This conventional story tells of how the EU enjoys reasonable throughput and output legitimacy but suffers from weak input legitimacy given its well-known 'democratic deficit'.[3] The EU's 'long decade of crisis', starting in 2008, has challenged this conventional wisdom regarding the EU's legitimacy, however. A post-crisis 'new orthodoxy' has emerged which sees the EU failing on all three metrics of legitimacy. However, what this 'new–old' orthodoxy fails to account for is the endurance and expansion of the EU during its long decade of crisis,[4] which is in tension with the narrative of collapse in the EU's legitimacy.

This chapter provides an outline of an alternative 'political realist' approach to the EU's legitimacy, based particularly on the work of Bernard Williams. This approach explains the tension between the 'new–old' orthodoxy's account of the

[1] D Easton, 'An Approach to the Analysis of Political Systems' (1957) 9 *World Politics* 383; VA Schmidt, 'Democracy and Legitimacy in the European Union Revisited: Input, Output and "Throughput"' (2013) 61 *Political Studies* 2.

[2] Schmidt, 'Democracy and Legitimacy' (n 1).

[3] F Scharpf, *Governing in Europe: Effective and Democratic?* (Oxford, Oxford University Press, 1999); G Majone, *Dilemmas of European Integration: The Ambiguities and Pitfalls of Integration by Stealth* (Oxford, Oxford University Press, 2005).

[4] For current purposes, the expansion is primarily linked to the innovations associated with the management of the COVID-19 pandemic involving coordination in procurement and the significant changes in EU fiscal policy. See S Wolff and S Ladi, 'European Union Responses to the COVID-19 Pandemic: Adaptability in Times of Permanent Emergency' (2020) 42 *Journal of European Integration* 1025; G Celi, D Guarascio and A Simonazzi, 'A Fragile and Divided European Union Meets COVID-19: Further Disintegration or "Hamiltonian Moment"?' (2020) 47 *Economia e politica industriale* 411. The EU's united response to the UK's departure also represents a significant development relevant to the EU's agency and legitimacy during this period. See B Laffan, 'How the EU27 Came to Be' (2019) 57 *Journal of Common Market Studies* 13.

EU's failing legitimacy and the persistent endurance and expansion of the polity by equating the 'new–old' orthodoxy with what Williams calls 'political moralism' – a view of political legitimacy which begins with a priori abstract values, neglects the role of authority and context in thinking about legitimacy in normative terms, and fails to accommodate disagreement about what normative legitimacy requires, particularly in a complex 'in-between' entity like the EU. It argues that Williams's political realist account provides a more satisfactory account of legitimacy in the EU through his focus on the 'first political question'[5] (FPQ) – the establishment of authority followed by the justification of that authority in normative terms. This approach offers an account of EU legitimacy that is free of the key tension in the 'new–old' orthodoxy by better encapsulating the reasons why the EU has endured the crises of the past decade as well as accommodating disagreement about both the nature of the EU and the normative values appropriate for it in managing the various crises.

These reasons relate primarily to the fact that the EU can still be said to provide a satisfactory answer to the FPQ of *supranational* politics – the securing of the conditions of supranational order, mutual trust and cooperation – as well as an adequate justification of its authority in the context of disagreement about the nature of the polity and the normative values most relevant to its context. Whereas this political realist account of legitimacy can explain the endurance and expansion of the polity in the face of the various recent crises, it also shows how the EU's legitimacy can be undermined. It concludes by identifying the EU's values-regression crisis in particular Member States as potentially posing the greatest of the current threats to the EU's legitimacy. This is due to the real risk of non-values regressing Member States taking unilateral action in the light of the EU's tolerance of representatives of authoritarian populist governments in EU decision-making and the impact of national authoritarian populist law and policies on EU citizens. Such unilateral 'civil disobedience' would undermine the EU's claim to provide a satisfactory answer to the FPQ of supranational politics, erode the foundations of the EU's legitimacy and seriously challenge the endurance of the polity.

## II. The Orthodoxy: Input, Output, Throughput

In perhaps the most well-known typology of legitimacy in the EU context, Fritz Scharpf, drawing on the work of systems theory,[6] posited two main types of legitimacy of governing regimes which were then applied to the EU: what he originally called 'input oriented legitimisation' and 'output oriented legitimisation', subsequently abbreviated to 'input' and 'output' legitimacy.[7] This typology built on the

[5] B Williams, 'Realism and Moralism in Political Theory' in G Hawthorn (ed), *In the Beginning Was the Deed: Realism and Moralism in Political Argument* (Princeton, Princeton University Press, 2005) 3.

[6] Easton (n 1).

[7] Scharpf, *Governing in Europe* (n 3); Schmidt,'Democracy and Legitimacy' (n 1).

work of political scientist David Easton, who,[8] in turn, took his benchmark of normative legitimacy from Abraham Lincoln's famous phrase from his Gettysburg address: 'government of the people, by the people, for the people'.[9] For Scharpf (and Easton), input legitimacy involved normative democratic ideals of government *by* the people, whereas output legitimacy reflected the normative ideals of government *for* the people.[10] Furthermore, input legitimacy related to political decision-making by representatives of the electorate, whereas output legitimacy related to political decision-making which effectively promoted the 'common good'.[11] Building on this dualistic typology of legitimacy in EU studies, Vivien Schmidt subsequently added the idea of 'throughput legitimacy'.[12] Encapsulating the ideal of government 'with the people',[13] throughput legitimacy related to the activities of governors in discharging their governing functions, such as formulating and executing policies, promulgating and enforcing legislation and so on. The key emphasis of throughput legitimacy relates to the question of *how* officials govern rather than *who* they are or who they represent.[14] Thus, while related to input and output legitimacy, throughput legitimacy entails a distinct and distinctive focus on five key values: efficacy, accountability, transparency, inclusiveness and openness.[15]

This framework of thinking about legitimacy has come to dominate appraisals of the EU's legitimacy.[16] What we can here call the 'orthodox' view, then, appraises EU legitimacy in the following terms: *input legitimacy* is weak due to the lack of a supranational demos, the weak powers of the European Parliament – most notably lacking the right of legislative initiative – and the (sometimes very) indirect nature of the expression of Member State democracies in EU institutions such as the European Council or Commission;[17] *throughput legitimacy*, while initially overlooked, or folded into input or output legitimacy, has, in more recent times, enjoyed a renewed focus, which has gone hand in hand with an improvement in the form of throughput legitimacy practiced by the EU and which therefore enjoys moderate throughput legitimacy;[18] while *output legitimacy*, more tolerant of 'weak collective identities',[19] has traditionally been seen as the EU's strongest legitimacy-related suit based on its achievements of market-making and economic growth.[20]

[8] Easton (n 1).
[9] ibid.
[10] Scharpf, *Governing in Europe* (n 3) 6.
[11] ibid 6.
[12] Schmidt, 'Democracy and Legitimacy' (n 1).
[13] ibid 15.
[14] VA Schmidt, *Europe's Crisis of Legitimacy: Governing by Rules and Ruling by Numbers in the Eurozone* (Oxford, Oxford University Press, 2020) 39.
[15] ibid.
[16] VA Schmidt, 'Democracy and Legitimacy in the European Union' in E Jones, A Menon and S Weatherill (eds), *The Oxford Handbook of the European Union* (Oxford, Oxford University Press, 2012); JHH Weiler, 'In the Face of Crisis: Input Legitimacy, Output Legitimacy and the Political Messianism of European Integration' (2012) 34 *Journal of European Integration* 825.
[17] Scharpf, *Governing in Europe* (n 3) 7–10.
[18] Schmidt, 'Democracy and Legitimacy' (n 1) 15.
[19] Scharpf, *Governing in Europe* (n 3) 12.
[20] ibid; Majone, *Dilemmas of European Integration* (n 3).

# III. *La Decandenza*

As Jean Monnet predicted, European integration would be forged in the crucible of crisis.[21] Crisis is, therefore, embedded in the EU's DNA.[22] However, the past long decade of crisis, beginning when the ink was barely dry on the Lisbon Treaty in 2007 (itself the product of the Constitutional Treaty's ratification crisis), arguably marks out perhaps the most existential period in European integration history. The intensity and relentlessness of crises – from the initial banking crisis to the fiscal crises of certain Member States; the euro crisis, which unleashed undiplomatic and public hostility between Member State governments as well as the large-scale mobilisation of public opinion hostile to the EU; the refugee crisis; the wave of populism which swept through the continent, resulting in the vote by a large member to leave the bloc in 2016 and a values-regression crisis in other Member States, all troublesomely cheered on by a populist US president;[23] the spreading of the first global pandemic in a century, swiftly followed by a geopolitical and security crisis caused by Russia's invasion and destruction of Ukraine; not to mention the ever-worsening climate crisis – permit the conclusion, without much exaggeration, that the EU is undergoing one of the most critical periods in its history. Never before has the future of the integration project seemed less assured. The EU's long decade of crisis has, unsurprisingly, prompted a serial re-evaluation of the EU's legitimacy. The general trend in the literature has been to reassess the results of the 'score card' outlined above – weak input, improving throughput and strong output – to an altogether more damning record of worsening input, worsening throughput and worsening output legitimacy in the EU's responses to the various crises.[24] For current purposes, we can briefly track the ways in which the eurozone crisis and the EU values-regression crisis have resulted in this general downgrading in the EU's legitimacy.

## A. The Eurozone Crisis

The measures taken to manage the eurozone crisis in the early 2010s have garnered a consensus among the orthodoxy that the EU is failing on all of the polity's conventional legitimacy indicators: input, throughput and output.[25] The EU's weak

[21] 'Europe would be built through crises, and that would be the sum of their solutions': J Monnet, *Memoirs* (R Mayne trans, Collins 1978) 417.

[22] Of course, the integration project itself began with a crisis with the failure of the European Defence Community in 1954.

[23] See generally J White, *Politics of Last Resort: Governing by Emergency in the European Union* (Oxford, Oxford University Press, 2019).

[24] See F Scharpf, 'Political Legitimacy in a Non-optimal Currency Area' in O Cramme and S Hobolt (eds), *Democratic Politics in a European Union Under Stress* (Oxford, Oxford University Press, 2014); Schmidt, *Europe's Crisis of Legitimacy* (n 14); Weiler (n 16).

[25] Schmidt, *Europe's Crisis of Legitimacy* (n 14); Weiler (n 16).

input legitimacy, primarily predicated on the democratic credentials of its Member States, with a supporting role for the European Parliament, has, it has been argued, been exacerbated in the aftermath of the eurocrisis.[26] With regard to the role of the European Parliament, it has been all but sidelined in eurozone decision-making.[27] Perhaps more egregiously, however, the EU's crisis management served to undermine whatever weak input legitimacy the EU enjoyed – primarily national democratic processes – by constraining the acts of Member State legislatures and policy-makers. In the barrage of post-euro crisis measures that were adopted, the freedom of action of national legislatures and policy-makers was increasingly constricted, in that they were forced to conform to the EU's crisis management playbook on pain of disavowing the integration project altogether.[28]

Furthermore, the messy and intransparent bailout negotiations, as well as the mechanisms through which bailouts occurred, impacted negatively on the EU's throughput legitimacy.[29] In particular, the lack of transparency and rule-following – key features of input legitimacy – particularly by the Commission and the European Central Bank (ECB) compromised the EU's throughput legitimacy.[30] With regard to the ECB, its acts and statements, not least the notorious 'whatever it takes' comments by its former president Mario Draghi,[31] are evidence of its lack of respect for legality in the view of many[32] – not least the German Federal Constitutional Court[33] – as it strayed well beyond its legally defined competences stipulated in the Treaties in an effort to manage the euro crisis.[34] Similarly, the Commission's legitimacy as a neutral arbiter of the European common good has, it has been alleged, been compromised by its complicity in imbalanced and asymmetrical eurozone governance vis-à-vis different Member States, such that it was increasingly seen as less neutral and more beholden to particular interests – not least those of the EU's largest Member State, Germany.[35]

Finally, the EU's output legitimacy – conventionally considered the most robust pillar of EU legitimacy – has fared little better. Scharpf notes that the EU's financial crisis management measures, while invasive and far-reaching, failed to

[26] Scharpf, 'Political Legitimacy' (n 24) 34; Schmidt, *Europe's Crisis of Legitimacy* (n 14).

[27] C Fasone, 'European Economic Governance and Parliamentary Representation. What Place for the European Parliament?' (2014) 20 *European Law Journal* 164.

[28] Scharpf, 'Political Legitimacy' (n 24) 20; F Scharpf, 'Monetary Union, Fiscal Crisis and the Pre-emption of Democracy' (2011) 9 *Zeitschrift für Staats- und Europawissenschaften* 163.

[29] C Kilpatrick, 'On the Rule of Law and Economic Emergency: The Degradation of Basic Legal Values in Europe's Bailouts' (2015) 35 *CJLS* 325; Schmidt, *Europe's Crisis of Legitimacy* (n 14) ch 5.

[30] Schmidt, *Europe's Crisis of Legitimacy* (n 14) 11–12; Scharpf, 'Political Legitimacy' (n 24) 38–39.

[31] A Tooze, *Crashed: How a Decade of Financial Crises Changed the World* (New York, Viking, 2018) ch 18.

[32] VA Schmidt, 'European Emergency Politics and the Question of Legitimacy' (2021) *Journal of European Public Policy* 1, 11.

[33] 'Special Section: "The German Federal Constitutional Court's PSPP Judgment"' (2020) 21 *German Law Journal* 944.

[34] Scharpf, 'Political Legitimacy' (n 24) 38; 'Special Section' (n 33).

[35] Scharpf, 'Political Legitimacy' (n 24) 39; see also U Beck, *German Europe* (Cambridge, Polity Press, 2013).

address economic decline and high unemployment in the worst-affected Member States.[36] As such, the EU failed a key test in its output legitimacy in managing the eurozone crisis: the test of competent management of a major financial crisis which would leave EU citizens better off than they would have otherwise been. The debasement of the EU's legitimacy post-euro crisis is clearly captured by Scharpf, who characterised the fate of EU citizens in the following, stark, terms: 'European citizens must suffer the impact of the crisis and of the depoliticized euro regime either in stoic acceptance or in helpless frustration … EMU and its defence have created problems for which there simply are no "good" solutions.'[37]

## B. The Values-Regression Crisis

Like the eurozone crisis, the EU's values-regression crisis has resulted in a downgrading of the EU's legitimacy. The regression in respect for EU values – particularly the rule of law and democracy – in certain post-2004 accession Member States have been a cause of concern for some time, coinciding with the rise of authoritarian populism both within Europe and beyond.[38] The EU's responses to these events within its borders has been the subject of sustained and trenchant criticism, particularly due to the inability[39] or unwillingness[40] of key bodies – notably the European Council and European Commission – to do what is necessary to stem the rise of authoritarian populist governments in EU Member States.[41]

With respect to considerations of input legitimacy, the rise of authoritarian populism in certain Member States poses problems for the EU's weak input

[36] Scharpf, 'Political Legitimacy' (n 24) 20; see also M Blyth, *Austerity: The History of a Dangerous Idea* (Oxford, Oxford University Press, 2013); A Mody, *Eurotragedy: A Drama in Nine Acts* (Oxford, Oxford University Press, 2018).

[37] Scharpf, 'Political Legitimacy' (n 24) 40–41.

[38] F Stengel, D MacDonald and D Nabers (eds), *Populism and World Politics: Exploring Inter- and Transnational Dimensions* (Berlin, Springer, 2019).

[39] The problems with triggering Art 7 TEU to sanction a regressing Member State have been well documented. See L Besselink, 'The Bite, the Bark, and the Howl: Article 7 TEU and the Rule of Law Initiatives' in A Jakab and D Kochenov (eds), *The Enforcement of EU Law and Values* (Oxford, Oxford University Press, 2017); B Bugarič, 'Protecting Democracy inside the EU: On Article 7 TEU and the Hungarian Turn to Authoritarianism' in C Closa and D Kochenov (eds), *Reinforcing Rule of Law Oversight in the European Union* (Cambridge, Cambridge University Press, 2016).

[40] RD Kelemen and L Pech, 'The Uses and Abuses of Constitutional Pluralism: Undermining the Rule of Law in the Name of Constitutional Identity in Hungary and Poland' (2019) 21 *Cambridge Yearbook of European Legal Studies* 59.

[41] For good overviews of the EU's value-regression crisis, see Closa and Kochenov (n 39); Jakab and Kochenov (n 39); KL Scheppele, DV Kochenov and B Grabowska-Moroz, 'EU Values Are Law, after All: Enforcing EU Values through Systemic Infringement Actions by the European Commission and the Member States of the European Union' (2020) 39 *Yearbook of European Law* 3. On 5 April 2022, the Commission initiated proceedings to withhold EU funding from Hungary based on rule-of-law concerns after the flawed Hungarian elections on 3 April 2022, which returned a resounding victory for the incumbent populist Fidesz party. See 'EU Launches Process to Slash Hungary's Funds over Rule-of-Law Breaches' *Politico* (5 April 2022) www.politico.eu/article/eu-commission-to-trigger-rule-of-law-budget-tool-against-hungary/.

legitimacy similar to those posed by the EU's post-crisis eurozone regulation. If national democratic processes are undermined, in this case by the manipulation of electoral democracy and the rule of law by authoritarian populists, then the EU's own (weak) input legitimacy suffers as a result in that the undermining of democratic values in individual Member States has a knock-on effect on the EU's claims to democratic legitimacy.[42]

The EU's failures in terms of throughput legitimacy can be understood by reference to the efficacy criteria of throughput legitimacy.[43] As Schmidt argues, the efficacy criteria of throughput legitimacy relates to the efficacy of the policy tools and processes employed by the EU to achieve its core objectives.[44] Whereas there have arguably been some successes in terms of efficacy with respect to rule-of-law questions – notably by the CJEU's innovative use of Article 19 TEU as a gateway to addressing rule-of-law issues in national judiciaries[45] – the Commission, in particular, has come in for considerable criticism in the policy choices and tools it has employed to address the values-regression crisis more generally.[46] Its strategy of tackling the backsliding of values through enforcement actions in discrete, and at times arcane, areas of EU law – such as tackling court-packing using age discrimination law – has been derided as a strategy of 'losing through winning':[47] while it may win cases in these discrete areas, such gains are having little impact on the broader trend in particular Member States towards further authoritarian populist government.[48]

Finally, and relatedly, the EU's output legitimacy is also undermined by the continuing backsliding of values within the EU's borders. Whereas output legitimacy in the EU has conventionally been considered in economic terms[49] – clearly articulated in Article 3(3) TEU – Article 3(1) TEU makes clear that another legally mandated 'output' of EU governance is the *promotion* of the EU's values contained in Article 2 TEU, and in particular *democratic* values.[50] Where the EU, and particularly the Commission in this case, fails to promote the EU's values by effectively tackling values-regression within its own Member States, comparable, say, to the extent to which it promotes the common market or the rules of the common currency, its output legitimacy is undermined.

[42] Scheppele et al (n 41) 15.
[43] Schmidt, *Europe's Crisis of Legitimacy* (n 14) 39.
[44] ibid 8.
[45] Case C-64/16 *Associação Sindical dos Juízes Portugueses v Tribunal de Contas* EU:C:2018:117; M Bonelli and M Claes, 'Judicial Serendipity: How Portuguese Judges Came to the Rescue of the Polish Judiciary' (2018) 14 *European Constitutional Law Review* 622.
[46] See generally Scheppele et al (n 41).
[47] ibid 42.
[48] Alternative policy tools have been promoted in the literature. See ibid.
[49] G Majone, *Rethinking the Union of Europe Post-Crisis: Has Integration Gone Too Far?* (Cambridge, Cambridge University Press, 2014) ch 1.
[50] C Hillion, 'Overseeing the Rule of Law in the EU: Legal Mandate and Means' in Closa and Kochenov (n 39); R Coman, 'Strengthening the Rule of Law at the Supranational Level: The Rise and Consolidation of a European Network' (2016) 24 *Journal of Contemporary European Studies* 171, 174.

## IV. Addressing the Elephant in the Room: The Crisis-Ridden EU's Endurance and Expansion

In reviewing the EU's legitimacy after its long (and ongoing) decade of crisis using the toolkit of what I have here called the 'orthodox view', we are left with a puzzle. If, on the orthodox view, the EU's (already shaky) legitimacy has been seriously compromised with regard to the eurozone, values-regression and other crises, why have other Member States not followed the path of the UK and left? Why has the EU not collapsed? Not only have other Member States not left the bloc during the long decade of crisis, but Eurobarometer polls, such as they are, have rebounded significantly since the lows at the peak of the euro crisis.[51] Furthermore, advances in European cooperation to jointly manage the COVID-19 pandemic, as well as the united front in managing the departure of the UK from the Union,[52] speak to the strengthening of the EU's agency rather than the weakening that would be associated with a collapse in its legitimacy. Even if we acknowledge that there are complex reasons for the endurance of the EU as well as fluctuations in Eurobarometer results, we cannot discount the fact that legitimacy plays a significant role in the EU's endurance, expansion and enhanced agency during this period. In responding to the 'new–old' orthodoxy's dire prognostications surrounding the EU's legitimacy, then, we can problematise their conclusions, paraphrasing Galileo, with the response: *eppur esiste!*[53]

That is, notwithstanding the various crises buffeting the EU during this long decade, it has endured. This alerts us to the fact that the orthodox approach to legitimacy in the EU context can provide, at best, a *partial* view of legitimacy in the EU, elucidating legitimacy failures and deficits in discrete areas of law and policy based on given benchmarks, rather than an overall, holistic, all-things-considered view of the EU's legitimacy, given that it cannot account for a significant legitimacy-relevant fact about the EU's long decade of crisis: its endurance and expansion. A more general consideration of the EU's overall legitimacy should be able to account for the fact that the EU has endured and expanded during the long decade of crisis. Bernard Williams's 'political realist' account of political legitimacy provides just such an account.

[51] It is striking that, according to a Eurobarometer poll from December 2021, 73% of respondents *in Greece* believe that the euro is a good thing *for Greece*. Flash Eurobarometer 501, 'The Euro Area' (December 2021) https://europa.eu/eurobarometer/surveys/detail/2289.

[52] See above (n 4).

[53] A popular account of Galileo's appearance before the inquisition for propagating the heliocentric view of the solar system has Galileo denouncing the idea that the earth moves around the sun followed by a subtle retraction of that denunciation by uttering the words '*eppur si mouve*'; 'and yet it [the earth] moves [around the sun]'. The story is widely believed to be apocryphal. See 'Galileo Galilei' in S Radcliffe (ed), *Oxford Essential Quotations* (Oxford, Oxford University Press, 2016).

## V. Williams's Political Realism and EU Legitimacy

In developing a political realist account of political legitimacy, the English moral philosopher Bernard Williams tried to map out a course between a non-normative account of power and the idealised moral prescriptions of much contemporary political philosophy. In attempting to provide a *normative* realist account of legitimacy, he attempted to navigate a middle course between the poles of political science, which tends to characterise politics in terms of mere power and interests, and idealised political theory which views politics as an activity guided by 'autonomous products of moral reason'.[54] In developing his particular account of political realism, he contrasted his political realist approach with what he called 'political moralism,'[55] an approach exemplified in two popular models of political legitimacy: an 'enactment model', which holds that political legitimacy is based on the achievement of particular 'principles, concepts, ideals and values[56] by political actors; and a 'structural model',[57] where the 'moral conditions of coexistence under power'[58] purport to establish when power can be 'justly exercised',[59] such as in the political liberalism of John Rawls.[60] While these models have important differences, what they share is a view of political legitimacy that prioritises 'the moral over the political',[61] what Guess has called an 'ethics first' approach to political legitimacy.[62] For the enactment model, prior moral values provide the goals that legitimate government should pursue;[63] for the structural model, prior moral values provide the constraints on 'what politics can rightfully do'.[64] However, in both cases, political legitimacy is presented as 'something like applied morality'.[65] The problem with political moralist accounts of legitimacy, Williams argued, was the political moralist lack of attention to the question of authority and historical context in the articulation of normative values as well as the endemic disagreement in politics around questions of normative value.[66] In short, political moralism leaves little room for *politics* in their accounts of legitimacy.

[54] Williams, 'Realism and Moralism' (n 5) 12.
[55] ibid 3.
[56] ibid 1.
[57] ibid.
[58] ibid.
[59] ibid.
[60] ibid.
[61] ibid 2.
[62] R Geuss, *Philosophy and Real Politics* (Princeton, Princeton University Press, 2008) 8.
[63] Williams, 'Realism and Moralism' (n 5) 1.
[64] ibid 2.
[65] ibid 2.
[66] E Hall, 'The Limits of Bernard Williams's Critique of Political Moralism' (2013) 20 *Ethical Perspectives* 217; M Sleat, 'Bernard Williams and the Possibility of a Realist Political Theory' (2010) 9 *European Journal of Political Theory* 485, 503; C Mac Amhlaigh, 'Friend or Foe?: Bernard Williams and Political Constitutionalism' (2021) 27 *Res Publica* 219.

Political realism, on the other hand, takes more seriously the autonomy of 'distinctively political thought'[67] and does not equate political thought with moral thought. Political realism as a theory of political authority, for Williams, *begins* with the question of authority, the FPQ involving the securing of 'order, protection, safety, trust, and the conditions of cooperation'.[68] The FPQ is the paramount question of politics for Williams, in that its resolution is a necessary condition of posing and resolving other political questions, including questions of *value*.[69]

A satisfactory response to the FPQ is a necessary but not a sufficient condition for the legitimacy of authority, however.[70] Unlike Hobbes, who assumed that the resolution of the FPQ was all there was to the question of authority, Williams argued that a satisfactory response to the FPQ must also satisfy what he called the 'basic legitimation demand', or BLD.[71] The BLD requires that the resolution of the FPQ be an '*acceptable*' one; that is, that the authority offers a justification of its power '*to each subject*' (emphasis added).[72] Thus, Williams's account of legitimacy involves the requirement that a governing regime can justify its authority and legitimacy to each of its subjects through the resolution of the FPQ in an 'acceptable'[73] way. The BLD requires, at a minimum, that an authority protect 'radically disadvantaged groups'.[74]

For Williams, the BLD is not satisfied where citizens are in a state of fear of harms such as 'coercion, pain, torture, humiliation, suffering [or] death'.[75] This fails as an account of legitimacy because a satisfactory answer to the FPQ is inherent in taking individuals out of a situation where they can fear these degradations. Legitimacy on this account requires that '*something*' is said to the governed which explains the difference between 'the solution and the problem' (original emphasis).[76] A failure to justify authority in this way is not, for Williams, then a *political* situation, but one of coercion *tout court*.[77] As Williams pithily puts it:[78] 'The situation of one lot of people terrorising another lot of people is not per se a political situation: it is, rather, the situation which the existence of the political is in the first place supposed to alleviate (replace).'

Furthermore, to this specification of the BLD, Williams adds what he calls a critical theory principle.[79] Not just any attempted justification of authority counts for the BLD. According to the critical theory principle, a subject's acceptance of

[67] Williams, 'Realism and Moralism' (n 5) 3.
[68] ibid.
[69] ibid.
[70] ibid.
[71] ibid 4.
[72] ibid.
[73] ibid 5.
[74] ibid 4.
[75] ibid.
[76] ibid 5.
[77] ibid 4.
[78] ibid 5.
[79] ibid 5.

the justification of an authority 'does not count if the acceptance itself is produced by the coercive power which is supposedly being justified'.[80] That is, the authority cannot use coercion as a substitute for justification, and the acceptance of the justification of the authority must be freely and independently entered into by the subject of the authority.

Significantly, on Williams's account, historical context is important to thinking about legitimacy in a given setting. He uses the idea of 'making sense' as a way of emphasising the fact that the extent to which a political structure is intelligible as an authoritative order will in part depend upon 'historical and cultural circumstances'.[81] Williams's emphasis on the role of historical context in articulating normative values permits the possibility that the BLD can be satisfied in different ways. Thus, even if, as Williams himself concedes, liberalism has become the dominant mode of legitimation in our historical condition of modernity,[82] this does not mean that there is only one form or one interpretation of liberal value that can satisfy the requirements of the BLD. The 'ambiguities' of liberalism, Williams writes, indicate 'a range of options which make political sense in the modern world'.[83] They are all, for example, compatible with a '*Rechtstaat*' and they can 'vary depending on how much emphasis is put on welfare rights and the like'.[84] In this way, Williams's account of political realism leaves room for disagreement about how the requirements of the BLD can be satisfied in a given political context.

## VI. Political Realism and the European Union

Applying Williams's typologies of legitimacy to the orthodox approach to EU legitimacy, we can argue that the forms of input, throughput and output constitute forms of *political moralism*. Input and throughput legitimacy look a lot like the *structural* model of political moralism, where legitimacy stems from politics operating within predetermined (and putatively pre-political) values. Both input and output legitimacy rely on (particularly liberal-inspired) assumptions about legitimacy (governing of and by the people) – majoritarian representative liberal democracy and values of procedural liberalism, such as transparency, fairness, accountability and openness[85] – which assume a decontextualised normative value prior to, and above, politics. In a similar way, output legitimacy is analogous

[80] ibid 6.
[81] ibid 11.
[82] Which he aphoristically captures in the slogan 'Leg[itimacy] + Modernity = Liberalism', ibid 9. See also B Williams, 'Modernity and the Substance of Ethical Life' in G Hawthorn (ed), *In the Beginning was the Deed* (Princeton, Princeton University Press, 2005).
[83] Williams, 'Realism and Moralism' (n 5) 9.
[84] ibid.
[85] J Rawls, *Political Liberalism* (New York, Columbia University Press, 1993) Lecture VI 'The Idea of Public Reason'.

to the *enactment* model of political moralism. Here, rather than predetermined, pre-political values providing the *boundaries* within which legitimate politics can operate, the values are posited at the outset as the teleology of legitimate politics. In the EU context, the teleology of a European common good, particularly in terms of economic considerations as exemplified by the promotion of the common market,[86] provide the benchmark against which legitimate EU governance is assessed.[87]

Recasting the orthodox view of legitimacy as forms of political moralism helps us understand the tensions between the conclusions of the 'new–old' orthodox view and the realities of the EU's endurance and expansion. First of all, as political moralism more generally ignores the problem of authority, its expression in the orthodox account cannot provide an answer to the 'Galileo gambit': that, notwithstanding the poor legitimacy record in handling the various crises according to the orthodox view, the EU not only endures, but is also expanding, including for legitimacy-related reasons. If, on the other hand, we approach the 'Galileo gambit' starting with the question of authority – Williams's FPQ – we can argue that the EU's legitimacy, and its endurance and expansion during the long decade of crisis, can be understood in terms of its ability to (continue to) provide a solution to the FPQ of *supranational* politics; that is, the securing of 'order, safety, trust and the conditions of cooperation'[88] in respect of those aspects of politics which are not reducible to, nor can be contained purely within, the political orders of states (ie Member States' own answers to the FPQ of *national* politics).[89] Thus, in thinking about political realism in the EU context, it is the achievement of a satisfactory answer to the FPQ of supranational politics that provides the first necessary condition of the EU's legitimacy, which helps explain its endurance and expansion during the long decade of crisis.

Secondly, a political realist approach to EU legitimacy leaves room for disagreement about the ways in which the subsequent condition of political realism – the BLD – can be satisfied. 'Where the action is' in thinking about disagreement about legitimacy in the EU context on a political realist account, then, is with respect to the ways in which the EU satisfies the BLD using 'first-order discussions using our political, moral, social, interpretive and other concepts'.[90] However, if it is the case, as Williams suggests, that disagreement exists even where we limit our normative values to *liberal* values in modernity in the *state* context,[91] then we can expect disagreement to be even more intense, in relation to the legitimation of a complex 'in-between' governing entity such as the EU, between a federal-constitutional structure and a classic international organisation, implicating both constitutional

[86] Art 3(3) TEU.
[87] Majone, *Rethinking the Union* (n 49).
[88] Williams, 'Modernity and the Substance of Ethical Life' (n 82) 3.
[89] See R Dworkin, 'A New Philosophy for International Law' (2013) 41 *Philosophy and Public Affairs* 2, 18.
[90] Williams, 'Realism and Moralism' (n 5) 11.
[91] ibid 4.

(domestic and state law-based) and international (diplomatic and international law-based) methods and structures of governing.[92]

That this level of disagreement is influential in the EU's responses to the various crises and its overall legitimacy is clear in Schmidt's account of the EU's initial response to the eurozone crisis, which betrayed 'Differing perceptions of the causes of the crisis, conflicting ideas about how to govern the European economy, divergent preferences for courses of action, and differing normative orientations regarding the EU and what it is or should become'.[93] Moreover, these 'differing perceptions' – in short, *disagreements* about the crisis, the values relevant to it and the EU's role in managing it – tended to track national Member State boundaries, reflecting the complex 'in-between' nature of EU governance.[94]

The satisfaction of the BLD in the EU context will entail disagreement about different models of liberal democracy, but also disagreement about the nature of the EU as an 'in-between' governing entity and what is appropriate and can be expected in terms of its legitimation.[95] Thus, an important feature of thinking about legitimation in the EU is the idea of what 'makes sense' as authoritative order in an 'in-between' quasi-international, quasi-federal entity such as the EU, which is likely to differ, sometimes significantly, from the political-moralist assumptions of the orthodox approach. Williams's political realism therefore also leaves room for the historical context of the development of the EU in a way which does not make demands in terms of normative legitimacy which ignore the complex evolutionary nature of the EU and its 'in-between' character.

A political realist account of EU legitimacy shows the ways in which the EU's legitimacy endures even in the light of disagreements and individual policy failures, which is a missing piece of the political moralist calculus: the EU's continued ability to provide a satisfactory response to the FPQ of supranational politics accompanied by its satisfaction of the BLD in a way which 'makes sense' in a part-constitutional, part-diplomatic/international political entity. Moreover, as a *political* conception of legitimacy, the ways in which the EU secures its legitimacy on the political realist account will evolve over time, responding to historical events and circumstances such that what 'makes sense' in one period of integration may not in another. One example of this is the evolution of fundamental rights law in the EU context.[96] Whereas the EU's (and its predecessors') legitimation may have

[92] D Curtin and I Dekker, 'The EU as a "Layered" International Organization: Institutional Unity in Disguise' in P Craig and G De Búrca (eds), *The Evolution of EU Law* (Oxford, Oxford University Press, 1999).

[93] Schmidt, *Europe's Crisis of Legitimacy* (n 14) 9.

[94] ibid 9: 'What needed to be done to solve the crisis was extremely unpopular with voting publics of the core member states in Northern Europe – not only Germany but also The Netherlands, Austria, Finland, and even Latvia … At the same time, what was imposed on member states in the periphery in terms of austerity and structural reform was equally unpopular, and often seen as unjustly forcing the debtor countries to pay for the risky loans of creditor country bank[s].'

[95] See Z Bankowski and E Christodoulidis, 'The European Union as an Essentially Contested Project' (1998) 4 *European Law Journal* 341.

[96] G de Búrca, 'The Road Not Taken: The European Union as a Global Human Rights Actor' (2011) 105 *The American Journal of International Law* 649.

'made sense' in the early days of integration without a robust system of judicially protected fundamental rights, it is arguably inconceivable that the BLD could be satisfied in the absence of such protection in the contemporary EU.

## VII. W(h)ither the Normative Bite in Political Realism?

In thinking about how a political realist assessment approaches the legitimacy of the EU, it is important to emphasise, as Williams was at pains to do, that political realism is a *normative* theory of legitimacy, and not a justification of pure power or an apology for the status quo. As a normative theory, it does have critical bite in the normative demands made in answering the FPQ and the BLD. As much is clear in the normativity inherent in Williams's account of politics,[97] which insists that an arrangement of coercion of the whole or part of the governed is not a political situation,[98] and in the way in which he equates, more or less, the satisfaction of the BLD with the normative demands of liberalism in modernity, which, of course, includes their articulation as EU values in the EU Treaties.[99]

Thus, thinking about EU legitimacy from a political realist approach does not assume that the EU has not suffered from legitimacy problems during the long decade of crisis, nor that nothing should be done to improve the EU's legitimacy in the context of eurozone governance or the values-regression crisis. Rather, political realism reminds us to take more seriously the 'platitude'[100] of the relevance of authority to political legitimacy as well as the disagreement inherent in considerations of normative value in addressing the *normative* legitimacy of the EU – not least given its complex 'in-between' character.

For the crises considered here, then, we can, from a political realist approach, conclude that while the eurozone crisis presented acute challenges to the EU, its overall legitimacy remained intact due to the fact that during the crisis, the EU proved capable of responding to the FPQ of supranational politics in providing the conditions for supranational management of a supranational crisis, even when the legitimacy of individual measures to deal with the crisis were bitterly contested. Moreover, arguably the power asymmetries as well as the demands made by the more powerful actors in terms of austerity were tolerated (as evidenced by the lack of an exit by a Member State on the grounds of the EU's eurozone management) not because of their normative 'correctness', but because they 'made sense' in the political context in which they were applied. In such a context, what would be unacceptable in, say, a unitary state context was at least tolerated in a complex 'in-between' political entity, where questions of solidarity (or the lack thereof) were compensated by the quasi-international, quasi-interstate bargaining of elements

[97] Mac Amhlaigh (n 66) 231.
[98] Williams, 'Realism and Moralism' (n 5) 5.
[99] ibid 9.
[100] ibid 13.

of the management of the eurozone bailouts. Whatever the rights and wrongs of austerity and individual bailout programmes,[101] they were not such as to cause the collapse of the legitimacy of the EU as a whole.

The values-regression crisis, on the other hand, poses a potentially bigger challenge to the EU's legitimacy on a political realist reading. This has to do with the risks of individual Member States reacting to the deteriorating situation in regressing Member States, particularly Poland and Hungary. A political moralist view of the rule-of-law crisis, as we have seen, would conceive of the EU's inaction with respect to values-regression within its own borders as per se undermining the EU's legitimacy.[102] However, this fails to capture the fact that the EU has endured and expanded through over 10 years of values-regression in particular Member States. Rather, on a political realist reading, a satisfactory answer to the FPQ of supranational politics as well as a satisfactory answer to the BLD *by the EU* – as opposed to regressing Member State governments, who arguably do not provide a satisfactory justification under the BLD[103] – have sustained the EU's legitimacy over the period of this particular crisis. Moreover, as with the eurozone crisis, disagreement affects the question of what the EU should be doing to tackle values-regression within its borders based on the legal powers the different institutions enjoy under the Treaties.[104] On a political realist reading, the real threat to legitimacy posed by the values-regression crisis is the undermining of the EU's ability to answer the FPQ in a satisfactory way due to the activities of *other* non-regressing Member States. Where a failure to tackle EU values-regression in certain Member States leads to unilateral action by other Member States, starting as a form of 'self-help'[105] in the form of 'counter-measures'[106] to counter the acts of backsliding Member States' failure to respect the EU Treaties, the EU's legitimacy could be destroyed, potentially precipitating the disintegration of the polity. This is because a trend in unilateral Member State action to counter values-regression in other Member States would destroy the EU's capacity to answer the FPQ of supranational politics

[101] Even the Commission itself subsequently admitted that austerity had been a 'mistake'. 'Austerity Was a Mistake, Says EU Economy Commissioner' *Irish Times* (20 September 2021) www.irishtimes.com/business/economy/austerity-was-a-mistake-says-eu-economy-commissioner-1.4678260. See also Blyth (n 36); Mody (n 36).

[102] See generally W Schroeder (ed), *Strengthening the Rule of Law in Europe: From a Common Concept to Mechanisms of Implementation* (Oxford, Hart Publishing, 2016).

[103] An argument could be made that the EU could fail to respond to the FPQ of supranational politics in a satisfactory way in the face of Member State values-regression if we understand part of the FPQ of supranational politics as including keeping states on the democratic 'straight and narrow'. Whereas I can see the logic of this argument, I am not convinced that we are at a stage whereby we can unambiguously say that the EU intervening in Member States to tackle regression in a general way – as opposed to specific ways under discrete provisions of EU law – makes sense in terms of the legitimacy of its authority. I would suggest that the disagreement on this point is evidence of this.

[104] Contrast, eg JW Müller, 'Should the EU Protect Democracy and the Rule of Law inside Member States?' (2015) 21 *European law Journal* 141; Hillion (n 50).

[105] Scheppele et al (n 41) 5.

[106] For discussion of the possibility under EU law, see B Simma and D Pulkowski, 'Of Planets and the Universe: Self-Contained Regimes in International Law' (2006) 17 *European Journal of International Law* 483, 516–19.

and thus provide the relevant conditions of supranational order, trust and mutual cooperation that are a necessary condition of the EU's legitimacy.

## VIII. Conclusion

The EU's long decade of crisis has tested the integration project in a manner arguably unseen in its previous 50-year history. There has been no shortage of analysis undertaken, and solutions proposed, to the EU's crisis of legitimacy during this period. The preponderance of these analyses and solutions, however, rely on a political moralist approach to thinking about political legitimacy in the EU context in a manner which does not take seriously the EU's role in answering the FPQ of supranational politics and ignores disagreement about the nature and relevance of normative values in the context of a complex 'in-between' polity. This could lead, somewhat ironically, to the undermining of the EU's legitimacy where the prescriptions of political moralist approaches undermine the EU's ability to answer the FPQ of supranational politics.[107] Rather, a political realist approach to EU legitimacy, based on Bernard Williams's approach, provides a more fruitful way of thinking about EU legitimacy to manage the current and undoubted future crises which will buffet this crisis-ridden, if resilient, supranational authority.

[107] Something along these lines seems to be implicit in Weiler's cautioning against ignoring the EU's evolutionary *Sonderweg* in thinking about institutional reforms to enhance its legitimacy. He cautioned against both the formal constitutionalisation of the polity in the attempt to draft a constitutional treaty in the 2000s as well as the 'full democratisation' of the EU, both of which, he argues, could undermine the EU's authority. See JHH Weiler, 'In Defence of the Status Quo: Europe's Constitutional Sonderweg' in JHH Weiler and Marlene Wind (eds), *European Constitutionalism beyond the State* (Cambridge, Cambridge University Press, 2003); JHH Weiler, *The Constitution of Europe* (Cambridge, Cambridge University Press, 1999) 264.

# 10

# As Beyond, So Below: European Sovereignty and Economic Globalisation

DANIEL AUGENSTEIN

## I. Sovereignty under Siege?

The corrosive effects of so-called neoliberal- or hyper-globalisation on sovereign statehood have long been a common theme across the social sciences.[1] As far as the internal dimension of sovereignty (political self-determination qua popular sovereignty) is concerned, globalisation erodes the substance of legal and political authority that states wield over their territory and citizenry. Global economic integration creates increasing gaps between the regulatory capacity of territorial states and the operational capacities of global business enterprises. Global economic competition pushes for a privatisation of state functions that shifts powers and responsibilities from governments to the market. The ensuing difficulties experienced by many states in exercising effective democratic control over their domestic economies goes hand in hand with a shrinking capacity to deliver on social justice.

As far as the external dimension of sovereignty (political independence qua sovereign state equality) is concerned, global economic integration and competition transforms states' international relations with one another. Globalisation asserts pressure on capital-exporting states to create a global 'level playing field' for their national industries by further dismantling barriers to trade liberalisation. At the same time, capital-importing states have proven unable and/or unwilling to raise national standards of social protection for fear of losing their competitive advantage in global markets. Taken together, these developments destabilise territorial demarcations between the 'domestic' and the 'foreign' constitutive of the Western/Westphalian conception of sovereign statehood,[2] and upset the capitalist

[1] From the burgeoning literature, see Q Slobodian, *Globalists: The End of Empire and the Birth of Neoliberalism* (Cambridge, MA, Harvard University Press, 2018); D Rodrik, *The Globalisation Paradox* (New York, Norton 2012); D Held et al, *Global Transformations* (Cambridge, Polity Press, 1999).

[2] B Kingsbury, 'Sovereignty and Inequality' (1998) 9 *European Journal of International Law* 599.

bargain of 'embedded liberalism', in which the commitment to international market liberalisation was balanced by an activist welfare state able to promote social and economic equality at the national level.[3]

Attempts to 'naturalise' and thus depoliticise these developments (the market as a naturally evolving order; the naturalistic 'no choice' rhetoric of financial crisis management; law and economics as a proxy for natural sciences) notwithstanding: The global implementation of the neoliberal policy triad of trade liberalisation, deregulation and privatisation heavily depends on political statecraft and legal engineering to underwrite *the other* new international economic order[4] and to implement domestic legal reforms conducive to global business operations.[5] Put crudely, what manifests itself as an external threat to state sovereignty is co-determined by internal transformations of statehood that respond to economic globalisation through its local re-enactment. This re-enactment injects into the Westphalian unity of government, territory and citizenry that represents the general interest of the state polity transnational legal and political authority that is bounded by the common goal of global market integration.

As a non-state polity, the European Union assumes a peculiar place in these transformations of statehood – not least because it needs to vindicate its internal and external sovereignty both inwards (in relation to the Member States and their citizenries) and outwards (in relation to third countries and international organisations). This twofold contingency of EU claims to sovereignty that require reciprocation from 'below' and 'beyond' has yielded competing interpretations of the role of European integration in processes of economic globalisation: as an erosion of Member State sovereignty that tames not only national self-interest but also state welfarism with a new supra- and transnational legal discipline;[6] as a pioneer of cosmopolitan citizenship that reclaims democratic control over global markets beyond the nation-state;[7] as a normative power that asserts global influence not by conquering territories but through regulating markets;[8] and as a role model for an international economic order that heeds the demands of universal human rights.[9] A common theme that animates these competing interpretations is whether Europe's 'economic constitution' places it at the vanguard of neoliberal globalisation, which juridifies markets to shield them from democratic

[3] JG Ruggie, 'International Regimes, Transactions, and Change: Embedded Liberalism in the Post-War Economic Order' (1982) 36 *International Organisations* 379.

[4] D Kennedy, 'Law and the Political Economy of the World' (2013) 26 *Leiden Journal of International Law* 7.

[5] K Pistor, *The Code of Capital: How Law Creates Wealth and Inequality* (Princeton, Princeton University Press, 2019).

[6] JHH Weiler, *The Constitution of Europe* (Cambridge, Cambridge University Press, 1999) 324–56; W Streek, *Buying Time: The Delayed Crisis of Democratic Capitalism*, 2nd edn (London, Verso 2017).

[7] J Habermas, *The Postnational Constellation* (Cambridge, Polity Press, 2001) 58–112.

[8] C Damro, 'Market Power Europe' (2012) 19 *Journal of European Public Policy* 682.

[9] EU Petersmann, 'Time for a United Nations "Global Compact" for Integrating Human Rights into the Law of Worldwide Organisations: Lessons from European Integration' (2002) 13 *European Journal of International Law* 621.

accountability, or whether the EU's value-based approach to market integration suggests a global maturation of post-national polities that emulate statist commitments to liberal democracy.

The aim of this contribution is to shed light on at least some of the assumptions about the internal and external dimensions of EU sovereignty borne out by these competing interpretations of the relationship between European integration and economic globalisation. More specifically, the contribution explores what the local re-enactment of economic globalisation entails for the role of sovereignty in the identify formation ('constitution') of the European Union at the interface of law, politics and social justice. To anticipate the overall argument: if Westphalian sovereignty was predicated upon the (more or less) exclusive unity between government, territory and citizenry, a distinguishing trait of post-Westphalian sovereignty is the functional delimitation and extension of state powers in a globalised liberal private sphere.

The next part of this chapter examines the texture of 'late sovereignty' in the European Union,[10] that is, the spatial, subjective and material dimensions through which it is claimed and enacted. It attributes to each of these dimensions a pair of relations: between territorial authority and functional integration; between national and market citizenship; and between democracy and human rights. The third part of the chapter complements this analysis by examining how the spatial, subjective and material dimensions of European sovereignty interact with economic globalisation in EU external relations. It discerns a reassembling of territorial authority at Europe's external borders that is justified in virtue of protecting the EU's value-based approach to internal market integration, while also justifying the projection of regulatory authority onto third states via global market actors.

## II. The Texture of European Sovereignty

Around the same time that the Maastricht Treaty integrated the European Economic Community into the newly founded European Union, IR scholar Susan Strange saw the state on the 'retreat' from economic globalisation: 'Where states were once the masters of markets, now it is the markets, which on many crucial issues, are the masters over the governments of states.'[11] Maastricht, it will be recalled, built on previous efforts to endow the European polity with more state-like features (strengthening the powers of the European Parliament; fashioning a European citizenship; committing the EU to respect fundamental rights) to 'create an ever-closer union among the peoples of Europe' (Article 1 TEU). These attempts to enhance the (direct) democratic credentials of an ever-broader

[10] N Walker, 'Late Sovereignty in the European Union' in N Walker (ed), *Sovereignty in Transition* (Oxford, Hart Publishing, 2003) 3–32.

[11] S Strange, *The Retreat of the State: The Diffusion of Power in the World Economy* (Cambridge, Cambridge University Press, 1996) 4.

integration project clashed with the ordo-liberal vision of a self-legitimising and self-delimiting European economic constitution, whose purpose was precisely to entrench a transnational division of labour between the two sides of the embedded liberalism bargain: European trade liberalisation and statist democratic legitimation and social protection.[12]

However, Maastricht was equally a response to the externalities of European market integration 'through law' on Member State democracies that eroded the Westphalian unity between government, territory and citizenry. It is thus tempting to read the 'leakages' of Europe's economic constitution in tandem with Strange's retreat of the state from globalisation that she deciphers less in terms of a quantitative loss of state power than in terms of a qualitative adjustment of the public functions that governments are still able or willing to perform. While, in some areas, the intervention of state authority into the daily lives of citizens is growing, the state has become 'less effective on those basic matters that the market, left to itself, has never been able to provide'.[13]

## A. Territorial Authority and Functional Integration

The partial 'liberation' of a functionally delimited and legally constituted sphere of global market integration from statist social democracy transforms sovereign statehood from within and without. It engineers a functional redefinition of public authority that attributes to state agencies a key role in the implementation of denationalised economic policies – the 'strategic places where many global processes take place are often national' – and 'the mechanisms through which the new legal forms necessary for globalisation are implemented are often part of state institutions'.[14] At the same time, it exposes state sovereignty to competing claims to ultimate authority. As Neil Walker says, while

> states in the age of late sovereignty still make claims to territorial authority *tout court* … non-state polities typically make claims to authority bounded by territory and function. In other words, the political *societies* which non-state polities claim to constitute are no longer just territorial communities but also functional communities.[15]

In the EU, both of these transformations were propelled by the European Court of Justice's early discovery of the individual as a rights-bearing subject of European legal ordering.[16] The confluence of direct effect and supremacy empowered private

[12] C Joerges, 'What Is Left of the European Economic Constitution?' (2004) EUI Law Department Working Paper No 13.

[13] Strange (n 11) 5.

[14] S Sassen, *Losing Control? Sovereignty in the Age of Globalisation* (New York, Colombia University Press, 1996) 29.

[15] Walker, 'Late Sovereignty' (n 10) 22.

[16] Case 26-62 *NV Algemene Transport- en Expeditie Onderneming van Gend & Loos v Netherlands Inland Revenue Administration* ECLI:EU:C:1963:1, [1963] ECR 1; Case 6-64 *Flaminio Costa v ENEL* ECLI:EU:C:1964:66, [1964] ECR 585.

(business) actors to claim their European market freedoms in national courts by invoking a public interest in vindicating the unity of the common/internal market under a transnational rule of law.[17] This co-opted the 'European citizen' as a vigilante of negative integration that forced Member State public authorities into compliance with the functional imperatives of EU market integration.[18] Conversely, the functional circumscription of the EC/EU legal order as an 'independent source of law' – the claim to rule over Member State citizens solely in their capacity as transnational market actors – allowed the CJEU to endow the European institutions with 'sovereign rights' enacted through the supremacy and direct effect of EC/EU law. Europe's economic constitution thus not only enabled competing claims to ultimate authority to coexist in the same territorial space; it also transformed the role of sovereignty in the identity formation of the state polity by steering the general interest of a territorially bounded citizenry towards the common goal of transnational market integration.

Rooting transformations of European sovereignty in the interplay between territorial state authority and functional market integration may give rise to various objections. It could thus be argued that the functional limitations of EU claims to sovereignty have become obsolete as the Union acquired competences and powers across a diverse range of policy areas formerly reserved to the Member States, and/or that they have become meaningless given the cross-sectoral impacts of market integration on policy areas still formally in the Member State domain.[19] Alternatively, it may be objected that the distinction between functional and territorial legal ordering is redundant because the former lays as much claim as the latter to political unity that is bounded in space (ie that takes place).[20]

It is possible to concede these objections without relinquishing the argument. My response to the first two objections is conceptual: as regards obsoleteness, the EU's aggregation of functions across different policy areas does not, and cannot, yield a representation of the general interest of the European polity. As regards meaninglessness, that market integration impacts on virtually all sectors of domestic policy (and that, inversely, virtually every domestic policy measure can be framed as a trade barrier) does not mean that the EU would lay claim to all-encompassing legal and political authority. While empirically valid, these objections put the cart before the horse. The transnational division of labour between European trade liberalisation and statist democratic legitimation and social protection is not simply a product of European integration; it is also the *premise* of EU claims to sovereignty. My response to the third objection

[17] JHH Weiler, 'Van Gend en Loos: The Individual as Subject and Object and the Dilemma of European Legitimacy' (2014) 12 *European Journal of International Law* 94, 96.

[18] F Scharpf, *Governing in Europe: Effective and Democratic?* (Oxford, Oxford University Press, 1999) 54–58.

[19] G de Búrca, 'Sovereignty and the Supremacy Doctrine of the European Court of Justice' in Walker, *Sovereignty in Transition* (n 10) 449, 457–59.

[20] H Lindahl, *Fault Lines of Globalisation: Legal Order and the Politics of A-Legality* (Oxford, Oxford University Press, 2013).

is substantive: that functional legal orders are spatially bounded says nothing about the composition of political unity represented in claims to functional sovereignty. Put differently, and turning to the subjective dimension of European sovereignty, it does not elucidate what functional claims to sovereignty entail for the representation of membership in the polity.

## B. National Membership and Market Citizenship

A perplexing feature of European citizenship long internalised by EU legal scholarship may still surprise more distant observers of the role of European integration in the 'disaggregation' of political rights from national membership:[21] while voting rights in national elections remain homeward-bound, European citizenship is commonly exercised abroad. Free movement and residence in the European legal space is not only a right of the citizens of the Member States, but also a condition for the enjoyment of European citizenship rights. Accordingly, both the acquisition of EU citizenship status (by nationals of the Member States) and the activation of EU citizenship rights (by crossing Member State borders) remain tethered to the Westphalian unity of government, territory and citizenry. At the same time, the EU's 'government of mobility' bonds a European citizenry of responsible market actors – measured by their past socio-economic conduct and prospective economic performance.[22] This places the European citizen at the intersection of territorial state authority and EU functional integration: what disaggregates political rights from national membership – the exercise of EU fundamental market freedoms – reaggregates the nationals of the Member States as 'market citizens' of the Union.[23]

To be sure, EU citizenship has made some inroads into Member State sovereignty, both in terms of regulating national membership (by protecting European citizens and residents against loss of nationality and expulsion from Union territory)[24] and in terms of assigning distributive obligations across national jurisdictions (by mitigating the conditionality of free movement rights upon economic self-sufficiency).[25] For the advocate generals in *Förster* and *Rottman*, these developments suggest an emancipation of the European citizenship status from the 'economic paradigm' and the emplacement of European citizenship rights in an autonomous EU 'political area'.[26] However, these same developments also remain

[21] S Benhabib, *The Rights of Others: Aliens, Residents and Citizens* (Cambridge, Cambridge University Press, 2004) 147–57.

[22] D Kramer, 'From Worker to Self-Entrepreneur: The Transformation of *Homo economicus* and the Freedom of Movement in the European Union' (2017) 23 *European Law Journal* 172.

[23] N Nic Shuibhne, 'The Resilience of EU Market Citizenship' (2010) 47 *CML Rev* 1597.

[24] Case C-135/08 *Janko Rottman v Freistaat Bayern* ECLI:EU:C:2010:104, [2010] ECR I-01449; Case C-34/09 *Gerardo Ruiz Zambrano v Office National de l'Emploi* ECLI:EU:C:2010:560, [2011] ECR I-01177.

[25] Case C-158/07 *Förster v IB-Groep* ECLI:EU:C:2008:630, [2008] ECR I-8507.

[26] Opinion of AG Mazák in *Förster* (n 25) para 54; Opinion of AG Maduro in *Rottman* (n 24) paras 16–24.

predicated on the distinction between transnational citizenship as an attribute of EU functional sovereignty and national membership as an attribute of territorial state sovereignty. As such, they are auxiliary to (a meaningful actual or potential exercise of) EU free movement rights, rather than intimating a more profound transformation of the European citizenship status that would transcend its origins in the internal market:

> A member state must therefore have the possibility … of refusing to grant social benefits to economically inactive Union citizens who exercise their right to freedom of movement solely in order to obtain another member state's social assistance although they do not have sufficient resources to claim a right to residence.[27]

Beggars can't be choosers: negotiating the boundaries between European market integration and statist social protection certainly allows for further fiddling at the margins of EU citizenship law. But a holistic reading of popular sovereignty and distributive justice that the Westphalian state rendered plausible through the representation of the citizenry as an exclusive territorial unity remains unavailable to the European Union. It would not only obfuscate the complementary role of EU citizenship (which should add to but not replace national membership) and upset the EU's constitutional architecture (competence creep through the backdoor of citizenship); it would also undermine the very premise of EU claims to functional sovereignty: that Member States have 'limited their sovereign rights … within limited fields'.[28]

This is not to succumb to a false dichotomy between economic integration and political participation, nor to deny that Europe's citizenry could reappropriate the constitutional foundations of the European polity through democratic reiterations.[29] It is only to maintain that such political participation and democratic reiteration is framed by EU claims to functional sovereignty that represent the European citizen in her partial subjectivity as a free-moving market participant in the liberal private sphere – as an investor, service provider, consumer, worker, caretaker, student, and so on. Correspondingly, in lieu of (re)distributive justice, the European citizen contends with 'social inclusion' into the EU market society, secured through non-discriminatory market access (including economic discrimination) and broadened legal responsibilities of collective private actors (including business enterprises).[30]

## C. Democracy and Human Rights

Beyond the doctrinal confines of European citizenship law, the functional coupling of national membership and EU fundamental market freedoms also circumscribes

[27] Case C-333-13 *Dano v Jobcenter Leipzig* ECLI:EU:C:2014:2358, [2014] ECR I-2358, para 78.
[28] *Van Gend en Loos* (n 16) 11.
[29] See, respectively, Nic Shuibhne (n 23) 1623–24; Benhabib (n 21) 176–83.
[30] HW Micklitz, *The Politics of Justice in European Private Law* (Cambridge, Cambridge University Press, 2018).

the scope of democracy and human rights as founding values of the European polity (the material dimension of EU sovereignty). Europe's economic constitution steered the integration project towards output legitimacy: the EU delivers not only an internal market, but also peace, prosperity and individual well-being *through* market integration. Whilst the post-World War II rediscovery of the 'sweetness of commerce' cushioned imperial sovereignty with common economic interests,[31] the 2008 financial crisis exposed the fragile social-democratic foundations of the European polity. Europe's austerity politics to save crisis-ridden Member States and their foreign creditors not only depleted the EU's social model,[32] but also eroded its cherished commitment to democratic government under the rule of law.[33] All appeals to an 'ever closer union among the peoples of Europe' (Article 1 TEU) notwithstanding, the main distributive battles over Europe's financial crisis management were fought outside EU law in state and intergovernmental fora – a poignant reminder of the limitations of a European polity that sought to decouple a legally constituted transnational market from supranational democratic legitimation and social protection.[34]

At the same time, EU functional sovereignty curbs ambitions to address the Union's democratic and social 'deficit' by shifting its political modus operandi from output legitimacy and negative integration towards input legitimacy and positive integration. If Maastricht sought to enhance the European Union's (direct) democratic credentials, the 2000 Lisbon Agenda marked the turn to 'new governance' and set the path for later attempts to reconcile trade liberalisation with social inclusion through promoting economic efficiency – 'smart, sustainable and inclusive growth'.[35] The twofold shift from democracy to governance and from distributive justice to social inclusion targeted the exposure of the national welfare state to economic globalisation without, however, emulating statist models of social democracy at the ('federal') European level.

As concerns input legitimacy, the democratic aspirations of EU multilevel and polycentric governance *sans* government remain too anaemic to transcend the functional limitations of EU claims to sovereignty over an ever closer union of peoples. The substitution of 'parliamentary' by 'participatory' democracy (political competition for governmental power by political participation in its execution),

[31] A Hirschman, *The Passions and the Interests: Political Arguments for Capitalism before Its Triumph* (Princeton, Princeton University Press, 2013).

[32] C Barnard, 'EU Employment Law and the European Social Model: The Past, the Present and the Future' (2014) 67 *Current Legal Problems* 193.

[33] C Kilpatrick, 'On the Rule of Law and Economic Emergency: The Degradation of Basic Legal Values in Europe's Bailouts' (2015) 35 *OJLS* 325.

[34] For a post-financial crisis assessment that posits the decline of output legitimacy (the rise of social and economic inequality) as a threat to democracy, see European Commission, 'An Ever Closer Union among the Peoples of Europe? Rising Inequalities in the EU and their Social, Economic, and Political Impacts' (Brussels, 2015) EUR 26814 EN.

[35] See, respectively, Presidency Conclusions Lisbon European Council (23–24 March 2000); European Commission, 'Europe 2020: A Strategy for Smart, Sustainable and Inclusive Growth' COM (2010) 2020 final; Micklitz (n 30) 180.

together with the self-referentiality of 'good governance' and 'better regulation' (good for whom; better for what?) bear resemblance with the neoliberal 'market polity' that demolishes collective political self-determination into an aggregation of private preferences.[36] It is, as Richard Bellamy argues, quite simply difficult to bootstrap European democracy from the protection of civic and economic liberties. Inversely, the EU-wide guarantee of citizens' private autonomy is insufficient to proffer a robust conception of the European public good that could override national self-interest.[37]

As concerns positive integration, the EU's social model has yet to redress the institutional imbalance between fundamental market freedoms and fundamental social rights. The free movement of workers, hitherto jealously guarded by sovereign borders, renders collective labour rights the battleground between Member States hoping to capitalise on their comparative trade advantages (low labour costs) and Member States aiming to protect their national industries by externalising their social protection standards.[38] Meanwhile, attempts to mitigate the adverse impacts of EU regulatory competition through social inclusion largely thrive on the logic of market failures:[39] environmental protection as compensation for negative market externalities or consumer protection and anti-discrimination legislation as means to redress information asymmetries and to ensure equal market access.[40] This revamping of the general interest under the guise of economic expediency borrows from neoliberal 'development' strategies of rebranding (local/Member State) political conflicts about distributive justice as (global/EU) policies for sustainable growth that penetrate sovereign territorial borders.[41]

Nevertheless, accounts that place European integration at the forefront of neoliberal globalisation neglect the distinctive role of democracy and human rights in legitimising its 'market polity' *from within* the functional constraints of EU claims to sovereignty. For neoliberals, Europe's economic constitution promised an excavation of the economy from the state polity that would shield the private sphere from public authority and insulate the market from democratic accountability.[42] The European Union, by contrast, promotes democracy and

[36] See Weiler (n 17) 100–01; S Garben, 'A Taste of Its Own Medicine: Assessing the Impact of the EU Better Regulation Agenda' (2020) 26 *European Law Journal* 83.

[37] R Bellamy, 'The Liberty of the Moderns: Market Freedom and Democracy within the EU' (2012) 1 *Global Constitutionalism* 141.

[38] C Barnard, 'Social Dumping or Dumping Socialism?' (2008) 67 *CLJ* 262.

[39] Critically, M Sandel, *What Money Can't Buy: The Moral Limits of Markets* (New York, Farrar Strauss & Giroux, 2012).

[40] See, eg A Somek, *Engineering Equality: An Essay on European Anti-discrimination Law* (Oxford, Oxford University Press, 2011).

[41] World Bank, *Governance and Development* (Washington, DC, World Bank Publications, 1992); World Bank, *Governance: The World Bank's Experience* (Washington, DC, World Bank Publications, 1994). Compare further Andrew Moravcsik's equation of common interest and economic efficiency with Milton Friedman's praise of market freedom as dispensing with the need for collective politics: A Moravcsik, 'In Defence of the Democratic Deficit: Reassessing Legitimacy in the EU' (2002) 40 *Journal of Common Market Studies* 603; M Friedman, *Capitalism and Freedom* (Chicago, University of Chicago Press, 2002).

[42] Slobodian (n 1) 182–217.

human rights to mainstream its value-based approach to market integration into Member State sovereignties. Rather than purporting to replicate the democratic self-enactment of the state polity ('We, the people of Europe'), positing democracy as a founding value of the European Union that is 'common' to the Member States (Article 2 TEU) ties the former's democratic aspirations to the latter's democratic credentials. This derivative legitimation of European integration has empowered the EU to generate political commonality between the Member States by tying the benefits of market access pre- and post-accession to their observance of democratic principles under the European rule of law.[43]

Similarly, 'valuing' respect for human rights does not project the EU's fundamental rights regime back onto the founding of the polity (the primordial manifestation of public autonomy) but embeds European market integration in the constitutional traditions of the Member States – where it is (supposed to be) 'turtles all the way down'. At the same time, fundamental rights vindicate the autonomy of EU law against competing claims to ultimate authority by rendering the unity of the market the unit of European values.[44] Elevating democracy and human rights to transnational legal constraints of unfettered trade liberalisation and authoritarian nationalism differs decisively from neoliberal aspirations to model democratic government on the principles of the market economy,[45] and to protect the 'rights of global capital' – freedom of contract and private property – against redistributive politics.[46]

## III. European Sovereignty Inside Out

The spatial, subjective and material dimensions of European sovereignty – market integration in the place of territorial acquisition; market freedom to justify transnational citizenship rights; and the unity of the market as the unit of European values – elucidate a distinctive trait of post-Westphalian sovereignty which, through the local re-enactment of economic globalisation, engineers a functional delimitation and extension of state powers that is exercised in and through a globalised liberal private sphere. As such, they not only mould the EU's constitutional identity,

[43] See, eg JW Müller, 'Should the EU Protect Democracy and the Rule of Law inside Member States?' (2015) 21 *European Law Journal* 141.

[44] D Augenstein, 'Disagreement – Commonality – Autonomy: EU Fundamental Rights in the Internal Market' (2013) 15 *Cambridge Yearbook of European Legal Studies* 1.

[45] *cf* M Foucault, *The Birth of Biopolitics: Lectures at the Collège de France 1978–1979* (New York, Palgrave Macmillan, 2010) 131: 'the problem of neoliberalism was not how to cut out or contrive a free space of the market within an already given political society, as in the liberalism of Adam Smith and the eighteenth century. The problem of neoliberalism [was] rather how the overall exercise of political power can be modelled on the principles of a market economy'.

[46] J Whyte, *The Morals of the Market: Human Rights and the Rise of Neoliberalism* (London, Verso, 2019).

but also shape its approach to 'managing' globalisation.[47] Next to a commitment to 'free and fair' global trade that should curb state protectionism, the EU's management of globalisation aims to establish, monitor and enforce a global order that should 'promote its values and interests and contribute to the protection of its citizens' (Article 3(5) TEU). This both particularises and universalises the texture of European sovereignty – with cognitive dissonances abound.[48]

On the one hand, the EU's value-based approach to internal market integration localises its claim to sovereignty in the constitutional traditions common to the Member States. This political commonality justifies a reassembling of territorial authority at the EU's external borders to protect its citizenry against unwarranted/unwanted external interference. On the other hand, the negative externalities of economic globalisation on people and planet require regulatory intervention that universalises the EU's value-based approach to international trade liberalisation. This (human rights) universalism justifies a functional extension of the territorial reach of EU law through which the Union injects its regulatory preferences into the domestic policies of third states.

## A. Territorial Authority and Functional Integration

Mark Pollack has traced the emergence of a 'new, new sovereigntism' in EU external relations that defends the autonomy of the EU legal order against neoliberal and illiberal encroachments from abroad.[49] European sovereignty seems to part ways with earlier (self-)perceptions of the European Union as a global actor committed to political multilateralism under a strong international rule of law. 'Normative power Europe', in Ian Manners's influential, if conflicted, narrative, placed universal norms and principles at the centre of the EU's internal and external relations to define what passes as 'normal' in international relations.[50] The new European sovereigntism, by contrast, shields EU fundamental rights and social and environmental regulation from (what is perceived as) an international legal order driven by a free-market ideology (investor protection in the TTIP and CETA (Transatlantic Trade and Investment Partnership and Canada–EU Trade Agreement)), captured by corporate interests (the Anti-Counterfeiting Trade Agreement's enforcement

[47] W Jacoby and S Meunier, 'Europe and the Management of Globalisation' (201) 17 *Journal of European Public Policy* 299.

[48] K Nicolaidis and R Howse, '"This is my EUtopia …": Narrative as Power' (2002) 40 *Journal of Common Market Studies* 767.

[49] M Pollack, 'The New, New Sovereigntism or How the European Union became Disenchanted with International Law and Defiantly Protective of its Domestic Order' in C Giorgetti and G Verdirame (eds), *Whither the West? International Law in Europe and the United States* (Cambridge, Cambridge University Press, 2021) 53–72.

[50] I Manners, 'Normative Power Europe: A Contradiction in Terms? (2002) 40 *Journal of Common Market Studies* (2002) 235, 239–41; critically, T Diez, 'Constructing the Self and Changing Others: Reconsidering "Normative Power Europe"' (2005) 33 *Millennium Journal of International Studies* 613.

of intellectual property rights at the expense of civil liberties) and reigned by technocracy instead of democracy (the rulings of the World Trade Organization (WTO) on hormone-treated beef and genetically modified organisms (GMOs)).

Pollack's main concern is to show how the EU's new sovereigntism and its commensurate defiance of international law bear structural similarities with old-style US sovereigntism. What goes unnoticed in this 'federal' comparison is that such a Westphalian reading of sovereignty presupposes a reassembling of territorial authority at the EU's external borders that represents the Union as a spatial unity – distinct not only from its Member States, but also from 'mere' international economic organisations such as the WTO. The territories of the Member States which the internal market sought to integrate become the territory of the Union in and through which the EU exercises its external sovereignty. At the same time, this re-territorialisation of functional sovereignty may signal less a retreat from the international rule of law than a transformation of international legal rule that responds to economic globalisation through its local re-enactment: from political multilateralism to unilateral regulation; from international agreements to domestic legislation with extraterritorial effect; and from contractual obligations (pacta sunt servanda) to global values.

Union territory not only shields EU sovereignty against external interference, but also supplies the jurisdictional nexus for a functional extension of the territorial reach of the EU.[51] Different from imperial sovereignty through territorial acquisition, the functional extension of EU law relies on markets to globalise the EU's regulatory preferences – thus externalising its value-based approach to *internal* market integration.[52] Yet, different from 'naked' market power, the EU also aspires to promote compliance by third states with *international* objectives and standards – thus consolidating Europe's legitimacy as a global regulator. As Joanne Scott notes:

> The EU is using the mechanism of territorial extension, in circumstances of inescapable interdependence, to gain regulatory traction in respect of activities that take place abroad but that also impact negatively upon the EU or upon globally shared resources … While many EU measures that create territorial extension are not based on pre-existing international standards, these measures nonetheless serve to address global or transboundary problems in relation to which international agreement on the importance of the underlying objective has been reached.[53]

Domestic legislation with extraterritorial effect superimposes a global (market-) value order upon the formal (liberal contractarian) constraints of sovereign state equality in delimiting states' rights and obligations in international law. Back in

[51] S Lavenex, 'The Power of Functionalist Extension: How EU Rules Travel' (2014) 21 *Journal of European Public Policy* 885; J Scott, 'Extraterritoriality and Territorial Extension in EU Law' (2014) 62 *American Journal of Comparative Law* 87.

[52] Damro (n 8) 685; A Bradford, 'The Brussels Effect' (2012) 107 *Northwestern University Law Review* 1, 39–43.

[53] Scott (n 51) 124–25.

the 1990s, Marti Koskenniemi would still frame environmental pollution as a boundary conflict between the territorial sovereignty of the source state and the target state: 'From the former's perspective, the conflict concerns its right to engage in economically beneficial activities within its own borders. The latter sees the issue in terms of its right to territorial integrity and inviolability.'[54] Once – as in legislative debates about the EU's carbon footprint – Europe's contribution to climate change is mapped onto global value chains,[55] a territory-based demarcation of (legal) responsibility loses much of its plausibility. At the same time, it is doubtful whether the regulatory pull of global value chains suffices to mitigate concerns about market hegemony and value imperialism in a post-Westphalian world order.

Scott emphasises that the territorial extension of EU law operates within the limits of prescriptive jurisdiction in international law and is used to promote internationally agreed objectives.[56] However, the constraints imposed on regulatory globalisation by international rules of jurisdiction are debatable, given that under conditions of global interdependency, establishing a territorial nexus or otherwise reasonable link with the regulating state will rarely prove challenging.[57] Relatedly, international objectives are generally too indeterminate to justify unilateral regulatory intervention into the domestic affairs of third states, absent political agreement on their proper implementation.[58] Where these constraints fail, the injection of functional sovereignty into territorial state sovereignty yields a global regulatory pluralism that transforms the international rule of law into a set of instrumental rules structured by hierarchies of transnational market power.

## B. National Membership and Market Citizenship

Within the internal market, the introduction of European citizenship mitigated the social edges of EU fundamental market freedoms by redirecting citizenship rights from demanding democratic accountability from Member State governments to governing the European market society. Similarly, in EU external relations, citizenship provides the material connection between the internal market and Europe's management of globalisation that should protect and promote the EU's '*acquis social*' within and beyond Union territory.

[54] M Koskenniemi, 'The Future of Statehood' (1991) 32 *Harvard International Law Journal* 397, 408.

[55] See, eg European Parliament Resolution of 22 October 2020 with recommendations to the Commission on an EU legal framework to halt and reverse EU-driven global deforestation, 2020/2006(INL), Recital 11, which justifies the need for EU regulation with the finding that 'the Union has the largest carbon footprint in the world due to its soy imports from Brazil'.

[56] Scott (n 51) 124–25.

[57] Similarly, BS Chimni, 'An Outline of a Marxist Course on Public International Law' (2004) 17 *Leiden Journal of International Law* 1, 19.

[58] Koskenniemi (n 54) 399; on the relationship between the EU and its Member States, see Augenstein (n 44).

The exercise of EU sovereignty to protect the European social model is commonly justified by sheltering domestic consumers against tainted products – from GMOs to forced labour and $CO_2$ emissions. Consumer protection translates into state 'protectionism', which conditions market access of foreign products and services on compliance with internal product and production standards.[59] This rebrands the EU consumer-citizen from a market actor to a political co-regulator of economic globalisation within the liberal private sphere. Yet it also predicates the protection of workers in global value chains upon the market preferences of European citizens and assimilates extraterritorial corporate human rights violations to internal market failures – qua distorted competition caused by misleading advertisement with fair global working conditions.[60]

EU functional sovereignty externalises social protection standards by imposing on business actors and activities within the internal market sustainability requirements that cascade into global value chains.[61] 'Corporate citizens' domiciled in EU territory become the transmission belt for the legal regulation of adverse human rights and environmental impacts in the lower tiers of global value chains. From an EU perspective, this regulatory modality of supply chain due diligence legislation is justified in virtue of international (soft) law standards that require home-states of global business enterprises to ensure corporate respect for human rights throughout their global operations.[62] From the perspective of the EU's trading partners, the ensuing 'Europeanisation' of global commerce may amount to little more than a market-based imposition of regulatory preferences to enhance the competitiveness of European industry.[63]

Either way, the EU's globalised market citizenship remains a far cry from cosmopolitan democracy and global distributive justice. Value chain due diligence legislation bypasses the legal segmentation of global business enterprises into separate legal persons endowed with multiple state nationalities (so-called multinational corporations).[64] Mapping corporate legal responsibilities for human

[59] See, eg the EU Conflict Minerals Regulation 2017/821 [2017] OJ L130; the EU Timber Regulation 995/2010 [2010] OJ L295; more generally, see L Ankersmit, J Lawrence and G Davis, 'Diverging EU and WTO Perspectives on Extraterritorial Process Regulation' (2012) 21 *Minnesota Journal of International Law* 14.

[60] For an illuminative example, see the ECCHR and Clean Clothes Campaign, 'Complaint re Fair Working Conditions in Bangladesh: Lidl Forced to Back Down', www.ecchr.eu/en/case/complaint-re-fair-working-conditions-in-bangladesh-lidl-forced-to-back-down/#case_case.

[61] See, recently, European Commission, 'Proposal for a Directive of the European Parliament and the Council on corporate sustainability due diligence and amending Directive (EU) 2019/1937' COM (2022) 71 final.

[62] Human Rights Council, 'Guiding Principles on Business and Human Rights: Implementing the United Nations' "Protect, Respect and Remedy" Framework' (2011) A/HRC/17/31; ETO Consortium, 'Maastricht Principles on Extraterritorial Obligations of States in the Area of Economic, Social and Cultural Rights' (2012) 34*Human Rights Quarterly* 1084.

[63] Bradford (n 52); S Seck, 'Unilateral Home State Regulation: Imperialism or Tool for Subaltern Resistance?' (2008) 46 *Osgoode Hall Law Journal* 565.

[64] See further J Zerk, *Multinationals and Corporate Social Responsibility* (Cambridge, Cambridge University Press, 2006) 49–54.

rights and environmental protection onto global value chains thus repatriates global business enterprises into the territorial jurisdictions of capital-exporting states. But it does little to redistribute political membership rights of natural persons born into subservience to sovereign statehood – perhaps most tragically illustrated by the plight of economic migrants drowning at the external borders of 'Fortress Europe'.[65]

Instead, globalised market citizenship transforms the attributes of membership within sovereign states by steering (re)distributive politics towards the functional imperatives of economic expediency – monetarisation in lieu of naturalisation. Decades of EU foreign trade policy – to make 'globalisation work for everyone'; to 'ensure trade for all'; etc – have sought to mitigate concerns about global (re)distributive justice simply by enlarging the pie, that is, by generating economic growth through trade liberalisation.[66] However, from the sweetness of commerce to the sweatshops of corporate stakeholder capitalism, delivering social justice through global markets represents the political citizen as an agent of economic globalisation. In more glamorous World Bank jargon: it 'promotes the productive use of the poor's most abundant asset – labour – through policies that provide opportunities and enable poor people to participate in economic growth'.[67]

## C. Democracy and Human Rights

The EU's faith in World Bank policy prescriptions and the political ambitions of 'Geneva school' neoliberalism notwithstanding,[68] European sovereignty has proven an awkward confederate of neoliberal globalisation. Internally, attempts to strengthen the EU's constitutional foundations by placing fundamental rights at the heart of the polity *also* aimed at re-embedding the functional spillovers of market integration into Member State societies. Externally, the unilateral regulation of global business enterprises with extraterritorial effect *also* seeks to redress the notorious imbalance between corporate rights and duties in international law by exercising legal authority over human rights and environmental harm in global value chains governed from and by (Western/Northern) home-states of corporate investment. A more balanced assessment of the relationship between EU functional sovereignty and economic globalisation reveals the systemic limitations of

[65] See, eg Amnesty International, 'The Human Cost of Fortress Europe: Human Rights Violations against Migrants and Refugees at Europe's External Borders' (2014) EUR 05/001/2014, www.amnesty.org/en/documents/eur05/001/2014/en/. On the involuntary nature of state membership as a prerogative to distributive justice, see T Nagel, 'The Problem of Global Justice' (2005) 33 *Philosophy & Public Affairs* 113.

[66] European Commission, 'Making Globalisation Work for Everyone: The European Union and World Trade' (2003) https://op.europa.eu/en/publication-detail/-/publication/d6ca59fb-5b06-4e81-8bd7-3ff5aa0658d8; European Commission, 'Trade for All: Towards a More Responsible Trade and Investment Policy' COM (2015) 497 final.

[67] World Bank, *Governance: The World Bank's Experience* (n 41) 53–54.

[68] Slobodian (n 1) 218–86.

globalising human rights through markets, as well as the limited capacity of the emerging global (market-)value order to resolve distributive conflicts between functionally integrated transnational political constituencies (consumers and workers; business enterprises and economic migrants; etc).

The European Union views trade liberalisation, value chain integration and sustainable development as mutually reinforcing. Value chain integration is central to trade liberalisation, which generates the resources necessary for sustainable development.[69] This builds a double conditionality into the EU's attempts to promote human rights through global markets: to trade 'freely' with the European Union, third countries must commit to human rights protection within their own territories; yet their capacity to protect said human rights depends on economic growth spawned through trade liberalisation across sovereign state borders. The mutual conditioning of human rights protection and global market integration becomes the more problematic the less likely the promised synergies are to materialise.

For example, global food supply chains may strengthen the competitiveness of export-oriented developing economies and cater to the eclectic tastes of European consumers. Yet they are hardly environmentally sustainable, nor do they necessarily contribute to enhancing global food security – especially where the benefits of trade liberalisation are extenuated by EU exports of CAP (Common Agricultural Policy)-subsidised surplus agricultural production (poultry, tomatoes, milk, sugar, etc).[70] Moreover, the integration of global food markets has yielded a concentration of market power in the upper tiers of the value chain that enables European retailers to generate economic growth by squeezing their suppliers for lower prices and faster manufacturing times.[71] Contrary to the World Bank's mantra of equitable development and poverty reduction, the human costs of trade liberalisation are often borne by smallholder farmers and food workers in the Global South – entrenching exploitation and structural discrimination in the lower tiers of the value chain.

The EU's regulatory odyssey into global trade sustainability continues unabated – from combating unfair trading practices in global value chains to strengthening the enforcement of labour provisions in EU free trade agreements.[72] However, the core challenge to the EU's management of globalisation is not a lack of economic efficiency or regulatory power, but its eschewal of democratic

[69] European Commission, 'Trade for All' (n 66).

[70] See, eg 'Report of the Special Rapporteur on the Right to Food, The Transformative Potential of the Right to Food' (2004) A/HRC/25/75, para 24; Human Rights Council, 'Application of the criteria for periodic evaluation of global development partnerships – as defined in Millennium Development Goal 8 – from the right to development perspective: the Cotonou Partnership Agreement between European Union and ACP countries' (2007) A/HRC/8/WG.2/TF/CRP.6.

[71] See, eg R Willoughby and T Gore, *Ripe for Change: Ending Human Suffering in Supermarket Supply Chains* (Oxford, Oxfam, 2018).

[72] Directive (EU) 2019/633 on Unfair Trading Practices in Business-to-Business Relationships in the Agricultural and Food Supply Chain [2019] OJ L111/59; European Commission, 'Trade Policy Review – An Open, Sustainable and Assertive Trade Policy' COM (2021) 66 final.

accountability. The injection of EU functional sovereignty into third state territories leaves the globalised political societies it claims to constitute with little hope for democratic contestation and legal remedies. 'Selling' human rights as market values shrinks the policy space of the EU's trading partners to (re)distribute wealth within their domestic economies. Inversely, foreign stakeholders of European business enterprises have no democratic stakes in the European Union, whose rules nevertheless co-govern their welfare.[73] Their prospects of access to justice in European courts for human rights violations linked to trade liberalisation and value chain integration remain equally limited.[74]

## IV. The End of Sovereignty

This chapter has scrutinised the spatial, subjective and material dimensions of European sovereignty in EU internal and external relations to elucidate a distinctive trait of post-Westphalian sovereignty which, through the local re-enactment of economic globalisation, engineers a functional delimitation and extension of state powers that is exercised in and through a globalised liberal private sphere. This local re-enactment injects into the Westphalian unity of government, territory and citizenry that represents the general interest of the state polity transnational legal and political authority that is bounded by the common goal of global market integration.

I have argued that EU functional sovereignty, despite family resemblances, differs significantly from neoliberal attempts to insulate the private sphere from public authority and to shield global markets from the onslaught of democratic majorities. Rather, the EU's value-based approach to internal market integration and international trade liberalisation seeks to compensate for the negative externalities of economic globalisation by imposing 'sustainability' requirements on transnational market actors and activities. At the same time, EU functional sovereignty points to the limitations of a global (market-)value order in enacting democracy and social justice. In the Western/Westphalian world, territorial state sovereignty was both an embodiment of collective political self-determination and an impediment to global (re)distribution.[75] The transformation of sovereignty wrought by economic globalisation does not redraw state borders but transcends them by delivering politics through markets – from democratic government to global governance, and from public (re)distributive justice to privatised social inclusion.

[73] G Davies, 'International Trade, Extraterritorial Power, and Global Constitutionalism: A Perspective from Constitutional Pluralism' (2012) 13 *German Law Journal* 1203, 1208.

[74] A Marx, C Bright and J Wouters, 'Access to Legal Remedies for Victims of Corporate Human Rights Abuses in Third Countries' (Strasbourg, European Parliament, 2019).

[75] On the former, see J Cohen, *Globalisation and Sovereignty* (Cambridge, Cambridge University Press, 2012); on the latter, see A Follesdal, 'Global Distributive Justice? State Boundaries as a Normative Problem' (2012) 1 *Global Constitutionalism* 261.

EU functional sovereignty may harness the political support of (some) transnational actors qua communities of values[76] and drive the functional extension of 'democratic governance norms' (of sorts) through international cooperation.[77] However, the EU's own experience with creating 'an ever-closer union among the peoples of Europe' should also caution against the risks of moulding a post-Westphalian world order in its own image. Supplanting statist democracy with transnational value communities can quell popular sovereignty by depoliticising human rights.[78] Transplanting democratic norms into the global economy can co-opt them as technologies of governance that convert accountability into accounting.[79]

At this point, the role of European sovereignty in the identity formation of the polity meets the future of EU constitutionalism. Internally, Europe's citizenry needs to reclaim the constitutional foundations of EU functional sovereignty to realign the economic benefits of having a common *market* with the democratic responsibilities of having a market *in common*. Externally, the intrusion of EU regulatory globalisation into sovereign state equality needs to be reciprocated by constitutionalising the rights of foreign citizens to claim democratic accountability in European courts.

Popular sovereignty is the political utopia of EU constitutionalism. Global business enterprises have had their share of political representation without taxation. Their (involuntary) 'stakeholders' should resist marketisation without democratisation. Otherwise, Europe will have once again embarked on a hegemonic trajectory, and the end of sovereignty remains out of sight.

[76] Manners (n 50) 251.

[77] Lavenex (n 51) 897–98.

[78] I Maus, 'From Nation-State to Global State, or the Decline of Democracy' (2006) 13 *Constellations* 465.

[79] K Davis, B Kingsbury and S Engle Merry, 'Indicators as Technology of Global Governance' (2012) 46 *Law & Society Review* 71.

# 11

# European Sovereignty and Extraterritorial Application of Foreign Legislation

KATARINA VATOVEC

## I. Introduction

The history with widening and deepening processes has shown that the European Union is a dynamic organisation constantly reforming or reflecting on its future. In 2021, the EU embarked on the latest process of rethinking its future development. Numerous crises and pressing challenges that the EU was facing in its inner area and outer surroundings and the changing international setting preceded and thus influenced the widespread debate on the future of European integration. The EU was heavily affected by financial and economic crisis. Moreover, it experienced difficulties with migration flows, and the refugee crisis flared. It is therefore no surprise that over the past decade trust in the EU and its institutions declined, while the EU is still trying to properly address the undermining of the rule-of-law standards in certain Member States. Climate change and environmental degradation are considered to be existential threats across the world. The pandemic of COVID-19 has caused distressing economic, health and social effects and severe impacts on human life of unmatched gravity in recent history. It has unveiled weaknesses in health systems, shortages in different supplies, shortfalls in medical equipment and dependence on certain value chains. In particular, the pandemic provoked insecurity, which has been deepened by the troubling situation outside the Union's borders. The complex situation, with the intensity of the recognised threats beyond the EU, was well captured in the opening sentences of the Global Strategy for the EU's Foreign and Security Policy, adopted in 2016.[1] In addition, the unprecedented armed attack by Russia on Ukraine not only worsened insecurities and intensified fear, but also forced the EU Member States to rethink their

[1] European Union Global Strategy, 2016. Shared Vision, Common Action: A Stronger Europe. A Global Strategy for the European Union's Foreign and Security Policy. Brussels: European External Action Service; https://eeas.europa.eu/sites/default/files/eugs_review_web_0.pdf, 10 June 2021, 13.

priorities. In so doing, they have tried to unify their interests and support in a common stance, while endorsing common values and demonstrating solidarity.

Against this backdrop and in the maelstrom of crises, variety of challenges, inner and outer incentives and complexity of international relations, one concept in particular (re)gained relevance: the concept of sovereignty. However, unlike in the past, when the concerns had concentrated on the protection and reinforcement of the sovereignty of the Member States, this time around the calls were made in favour of so-called European sovereignty. The latter has been sought across a whole range of areas, as European digital, strategic and technological sovereignty have become part of the quotidian European vocabulary. How can these many faces of European sovereignty be conceptualised? Is it at all possible to think about European sovereignty when the EU is merely an organisation composed of sovereign Member States? What is the contemporary relevance of European sovereignty talk?

This chapter will not seek to do justice to this big question as a whole. Rather, it will engage with the idea of European sovereignty in a very specific, but strategically highly important area – that of deterring third-state legislation with extraterritorial reach that imposes extraterritorial sanctions affecting the Union's economy and that has a direct impact on the Union's citizens and companies. The EU's response to these sanctions goes to the heart of its wider foreign policy role and importance in international relations. This chapter will therefore concentrate on two interrelated concepts: European sovereignty in the contemporary global environment, which moves beyond a state-based international system; and extraterritorial sanctions, which enable some but disable others from engaging globally. Is it possible to speak of European sovereignty at all, considering the mere existence of extraterritorial sanctions, never mind their application and possible impact? How should the EU approach the issue of deterrence of these measures and what steps should it take to foster and enhance its position internationally, including its values, free trade and the protection of its citizens and companies?

In attempting to respond to these questions, this chapter will examine the putative European sovereignty within the context of foreign legislation with extraterritorial reach. To do so, it will first analyse the changing paradigm of sovereignty, illustrated through the emergence of European sovereignty, and then assess the capacity of the hence putatively sovereign Europe to respond by way of its regulatory framework to the extraterritorial sanctions.

## II. Conceptualising European Sovereignty

### A. The Current Political Discourse within the European Union

In recent years, the political leaders and policy decision-makers in the EU have been vocal about European sovereignty. In 2017, French President Emmanuel

Macron started by proposing his initiative for a sovereign, united and democratic Europe.[2] He stated: 'Only Europe can, in a word, guarantee genuine sovereignty or our ability to exist in today's world to defend our values and interests. European sovereignty requires constructing, and we must do it.'[3]

He further advocated in favour of building 'the six keys to sovereignty': security (together with defence); protection of the borders and preservation of European values; foreign policy with clear priorities and increased development aid; ecological transition; digital technology transformation; and industrial and monetary economic power.[4] In his speech, he elaborated what each of the six elements mean and what they could encompass. Had he presented his ideas after the start of the coronavirus pandemic in March 2020, he would undoubtedly have advocated for a 'strategic health sovereignty' as well.[5] We can predict that the need for European energy sovereignty, which has accelerated with the Russian armed attack on Ukraine, would have similarly found its way onto the list of areas of European sovereignty. Macron continued to state:

> The real issue here is unity … In addition to these six battles for sovereignty, it is the battle for unity I want to lead. We will never have a strong, sovereign Europe if it is not united and coherent in itself.[6]

On a similar note, the European Council adopted a 2019–24 strategic agenda for the EU,[7] inter alia, emphasising specifically the digital sovereignty, but more broadly the need of the EU to improve its capacity to act autonomously on a global stage by protecting, upholding and promoting European interests and values, and by becoming more responsive and active.[8] Another example can be found in the 2022 adopted Versailles declaration, where the European Council, against a background of growing instability, security threats and strategic competition, decided to 'take further decisive steps towards building our European sovereignty'.[9]

The European Commission, too, has partaken in the narrative of European sovereignty. It was its former president, Jean-Claude Juncker, who, in 2018, noted that 'the time for European sovereignty has come'.[10] In her State of the Union

[2] E Macron, 'Initiative pour l'Europe, Discours du President de la Republique à la Sorbonne. Paris, 26 septembre 2017', www.diplomatie.gouv.fr/IMG/pdf/26.09_-_discours_du_president_de_la_republique_-_initiative_pour_l_europe_transcript__cle0cfdbe.pdf.

[3] ibid.

[4] ibid.

[5] See French–German Initiative for the European recovery from the coronavirus crisis, Paris, 18 May 2020, www.elysee.fr/en/emmanuel-macron/2020/05/18/french-german-initiative-for-the-european-recovery-from-the-coronavirus-crisis.

[6] Macron (n 2).

[7] European Council, 'A New Strategic Agenda 2019–2024', www.consilium.europa.eu/media/39914/a-new-strategic-agenda-2019-2024.pdf.

[8] ibid.

[9] Informal Meeting of the Heads of State or Government, Versailles Declaration, 10 and 11 March 2022, point 7, www.consilium.europa.eu/media/54773/20220311-versailles-declaration-en.pdf.

[10] 2018 State of the Union Address by President Juncker, Strasbourg, 12 September 2018, https://ec.europa.eu/commission/presscorner/detail/en/SPEECH_18_5808.

addresses, the standing president of the European Commission, Ursula von der Leyen, urged for more European sovereignty in different areas and called for empowerment of the EU in various fields. In September 2020, for example, she announced that Europe should pursue the path toward digital transformation and lead the reforms of the multilateral system.[11] A year later, she called for building the European Health Union as well as the European Defence Union, while simultaneously recalling the importance of investing in European technological sovereignty.[12] When stressing the need for the EU to be sovereign, the European Commissioner, Thierry Breton, sketched the idea of European sovereignty as encompassing: the defence of European strategic interests, rules and values; the confidence in European means; the protection of European companies 'against predatory and sometimes politically motivated foreign acquisitions'; the reduction of economic and industrial dependencies; and the development of European alternatives in key strategic technologies.[13]

The political discourse within the EU suggests that sovereignty has lately received intense focus in debates about the EU. The narrative of the European sovereignty has expanded horizontally to cover a wide range of policy issues. But what does this political discourse reveal about European sovereignty and how can this concept be best understood? Could there even be European sovereignty, as the EU is not a state and sovereignty – at least in its uncontested conventional conception – has been an exclusive characteristic of the state?

## B. The Evolutionary Conceptual Development of Sovereignty Through Scholarly Discourse

An historical overview reveals that sovereignty is a dynamic concept and a cross-disciplinary notion that reflects its evolutionary development based on the broader political and historical context. It is of medieval origin, linked with the sixteenth-century French jurist Jean Bodin, who emphasised the absolute nature of sovereign, its perpetual power and its unlimitedness in power, function and length of time.[14] He witnessed the medieval period of turmoil and, as Dunning put it, 'felt the need of a system that should embody somewhere a clear and unquestionable source of

[11] 2020 State of the Union Address by President von der Leyen at the European Parliament Plenary, Brussels, 16 September 2020, https://ec.europa.eu/commission/presscorner/detail/en/SPEECH_20_1655.

[12] 2021 State of the Union Address by President von der Leyen, Strasbourg, 15 September 2021, https://ec.europa.eu/commission/presscorner/detail/en/SPEECH_21_4701.

[13] Speech by Commissioner Thierry Breton at Hannover Messe Digital Days, European Commission, Brussels, 15 July 2020, https://ec.europa.eu/commission/presscorner/detail/en/SPEECH_20_1362.

[14] J Bodin, *On Sovereignty: Four Chapters from The Six Books of the Commonwealth* (Cambridge, Cambridge University Press, 1992) 1, 3. On Bodin's contribution to the concept of sovereignty, see, eg D Grimm, *Sovereignty: The Origin and Future of a Political and Legal Concept* (New York, Columbia University Press, 2015) 13–32.

authority'.[15] The supremacy of the sovereign over his own subjects, according to Bodin, derived from the superiority of power.[16] Sovereignty encompassed both 'the relation between a superior and an inferior – between the state and its subjects – [and] the relations subsisting between separate states',[17] known in theory as the internal and external dimensions of sovereignty.

Political scientist Stephen D Krasner addressed the 'problematic' notion of sovereignty, arguing that its meaning has not been uniform and it is proper to think of various kinds of sovereignty.[18] He first identified four different conceptions of conventional sovereignty based on the authority and ability to control activities within a state and/or cross-border activities: interdependence, domestic, international legal and Westphalian sovereignty.[19] According to Krasner, both international legal sovereignty and Westphalian sovereignty refer to authority, but do not involve control. Whereas international legal sovereignty means that recognition is extended only to judicially independent territorial entities, Westphalian sovereignty refers to the autonomy of domestic structures, with external actors being excluded from the state's territory.[20] Domestic sovereignty encompasses both the legitimated authority structure and its exercise of effective control within a state. Interdependence sovereignty, on the other hand, is concerned only with the state's control, ie its capacity to regulate different movements (of people, goods, capital, ideas).[21] In Krasner's subsequent writings, independence sovereignty becomes part of domestic sovereignty, which then comprises not only the state's authority, but also its effective control within its territory and across its borders.[22]

The existence of badly governed or fragile states provoked the need for departing from conventional concepts of sovereignty. Krasner argued for 'shared' sovereignty as a promising alternative.[23] According to this view, weak states, lacking certain capacities, would enter into contractual arrangements with external actors for an indefinite period in order to improve their domestic sovereignty. As Krasner explained: 'One core element of sovereignty, the ability to enter into voluntary international agreements, would be preserved, while at the same time

[15] WA Dunning, 'Jean Bodin on Sovereignty' (1896) 11 *Political Science Quarterly* 86. For more on Hobbes, who came after Bodin, see ibid 99–104.

[16] ibid 99.

[17] JW Garner, 'Limitations on National Sovereignty in International Relations' (1925) 19 *American Political Science Review* 1, 5.

[18] SD Krasner, 'Problematic Sovereignty' in SD Krasner (ed), *Problematic Sovereignty: Contested Rules and Political Possibilities* (New York, Columbia University Press, 2001); SD Krasner, *Sovereignty: Organized Hypocrisy* (Princeton, Princeton University Press, 1999) 3–4.

[19] ibid.

[20] ibid.

[21] ibid.

[22] SD Krasner, *Power, the State, and Sovereignty, Essays on International Relations* (London, Routledge, 2009) 15.

[23] SD Krasner, 'The Hole in the Whole: Sovereignty, Shared Sovereignty, and International Law' (2004) 25 *Michigan Journal of International Law* 1075, 1091–100; SD Krasner, 'Building Democracy after Conflict: The Case for Shared Sovereignty' (2005) 16 *Journal of Democracy* 69.

another core element, the principle of autonomy, would be ceded.'[24] It therefore seems that sovereignty is an umbrella concept, subdivided into many manifestations and meanings.

International legal scholars define sovereignty predominantly through the lenses of powers and rights the sovereign states should possess. Sovereignty includes, in particular, exclusive jurisdiction over a territory and the population living therein, and the duty of non-intervention of other states in the area of one state's exclusive jurisdiction, bearing in mind the limitations imposed by the international rules and standards to which the states have consented.[25]

The concept of sovereignty has changed over time, depending on the historical context, as well as the legal and socio-political realities.[26] With tight interconnectedness and interdependence in the contemporary international community, and the respect for human rights and fundamental freedoms written in legally binding international instruments, it is not possible to speak of absoluteness of sovereign. In the twenty-first century, it therefore goes by and large uncontested that absoluteness is not one of sovereignty's characteristics.

Moreover, sovereignty was conceptually elaborated with the state system in mind. New actors[27] in international relations and politics gaining importance, the changing of international settings and new developments, among others, have led to a growing 'complexity and heterogeneity',[28] and have brought about the need for sovereignty's redefinition[29] or re-envisioning.[30] Camilleri noted a variety of contemporary writings on sovereignty and grouped them in three categories: proponents of 'the centrality of sovereignty' on one side and those arguing for 'the end of sovereignty' on the other, with scholars pertaining to 'the qualification of sovereignty' between the two extremes.[31] As argued by Camilleri, the latter category encompasses differing notions that emphasise the lack of clarify in definition, purpose and norms, such as shared sovereignty, conditional sovereignty or post-statist sovereignty.[32] Therefore, in a multilayered setting, sovereignty need not be centred on one level. Pogge, for example, advocates for a 'vertical dispersal of sovereignty', in particular when dealing with specific transnational issues

[24] Krasner, 'The Hole in the Whole' (n 23) 1091.

[25] See, eg J Crawford, *Brownlie's Principles of Public International Law*, 9th edn (Oxford, Oxford University Press, 2019) 431; A Cassese, *International Law*, 2nd edn (Oxford, Oxford University Press, 2005) 49–52.

[26] For a historical overview, see Krasner, *Sovereignty: Organized Hypocrisy* (n 18).

[27] For example, international organisations, too, are subject of international law (see Advisory Opinion, 'Legality of the Use by a State of Nuclear Weapons in Armed Conflict' (1996) ICJ Reports 78, para 25).

[28] J Camilleri, 'Sovereignty Discourse and Practice – Past and Future' in T Jacobsen, C Sampford and R Thakur (eds), *Re-envisioning Sovereignty: The End of Westphalia?* (Aldershot, Ashgate, 2008) 33, 49.

[29] On developments that provoke redefinition of external sovereignty, see RA Brand, 'External Sovereignty and International Law' (1994) 18 *Fordham International Law Journal* 1685, 1691–96.

[30] Jacobsen et al (n28).

[31] Camilleri (n 28) 37.

[32] ibid 34, 40.

of great concern, such as peace and security, the reduction of oppression, global economic justice and ecology.[33]

There is thus an abundance of theoretical writings on sovereignty. With regard to European integration, sovereignty as a foundational concept has not disappeared or lost its relevance. In fact, quite the opposite. It is due to the establishment of the EU, and because of its ongoing development, that the prevalent idea of state sovereignty has been questioned[34] or has been 'posed in a new way'.[35] It was Jean Monnet in the 1970s who stated, in the last paragraph of *Memoirs*, that: 'The sovereign nations of the past can no longer solve the problems of the present: they cannot ensure their own progress or control their own future.'[36]

Having in mind different types of sovereignty, Krasner argued that the Member States of the EU have both international legal sovereignty and domestic sovereignty, but they compromised their Westphalian sovereignty as they voluntarily agreed for established supranational (EU) institutions to replace the authority of the Member State.[37] In fact, the EU is, as Krasner concluded, 'a product of state sovereignty because it has been created through voluntary agreements among its Member States'.[38]

Whereas it is hardly disputable that the EU is a product of its Member States' sovereignty, it is certainly question-begging whether the EU can be a holder of sovereignty in its own right. The EU is a unique polity, which simultaneously coexists with its Member States, which retain their own (state) sovereignty. The latter is hence not being eroded or displaced, nor should there be any concern about that happening. Contrary to some, who have argued that the growth of powers of the EU has decreased the sovereignty of its Member States, others have insisted that the EU has in fact empowered its Member States, so that their sovereignty has been strengthened simultaneously with the growing scope of the conferred powers.[39] Neil MacCormick, in particular, insisted that the Member States have not lost their sovereignty. Rather, it has been divided internally and enhanced externally towards the rest of the world.[40] Proceeding from the premises of constitutional pluralism, MacCormick advocated that different legal systems (of the EU and of its Member States) overlap and interact without any subordination or superiority.[41] The relationship between the state and non-state systems has thus been described

[33] For more on institutional cosmopolitanism in which sovereignty is distributed vertically, see TW Pogge, 'Cosmopolitanism and Sovereignty' (1992) 103 *Ethics* 48, 60.

[34] N MacCormick, *Questioning Sovereignty: Law, State, and Nation in the European Commonwealth* (Oxford, Oxford University Press, 1999).

[35] Grimm (n 14) 7.

[36] J Monnet, *Memoirs* (New York, Doubleday & Company, 1978) 524.

[37] Krasner, 'Problematic Sovereignty' (n 18) 2; Krasner, *Power, the State, and Sovereignty* (n 22) 17.

[38] SD Krasner, 'Think Again: Sovereignty, Foreign Policy', http://foreignpolicy.com/2009/11/20/think-again-sovereignty/.

[39] M Avbelj, 'A Sovereign Europe as a Future of Sovereignty' (2020) 5 *European Papers* 299, 301.

[40] MacCormick, *Questioning Sovereignty* (n 34) 133.

[41] N MacCormick, 'Beyond the Sovereign State' (1993) 56 *MLR* 1, 8.

as heterarchical.[42] As Walker noted, 'states are no longer the sole locus of constitutional authority'; rather, they are accompanied by other sites of constitutional authority, which include a supranational organisation.[43] When dealing with the EU as the 'post-state polity', Walker suggests the use of the concept of 'late sovereignty', as opposed to the 'early sovereignty' belonging to traditional state polities.[44] It is advocated that the EU is built on the pluralist understanding of sovereignty encompassing pluralities of autonomous legal orders, socio-political spaces and sovereigns.[45]

## C. The Concept of European Sovereignty in Political Discourse

What do these differing views and concepts of sovereignty reveal to us about the European sovereignty that has been lately so intensively relied upon in political rhetoric? Although the notion of sovereignty itself does not appear in EU primary law, that does not lead to the conclusion that it cannot be attributed to political entities such as the EU. As has been argued, in contemporary times, conceptualising sovereignty as only a state-linked doctrine would be neglecting the existence of the EU with its peculiarities. Schermers and Blokker described the most fundamental characteristics of supranational organisations as having: the power to take decisions binding on the Member States and their inhabitants; at least some independence (eg majority voting and specific composition) of the decision-making organs; the power to enforce its decisions; some financial autonomy; and incapacity of unilateral withdrawal.[46] Currently, there is no supranational organisation possessing all these powers and features, but the EU is the one with most of them.[47]

By signing and ratifying the Treaty establishing the European Economic Community in 1958, the Member States created, as the Court of Justice of the EU (CJEU) has consistently held, 'a new legal order for the benefit of which the States have limited their sovereign rights, in ever wider fields, and the subjects of which comprise not only Member States but also their nationals',[48] ie the Union's

[42] N Walker, 'Late Sovereignty in the European Union' in N Walker (ed), *Sovereignty in Transition* (Oxford, Hart Publishing, 2003) 3, 4; see also, eg M Avbelj, 'Theorizing Sovereignty and European Integration' (2014) 27 *Ratio Juris* 344, 358.

[43] Walker (n 42) 4.

[44] ibid 3–32.

[45] Avbelj, 'Theorizing Sovereignty' (n 42).

[46] HG Schermers and NM Blokker, *International Institutional Law: Unity within Diversity*, 5th edn (Leiden, Martinus Nijhoff Publishers, 2011) 56–57.

[47] ibid 57.

[48] See Opinion 1/91 *Agreement on the European Economic Area* ECLI:EU:C:1991:490, [1991] ECR I-6079, para 21. See settled case law of the CJEU, in particular, Case 6/64 *Costa v ENEL* ECLI:EU:C:1964:66, [1964] ECR 585; Case 26/62 *Van Gend en Loos* ECLI:EU:C:1963:1, [1963] ECR 1; Opinion 1/09 *Creation of a unified patent litigation system* EU:C:2011:123, para 65; Opinion 2/13 *Accession of the EU to the ECHR* ECLI:EU:C:2014:2454, para 157.

citizens. With the Treaty on European Union (TEU) in 1993, the Member States established the EU. With the entry into force of the Treaty of Lisbon in 2009, the EU replaced and succeeded the former European Community, and is now founded on two Treaties of the same legal value, ie the TEU, including the Charter of Fundamental Rights, and the Treaty on the Functioning of the EU (TFEU).[49] With the Treaties, certain powers of Member States have been gradually and extensively conferred upon the EU, so that the EU can now act in numerous areas (policies),[50] exercising its sovereign rights that affect both the Member States and the individuals directly. Many policies of the EU are subjected to the Community method and supranational decision-making. The legislature for the EU is the directly elected European Parliament and the Council of the EU, composed of Member State's representatives on a ministerial level. The Treaties provide for a predominantly double (ie qualified) majority voting system in the legislative procedure, whereas unanimous voting still remains in some areas. That signifies that the EU institutions can adopt binding decisions that are not necessarily agreed upon by all Member States. The EU represents a political authority, founded on common values. Needless to say, the EU is not a state, but a polity distinct from its Member States.[51] The primary and secondary law and the interpretative principles endorsed by the CJEU, such as the primacy of EU law and its direct effect, which are considered to be the 'essential characteristics' of the EU's legal order,[52] are part of the law of each of the Member States.[53]

Looking back to 1950, it was not state sovereignty that appeared in the seminal speech of the French Foreign Minister Robert Schuman, where he called for cooperation between European states. Instead, it was the idea of collaboration and connectivity that was strongly proclaimed. Keywords were solidarity, unification, elimination of conflicts, raising living standards, promoting peaceful achievement. The mistrust that was present among European states had to be overcome through coexistence, cooperation and, above all, interdependence. In recent years, however, in light of the crises, challenges and changes occurring in the contemporary international setting, it seems that the notion of European sovereignty occupies an important place in the Union's political discourse. As has been pointed out, though, its meaning is unclear and fluid, on some occasions signifying unity or solidarity, while on others deepened integration or more legislative harmonisation.[54] European sovereignty, as argued, is solely 'a discursive form' that calls for the EU to be transformed and adapted to the new international setting

[49] Consolidated version of the Treaty on European Union [2016] OJ C202/13, Art 1(3); Consolidated version of the Treaty on the Functioning of the European Union [2016] OJ C202/47, Art 1(2).

[50] EU Treaty, Art 1(1).

[51] EU Treaty, Art 2.

[52] See, eg Opinion 1/91 (n 48) para 21.

[53] See, eg MacCormick, *Questioning Sovereignty* (n 34) 115.

[54] Critically assessing the notion of European sovereignty, see, eg S Barbou des Places, 'Taking the Language of "European Sovereignty" Seriously' (2020) 5 *European Papers* 287, 290.

while at the same time preserving its own identity as an entity founded on the rule of law and rebuilt through law.[55]

There are nonetheless several distinct characteristics of the European sovereignty talk, with the previous theoretical background in mind. The reference to European sovereignty takes the form of a political narrative. It involves a high degree of symbolism. In the words of Koskenniemi, it 'points to the possibility, however limited or idealistic, that whatever comes to pass, one is not just a pawn in other people's games but, for better or for worse, the master of one's life'.[56] This could be understood as wishing the EU to be a polity that is autonomous (in legal terms), independent (in terms of gaining and maintain control over a variety of areas) and self-sufficient (relating to the Union's ability and capacity to act and to attain an acceptable and efficient level of functioning in these areas). This political narrative reflects a political commitment and, it would seem, wishes to contemplate and materialise the concerted political will, to stimulate the Union's ability and capacity in particular areas, and to gather widespread support for the EU's activities in these areas. The aim of the political discourse on European sovereignty seems to be to provoke the 'rally-around-the-flag' effect, and thus to reassure, in times of crisis, the public, ie the Union's citizens, but also the Member States, and to gather vast support in order to proceed with the steps necessary to acclaim sovereignty in certain areas.

MacCormick, alluding to a distinction between legal and political sovereignty, sees politics as mainly being concerned with power and the actual exercise of power, whereas the essence of law lies in the normative order, in rights and duties.[57] As he noted: 'Politics have legal backing and (often) a legal framework; law has political inputs and (usually) the support of political power.'[58] Although its current rhetoric is mainly of a political character, we should think of European sovereignty as an interdisciplinary concept. Its legal aspect should not be overlooked. As a legal concept, it translates what politicians articulate into the appropriate and effective regulatory framework. Being sovereign in certain areas, where particularly high interests are at stake – bearing in mind these areas change over time and in different political circumstances (currently, for example, digitalisation, technology, health, food) – presupposes not only a political wish, interest and political commitment, but also a legal commitment to establish a normative framework that confers the specific powers on the EU, if needed, prescribes legal rights and duties, and thus enhances the ability of the EU to perform in the specific areas in question in a wider setting.

The concept of European sovereignty, as mentioned by the European Commission's president when discussing the European technological sovereignty,

[55] ibid.

[56] M Koskenniemi, 'What Use for Sovereignty Today?' (2011) 1 *Asian Journal of International Law* 61, 70.

[57] MacCormick, 'Beyond the Sovereign State' (n 41) 11.

[58] ibid; MacCormick, *Questioning Sovereignty* (n 34) 11–12.

'is not defined against anyone else', but is instead the concept that focuses 'on the needs of Europeans'.[59] Understanding the notion of European sovereignty as such moves it away from its relational nature. However, bearing in mind the theoretical difference between internal and external sovereignty, the notion of European sovereignty predominantly relates to its external aspect. The political rhetoric seeks to address in particular the relationship between the EU (composed of its Member States and the Union's citizens) and third states, by emphasising that no third state will intervene in the EU's inner circle by prohibiting, disabling or conditioning European sovereignty in specifically mentioned areas, and by stressing that the EU's functioning must not be dependent on third states. Overall, the rhetoric of European sovereignty also adds to the momentum of the widespread debate on the future of the EU to generate public support and empower the functioning of the EU.

The relevance of European sovereignty discourse is thus multifaceted. For example, as theory has argued, the EU is a 'social environment', and as such has an important socialising role.[60] In this context, the European sovereignty rhetoric serves as a socialiser and unifier by connecting citizens and Member States, socialising them to identify with a common good, while also stimulating interactions across the EU. According to Wendt, 'sovereignty is a social identity'.[61] Talk on European sovereignty can, then, help with 'collective identity formation'.[62] The international relations perspective places particular emphasis on the need of the EU to act as a sovereign actor externally, to enhance its role in the international setting and to efficiently address the transnational challenges.[63] From the legal point of view, it seems important that the rhetoric translates into a regulatory framework and that European sovereignty becomes feasible and visible. The discourse on European sovereignty also has a strong symbolic function as it stimulates the unity of citizens and Member States within the EU, and encourages shared values and common preferences in a fragmented and vulnerable world in these very fragile times. European sovereignty could thus be described as an umbrella concept offering guidance to decision-makers by addressing specific areas in which the EU needs to gain autonomy, independence and self-sufficiency.

[59] European Commission, *Shaping Europe's Digital Future* (Luxembourg, Publications Office of the European Union, 2020) 3.

[60] JT Checkel, 'International Institutions and Socialization in Europe: Introduction and Framework' (2005) 59 *International Organization* 801. See also, eg MN Barnett and M Finnemore, 'The Politics, Power, and Pathologies of International Organizations' (1999) 53 *International Organization* 699; AI Johnston, 'Treating International Institutions as Social Environments' (2001) 45 *International Studies Quarterly* 487.

[61] A Wendt, 'Collective Identity Formation and the International State' (1994) 88 *American Political Science Review* 384.

[62] ibid; see also A Wendt, *Social Theory of International Politics* (Cambridge, Cambridge University Press, 1999).

[63] On elements of actorness, see C Bretherton and J Vogler, *The European Union as a Global Actor*, 2nd edn (London, Routledge, 2006) 12–36; M Telò, 'Introduction: The EU as a Model, a Global Actor and an Unprecedented Power' in M Telò (ed), *The European Union and Global Governance* (London, Routledge, 2009) 1; JU Wunderlich and DJ Bailey, *The European Union and Global Governance: A Handbook* (London, Routledge, 2011).

# III. Extraterritorial Legislation and Sanctions

## A. Conceptualisation of Extraterritorial Sanctions

I will now turn to the extraterritorial application of foreign legislation, which provides for the colloquially called extraterritorial sanctions (also known as secondary sanctions). These sanctions and their deterrence are the focus of this chapter, so a further clarification of the concept is required. I will first briefly explain both concepts separately, and then consider them together as a phrase.

The concept of extraterritoriality is widely perceived to derive from the international law discipline,[64] where it is principally attached to either jurisdiction or obligation, and even to imperialism.[65] As for extraterritorial jurisdiction, this is considered as an exception to the rule (ie that a state exercises its authority and power on its territory), and refers to the application of a state's laws beyond its territory.[66] The meaning of extraterritorial obligations is tightly connected to human rights and fundamental freedoms, and departs from the traditional human rights paradigm by emphasising that human rights obligations of states when imposing sanctions are not constrained by territorial boundaries.[67]

Turning to sanctions, it can be agreed that these measures, adopted on different legal bases either within the multilateral environment (United Nations or regional organisations) or unilaterally by states, are widely used in contemporary international relations. The conceptualisation of sanctions is not uniform and points to a variety of different approaches, eg purpose-oriented, author-oriented or object-oriented.[68] Although the United Nations Charter does not use the term 'sanctions', the concept does refer to 'measures not involving the use of armed force' taken by the Security Council under Chapter VII of the United Nations Charter, thus in response to a threat to peace, a breach of peace or an act of aggression.[69]

[64] For more on extraterritoriality and extraterritorial regimes, see DS Margolies, U Özsu, M Pal and N Tzouvala, *The Extraterritoriality of Law: History, Theory, Politics* (New York, Routledge, 2019).

[65] Historically, the role of extraterritoriality could also be considered as an 'instrument of power' and 'imperialist mechanism of imposed control', as argued by K Miles, '"Uneven Empires": Extraterritoriality and the Early Trading Companies' in Margolies et al (n 64) 87–103. On the US approaches to sovereign jurisdiction in territorial and extraterritorial spaces, see DS Margolies, 'Imperial Reorderings in US Zones and Regulatory Regimes, 1934–50' in Margolies et al (n 64) 151–66.

[66] See, eg MN Shaw, *International Law*, 8th edn (Cambridge, Cambridge University Press, 2017) 515; Crawford (n 25) 440–48.

[67] See, in particular, M Gibney, GE Türkelli, M Krajewski and W Vandenhole (eds), *The Routledge Handbook on Extraterritorial Human Rights Obligations* (London, Routledge, 2022); JG Ruggie, *Just Business: Multinational Corporations and Human Rights* (New York, WW Norton, 2013); M Langford, W Vandenhole, M Scheinin and W van Genugten (eds), *Global Justice, State Duties: The Extra-territorial Scope of Economic, Social and Cultural Rights in International Law* (Cambridge, Cambridge University Press, 2013).

[68] T Ruys, 'Sanctions, Retortions and Countermeasures: Concepts and International Legal Framework' in L van den Herik (ed), *Research Handbook on UN Sanctions and International Law* (Cheltenham, Edward Elgar Publishing, 2017) 19, 19–23.

[69] See UN Charter, Art 41; R Gordon, M Smyth and T Cornell, *Sanctions Law* (Oxford, Hart Publishing, 2019) 11–34; TJ Biersteker and Z Hudáková, 'UN Targeted Sanctions: Historical

The idea of sanctions is also frequently used in the vocabulary of the EU in referring to restrictive measures under EU law,[70] ie a foreign policy tool, tailored to the specific situation, mainly targeted (ie directed at a specific person or entity, as opposed to the prevalent comprehensive sanctions of the past) and involving a variety of categories, such as travel bans, arms embargoes, asset freezes, trade embargoes and other prohibitions of goods and services.

Foreign legislation with extraterritorial reach imposing extraterritorial sanctions is the reality of contemporary international relations and involvement in transnational activities. Extraterritorial sanctions are specific measures, as explained by Ruys, which

> expose natural and legal persons in third countries to sanctions in respect of certain actions that take place outside the jurisdiction of the State imposing the sanctions, notably when they conduct business with individuals, groups, regimes or countries that are the target of the 'primary' sanctions regime.[71]

Sanctions regimes are thus expanded beyond conventional jurisdictional boundaries.[72] Extraterritorial laws are considered to be legal obligations that companies must comply with or they will be subject to legal proceedings in a foreign country and consequently penalised. The extraterritorial sanctions attempt to restrict or even prohibit economic dealings between the target and third parties, so they have strong business implications and consequences. These measures do not involve the use of armed force, but are nonetheless coercive as they are unilaterally used by a state in order to enforce its decisions on a territory outside its own, and for actions that are committed outside its territory by individuals and companies from other countries.

## B. EU Response to Extraterritorial Sanctions

The practice of unilateral sanctions with extraterritorial reach has a history that is most notably closely connected with the USA.[73] Joy Gordon differentiates between

Development and Current Challenges' in PAG van Bergeijk (ed), *Research Handbook on Economic Sanctions* (Cheltenham, Edward Elgar Publishing, 2021) 107–24.

[70] See TFEU, Arts 215 and 275(2). For more on EU sanctions, see Gordon et al (n 69) 35–55.

[71] Ruys (n 68) 28. Secondary sanctions can be considered as supplementary to primary sanctions, which relate to the relationship between an imposing state (and its individuals and companies) and a target of the sanctions: see, eg M Sossai, 'Legality of Extraterritorial Sanctions' in M Asada (ed), *Economic Sanctions in International Law and Practice* (London, Routledge, 2020) 62, 63.

[72] Gordon et al (n 69) 114.

[73] For an historical overview, see C Beaucillon, 'Practice Makes Perfect, Eventually? Unilateral State Sanctions and the Extraterritorial Effects of National Legislation' in N Ronzitti (ed), *Coercive Diplomacy, Sanctions and International Law* (Leiden, Brill, 2016) 103. On the EU's practice of extraterritorial sanctions, which is not addressed in this chapter, see C Beaucillon, 'The European Union's Position and Practice with Regard to Unilateral and Extraterritorial Sanctions' in C Beaucillon (ed), *Research Handbook on Unilateral and Extraterritorial Sanctions* (Cheltenham, Edward Elgar, 2021) 110.

two 'generations' of the adopted US extraterritorial sanctions.[74] The main characteristics of the 'first generation' of these sanctions, introduced in the 1990s, are their broad range and simultaneously their relative precision in their scope and enforcement.[75] At that time, several legislative acts were adopted against Cuba, Iran and Libya. The extraterritoriality of the sanctions imposed on Cuba by the Cuban Democracy Act, passed in 1992,[76] and the Cuban Liberty and Democratic Solidarity (Libertad) Act, enacted in 1996,[77] was reflected, for example, in losses of foreign investment in Cuba and interference in its trade with third-state companies.[78] Similarly, under the Iran and Libya Sanctions Act of 1996, the USA prohibited foreign persons or companies (with no jurisdictional nexus with the USA) from doing business with Iran and Libya.[79]

The extraterritorial sanctions of the 'second generation', imposed in the last decade and particularly affecting financial transactions and the banking sector, are more extensive in scope and more costly, thus causing a 'chilling effect', evident when companies decline to engage in legally permissible activities simply because they are afraid of the potential consequences these measures would bring down upon them.[80] The problematic nature of extraterritorial sanctions was again brought to the surface with the US withdrawal from the Iranian nuclear agreement, ie the Joint Common Plan of Action (JCPOA), in May 2018.[81] Subsequently, the USA reimposed sanctions against Iran and adopted extraterritorial sanctions on foreign companies that do business with Iran.[82] Costly financial penalties or settlement payments amounting to hundreds of millions of dollars were imposed on the EU's companies and investors for violating the US extraterritorial legislation.[83] The EU's companies are indeed effectively caught between a rock and a hard place;[84] they are confronted by, on the one hand, the possibility of being subjected to costly extraterritorial sanctions imposed by the USA should

[74] J Gordon, 'Extraterritoriality: Issues of Overbreadth and the Chilling Effect in the Cases of Cuba and Iran' (2016) 57 *Harvard International Law Journal*, 1.

[75] ibid 6.

[76] Cuban Democracy Act of 1992, 22 USC 69 § 6001-10.

[77] Cuban Liberty and Democratic Solidarity (Libertad) Act of 1996, 22 USC 691 § 6021-91.

[78] Gordon (n 74) 2–6.

[79] Iran–Libya Sanctions Act (1996 & Supp III 1997), 50 USC § 1701.

[80] Gordon (n 74) 6–11; see also Sossai (n 71) 65–67.

[81] Describing the US withdrawal from the JCPOA, see J Galbraith, 'Contemporary Practice of the United States Relating to International Law' (2018) 112 *American Journal of International Law* 487, 514–22.

[82] Iran Freedom and Counter-Proliferation Act of 2012; see, eg GC Hufbauer and E Jung, 'Economic Sanctions in the Twenty-First Century' in van Bergeijk (n 69) 34.

[83] BR Early and KA Preble, 'Going Fishing versus Hunting Whales: Explaining Changes in How the US Enforces Economic Sanctions,' (2020) 29 *Security Studies* 231; Gordon (n 74) 7; S Emmenegger, 'Extraterritorial Economic Sanctions and Their Foundation in International Law' (2016) 33 *Arizona Journal of International and Comparative Law* 631.

[84] C Van Haute, S Nordin and G Forwood, 'The Reincarnation of the EU Blocking Regulation: Putting European Companies between a Rock and a Hard Place' (2018) 13 *Global Trade and Customs Journal* 496.

they continue investing in Iran, and, on the other hand, the explicit prohibition of complying with such sanctions that is written into the EU's legislation.

The application of the US legislation, with its extraterritorial effects and aggressive sanction regimes, has been vigorously contested.[85] Scholars overwhelmingly consider these measures controversial, even though they have differing views on their legality.[86] It has even been argued that extraterritorial sanctions undermine or endanger international law.[87] Extraterritoriality has been connected to an empire-building strategy, rather than a strategy of law.[88] It has even been seen as 'evidence of a hegemonic state seeking to exempt itself from the international legal system'[89] and therefore imposing its foreign policy and its own interests on others. At the same time, these measures call for a reciprocal answer, which could mean entering into a vicious circle creating not fewer, but more and new problems, aggravating an already unsustainable situation. A sustained argument against extraterritorial sanctions maintains that 'global challenges often require comprehensive responses, while extraterritorial regulation generally leads to piecemeal fragmentation and short-term responses',[90] importantly leading to the reduced relevance of the country imposing these sanctions in solving existing multiple transnational problems.[91] Instead of a return to unilateralism, responsible, multilateral relations should be practised.

The extraterritorial sanctions adopted by the USA provoked not only a scholarly response, but also reactions by third states and the EU. The latter has protested against such laws in the past and continues to contravene them in the present.[92] Given the discussion on European sovereignty earlier in the chapter, it is therefore no surprise that European sovereignty rhetoric has also been used in the context of extraterritorial sanctions.[93] Politicians at the highest level stated their commitment to adopt instruments in the Union's trade and competition policy that will 'protect

[85] Early and Preble (n 83) 182.

[86] R Higgins, *Problems and Process: International Law and How We Use It* (Oxford, Clarendon Press, 1995) 74; Gordon et al (n 69) 115; Sossai (n 71) 62. Challenging the general view on the illegality of all extraterritorial measures, see, JA Meyer, 'Second Thoughts on Secondary Sanctions' (2009) 30 *University of Pennslyvania Journal of International Economic Law* 905, 905.

[87] AL Parrish, 'The Interplay between Extraterritoriality, Sovereignty, and the Foundations of International Law' in Margolies et al (n 64) 177.

[88] ibid 179.

[89] ibid 177.

[90] ibid 177–78.

[91] ibid 178.

[92] For the past protests, see, eg Crawford (n 25) 447–48. See General Secretariat of the Council, 'Guidelines on Implementation and Evaluation of Restrictive Measures (Sanctions) in the Framework of the European Union Common Foreign and Security Policy' (Brussels, 2018) 5664/18, para 52: 'The EU has condemned the extra-territorial application of third country's legislation imposing restrictive measures which purports to regulate the activities of natural and legal persons under the jurisdiction of the Member States of the European Union, as being in violation of international law.'

[93] E Geranmayeh and M Lafont Rapnouil, 'Meeting the Challenge of Secondary Sanction', European Council on Foreign Relations Policy Brief, 25 June 2019.

from coercive measures by third countries'.[94] Deterring extraterritorial sanctions and better protecting EU individuals and companies from these sanctions by reinforcing the legislative framework was noted as an EU legislative priority.[95] This rhetoric is clearly reminiscent of the political discourse on European sovereignty addressed in the previous section. As has been argued, the extraterritorial sanctions by the US have seriously affected the EU, its Member States and its citizens. They interfere in the Union's ability to advance foreign policy objectives, and they provide negative impact on the EU's decisions on conducting agreements and managing its own bilateral relations. In other words, extraterritorial sanctions do undermine European sovereignty. However, in order to deter extraterritorial sanctions and enhance not only the EU's foreign policy role, but also its leadership in advancing multilateral contexts, the political rhetoric does not suffice. This political talk must translate into strong legal commitments allowing the EU to properly respond and protect its citizens, companies and values, and thus gain sovereignty in this particular area.

The EU has decided to confront these measures in the 'legal terrain'.[96] By opposing the adoption of the 'first generation' extraterritorial sanctions concerning Cuba, Iran and Libya, the EU most notably adopted a legislative mechanism – the Blocking Statute.[97] This 1996 blocking regulation forbids the Union's individuals and companies from complying by exploring ways to circumvent the extraterritorial sanctions, thus undermining their extraterritorial reach. This regulation was amended when the 'second generation' of extraterritorial sanctions was adopted by the USA.[98] However, as has been pointed out by Daniel Ventura, it is striking that the European Commission did not decide to include in the amended version of the Blocking Statute, among the foreign laws with extraterritorial effect, the Countering America's Adversaries Through Sanctions Act,[99] passed in 2017, which adopted sanction regimes concerning Iran (and also Russia and North Korea).[100]

The EU is unequivocal in its stance that extraterritorial sanctions violate international law and impede the attainment of free movement of capital between

[94] Informal Meeting of the Heads of State or Government, Versailles Declaration, 10 and 11 March 2022, point 23, www.consilium.europa.eu/media/54773/20220311-versailles-declaration-en.pdf.

[95] Joint Declaration of the European Parliament, the Council of the European Union and the European Commission, 'EU Legislative Priorities for 2022' (2021/C 514 I/01) UL C514, point 4.

[96] Sossai (n 71) 69.

[97] Council Regulation (EC) No 2271/96 of 22 November 1996 protecting against the effects of the extra-territorial application of legislation adopted by a third country, and actions based thereon or resulting therefrom [1996] OJ L309 (Blocking Regulation).

[98] Regulation (EU) No 37/2014 of the European Parliament and of the Council of 15 January 2014 amending certain regulations relating to the common commercial policy as regards the procedures for the adoption of certain measures [2014] OJ L18; Commission Delegated Regulation (EU) 2018/1100 of 6 June 2018 amending the Annex to Council Regulation (EC) No 2271/96 protecting against the effects of extra-territorial application of legislation adopted by a third country, and actions based thereon or resulting therefrom [2018] OJ L199I.

[99] Countering America's Adversaries through Sanctions Act, 22 USC 9401 et seq.

[100] D Ventura, 'Contemporary Blocking Statutes and Regulations in the Face of Unilateral and Extraterritorial Sanctions' in Beaucillon, *Research Handbook* (n 73) 221, 224.

Member States and third countries.[101] The Blocking Statute is considered to be 'a defensive mechanism'[102] aimed at protecting the established legal order, the interests of the Union, and the interests of natural and legal persons exercising rights under the TFEU against the adverse effects of extraterritorial sanctions, as well as counteracting the effects of those sanctions through a number of specific measures.[103]

The regulatory framework provides, firstly, a procedure to be followed when the threshold is reached (ie the economic and/or financial interests of persons and companies affected, directly or indirectly, by listed extraterritorial legislation), which involves providing the European Commission with all the relevant information within the prescribed time frame.[104] Secondly, it provides for the non-recognition and non-enforceability of a foreign court or tribunal judgment and of a foreign administrative decision giving effect to extraterritorial sanctions.[105] Thirdly, the Blocking Statute also establishes a 'clawback' provision that allows for the recovery of damages (including legal costs) caused by the application of extraterritorial sanctions.[106] Fourthly, Member States are responsible for implementing the Blocking Statute and imposing penalties for compliance with foreign extraterritorial legislation. These penalties may vary by Member State, but they must be effective, proportionate and dissuasive.[107] Although the Blocking Statute generally (by rule) prohibits compliance with extraterritorial legislation, it allows an exception by providing for a procedure where the non-compliance 'would seriously damage' the interests of individuals, companies or the EU.[108] Having in mind the principle of legal certainty and the effective implementation of the Blocking Statute, the European Commission adopted an Implementing Regulation providing the burden of proof and the criteria for the application of this exception.[109] The applicant must provide sufficient evidence that non-compliance would cause serious damage to at least one protected interest.[110]

There are, however, some deficiencies in the EU's blocking regulation that arguably undermine its effectiveness and deterrent nature.[111] Several provisions

[101] Council Regulation (EC) No 2271/96 (n 97) second and fourth recitals.
[102] European Commission, 'Proposal for a Council Regulation (EC) protecting against the effects of the application of certain legislation of certain third countries, and actions based thereon or resulting therefrom' (Explanatory Memorandum) COM (96) 420 final, 1.
[103] Council Regulation (EC) No 2271/96 (n 97) fifth recital, Art 1(1).
[104] ibid Art 2.
[105] ibid Art 4.
[106] ibid Art 6.
[107] ibid Art 9.
[108] ibid Art 5.
[109] Commission Implementing Regulation (EU) 2018/1101 of 3 August 2018 laying down the criteria for the application of the second paragraph of Article 5 of Council Regulation (EC) No 2271/96 protecting against the effects of the extra-territorial application of legislation adopted by a third country, and actions based thereon or resulting therefrom, fifth recital.
[110] Council Regulation (EC) No 2271/96 (n 97) Art 3(3).
[111] See, eg Ventura (n 100) 221.

of the legislative text seem unclear or ambiguous.[112] This was vividly demonstrated in a case that came through the preliminary reference procedure before the CJEU, which gave the Court the opportunity, for the first time since the adoption of the Blocking Statute in 1996, to interpret its provisions.[113] The case at issue concerned a dispute between a bank owned by the Iranian state which has a branch in Germany, Bank Melli Iran, and the German telecommunications provider Telekom Deutschland. With the US withdrawal from the JCPOA, Bank Melli Iran was again included on the list of blocking entities, and therefore prohibited from trading with foreign companies. Telekom Deutschland notified the Iranian bank of the termination of all of the contracts between them, but Bank Melli Iran challenged that decision before the German courts, arguing that the termination was the consequence of the US reimposing sanctions against Iran and prohibiting non-US companies from trading with Iranian companies. It is important to note that approximately half of the turnover of Telekom Deutschland is derived from its business in the USA.[114]

The main proceedings before the German courts revealed difficulties and doubts concerning the interpretation of the rule prohibiting compliance with extraterritorial legislation, determined in Article 5(1) of the Blocking Statute. The referring court addressed several questions to the CJEU. With regard to the application of Article 5(1), the Court endorsed a broad understanding of this provision explaining that it covers not only actions taken in response to the orders or instructions of an administrative or judicial authority, but also any action taken to comply with extraterritorial sanctions.[115] It clarified that the words 'any requirement or prohibition' in this provision are 'the result not only of an act of an individual nature or a collection of individual decisions, but also of an act of a general and abstract nature'.[116] The affected company may thus bring civil proceedings referring to Article 5(1) of the Blocking Statute, as was the case at issue. The Court further explained that a person may terminate the contract it has agreed with a person on the sanction's list without providing reasons for that termination.[117] However, in order to ensure that the rule prohibiting compliance with extraterritorial sanctions is indeed fully effective, the Court held that where, in civil proceedings, all the evidence available to a national court tends to indicate prima facie that an individual or a company has complied with the extraterritorial legislation, it is for the person to demonstrate that their conduct did not seek to comply with that legislation.[118] That means the EU individuals or companies bear the burden of proof in such disputes.

[112] See also Van Haute et al (n 84).
[113] C-124/20 *Bank Melli Iran v Telekom Deutschland GmbH* ECLI:EU:C:2021:1035 [2021].
[114] ibid para 16.
[115] ibid para 45.
[116] ibid para 46.
[117] ibid para 63, 68.
[118] ibid para 67, 68.

Moreover, at the EU level, there is no harmonisation of sanctions that are imposed in the event of a breach of any of the provisions of the Blocking Statute.[119] The choice of sanctions remains in the hands of the Member States, as long as these sanctions are 'effective, proportional and dissuasive'[120] and 'in accordance with EU law and its general principles … of which fundamental rights and freedoms form part'.[121] This could be problematic, as the Member States' regimes vary.[122] Under German law, for example, the sanction for such a breach could be that a contract is devoid of legal effects. The CJEU concluded that the annulment of the termination of contracts is not precluded, provided that the annulment does not entail disproportionate effects for that person having regard to the objectives of the Blocking Statute (ie the protection of the established legal order and the interests of the EU in general).[123] When assessing proportionality, the national court must strike a balance between, on the one hand, the pursuit of these objectives of the Blocking Statute, and on the other, the probability that the company concerned (in this case, Telekom Deutschland) would be exposed to economic loss, as well as the extent of that loss if the company was unable to terminate its commercial relationship with the person covered by the extraterritorial sanctions.[124] The Court also indicated that a relevant element of this assessment would be whether the company applied to the European Commission for an authorisation to derogate from the Blocking Statute.[125] In the case at issue, Telekom Deutschland had not applied for the exemption.

A recent study showed that the Union's individuals and companies prefer to quietly abide by extraterritorial sanctions because of their costly, negative impacts.[126] Arguably, then, the Blocking Statute does not offer a powerful enough instrument to avert EU individuals and companies from complying with foreign extraterritorial legislation; there is insufficient help and a lack of involvement in foreign litigations at the EU level in support of the companies, and no functioning mechanism of compensation for those who have suffered from extraterritorial sanctions. It is precisely because of these deficiencies that the call for European sovereignty in deterring extraterritorial sanctions is not without merits.

The EU institutions are well aware of these legislative deficiencies and real or potential implementation problems. In January 2021, the European Commission called for 'a general reflection on policy options' to further deter and counteract extraterritorial sanctions by amending the Blocking Statute.[127]

[119] See Council Regulation (EC) No 2271/96 (n 97) Art 9.
[120] ibid
[121] *Bank Melli Iran* (n 113) para 72.
[122] Ventura (n 100) 226–27.
[123] *Bank Melli Iran* (n 113) para 95.
[124] ibid para 95.
[125] ibid para 93.
[126] T Stoll et al, *Extraterritorial Sanctions on Trade and Investments and European Responses* (Brussels, European Parliament, 2020).
[127] European Commission, 'The European Economic and Financial System: Fostering Openness, Strength and Resilience' (Communication) COM (2021) 32 final, 19.

## IV. Concluding Remarks

This chapter has focused on European sovereignty in the context of foreign legislation with extraterritorial reach imposing unilateral extraterritorial sanctions. The essential question is how to deter these measures and simultaneously protect the EU and ensure its sovereignty in this particular area. There are several suggestions as to how to proceed and what is a proper response to extraterritorial sanctions. Arguably, two considerations seem to be relevant in identifying the best possible approach.

Firstly, the reflection within the EU needs to focus on the need of future legislative changes of the Blocking Statute to be better equipped for challenges posed by extraterritorial sanctions. It is worth recalling the observations made by the Advocate General Hogan in the case *Bank Melli Iran*:

> As the facts of this case have highlighted, the EU blocking statute is a very blunt instrument, designed as it is to sterilise the intrusive extraterritorial effects of US sanctions within the Union. This sterilisation method will inevitably bring casualties in its wake and many may think that Telekom Deutschland will be among the first to suffer, not least given its large US operations. As I have already hinted, these are matters which the EU legislature may well wish to ponder and consider.[128]

There is little room for state sovereignty when elaborating on how to proceed with a common stance and enhance blocking regulatory framework should the deterrence of the extraterritorial sanctions be successful, coherent and efficient. Emphasising Member States' sovereignty would have a detrimental effect on the EU as a whole. Back in 1996, the European Commission advocated for adopting blocking legislation at the Community level for various reasons. It observed, inter alia, that addressing this issue at the Community level

> would also achieve a level of protection that could not be obtained through identical or comparable (co-ordinated) national measures, not least because certain Member States have indicated that they would have difficulty in introducing such legislation at national level, or in introducing it rapidly.[129]

In addition, in a globally interconnected world, no Member State of the EU is powerful enough to lead by itself. This speaks in favour of common EU action. Clearly, the area in question encroaches upon European sovereignty as addressed in the context of this chapter. The talk of European sovereignty has to translate into a comprehensive and efficient normative response. Not only has the EU to be aware of particular problems its companies face when engaging in global relations, it also needs to listen to experts and companies when preparing legislative changes to blocking regulations.

[128] Opinion of Advocate General Hogan, delivered on 12 May 2021, Case C-124/20 *Bank Melli Iran v Telekom Deutschland GmbH* ECLI:EU:C:2021:386, para 136.

[129] European Commission, Explanatory Memorandum (n 102) 1.

A second observation is equally imperative: the adoption of legislation with extraterritorial reach by the EU, including similarly blunt and costly sanctions producing counter effects to the USA, would be neither productive nor wise. It might provoke additional negative effects on the already fragile and fragmented global international setting. If the EU wishes to enhance its global role, and stay committed to its proclaimed values in ensuring peace and sustainable security, then it should lead by example, act responsibly and opt for a global dialogue on extraterritorial sanctions, their intended and unintended effects, and thus interact globally in order to address this problem on a multilateral level and properly avert it. This would also be in the best interests of the international community as such.

Turning finally back to the concept of European sovereignty: at the time of writing this chapter, the EU is facing perhaps the most strenuous situation in its history, provoked by an armed attack of the Russian Federation on Ukraine. This is the Union's ultimate test and a real challenge of its capacity to act effectively as an actor in international relations and of European sovereignty. Only time will tell whether European sovereignty is indeed a feasible and sustainable concept in the future of EU constitutionalism.

# INDEX

**Introductory Note**

References such as '178–79' indicate (not necessarily continuous) discussion of a topic across a range of pages. Wherever possible in the case of topics with many references, these have either been divided into sub-topics or only the most significant discussions of the topic are listed. Because the entire work is about the 'EU constitutionalism', the use of this term (and certain others which occur constantly throughout the book) as an entry point has been restricted. Information will be found under the corresponding detailed topics.

www.ingramcontent.com/pod-product-compliance
Ingram Content Group UK Ltd.
Pitfield, Milton Keynes, MK11 3LW, UK
UKHW020818290926
15470UKWH00003B/1232

9 781509 962860